darfur diaries

darfur diaries

stories of survival

by Jen Marlowe with Aisha Bain and Adam Shapiro

Preface by Paul Rusesabagina

Foreword by Dr. Francis Mading Deng

NATION BOOKS
NEW YORK

DARFUR DAIRIES: STORIES OF SURVIVAL

Published by Nation Books
An Imprint of Avalon Publishing Group
245 West 17th St., 11th Floor,
New York, NY 10011

AVALON

Nation Books is a co-publishing venture of the Nation Institute
and Avalon Publishing Group Incorporated.

Library of Congress Cataloging-in-Publication data is available.

ISBN-10: 1-56025-928-0
ISBN-13: 978-1-56025-928-2

9 8 7 6 5 4

Book design by Pauline Neuwirth, Neuwirth & Associates, Inc.

Printed in the United States of America
Distributed by Publishers Group West

Darfur Diaries: Stories of Survival is dedicated to the children, women and men of Darfur, especially all those who shared their stories and lives with us.

The book is also dedicated to the children in our lives who remind us to smile on a daily basis: Alex, Gizelle, Maya, Renée and Sophie.

contents

acknowledgments

THERE ARE MANY people without whom the film, and subsequently this book, could not have been made. They include dozens of people who helped us with contacts, logistics, translation, and funds. They are Darfurians and internationals, located in the U.S. and in Chad and Darfur, and are listed on the film credits. Kolude Doherty stands out among the many United Nations and NGO staff that came to our assistance.

Amna Ibrahim stepped in to assist with last minute translation and analysis. Deborah Harris, Tovah Lazaroff, Wendy Pearlman, and Carol Grosman generously offered crucial advice on the book proposal in its early stages. Wendy Pearlman, Blackbird Willow, and Julie Flint provided an extremely helpful outside set of eyes for the manuscript as it developed, posing all the right questions as we ploughed through. Doreen Shapiro probably knows this book better than we do! Every word, comma, and dash underwent her loving scrutiny—multiple times.

Beth Martin Quittman and George Greenfield from CreativeWell, Inc. guided us through the bewildering process of finding a publisher with constant encouragement, all the time expressing their faith that this book should and could be published. Carl Bromley and Ruth Baldwin at Nation Books believed that this story should be told and took the risk to publish it.

Last but not least, a thank you to Julia and all the Marks family, without whose support, home, and threats to staple me to the chair, this book could not have been written.

We give you all our deepest appreciation.

—AISHA BAIN, JEN MARLOWE, ADAM SHAPIRO

authors' notes

WE HAVE USED first names only of Darfurians to protect their identity. Names of U.N./NGO staff were altered if we were not able to obtain their permission to be quoted. Unless otherwise indicated in the manuscript, the interviews with Darfurians are based on the accurate post-filming translation of our footage. Informal conversations are based on our memory. We have made every attempt at accuracy, with our first priority remaining an honest reflection of the history, experiences, and reality of the Darfurians we met, as they understood and expressed it to us.

A portion of the proceeds of Darfur Diaries: Stories of Survival *will go to rebuild schools in the destroyed villages of northern Darfur that are described in the book.*

For more information about the complete Darfur Diaries project, please visit www.darfurdiaries.org

preface

by Paul Rusesabagina

IN 1994, DURING the one hundred days of the Rwandan genocide, I tried everything to get the international community to listen, to respond, to help—but nobody was ready to see, hear or, most importantly, to act. Four months later, when it was finally acknowledged that nearly one million men, women, and children had been murdered during those one hundred days, I was angry and bitter. Close to one million people, fifteen percent of a nation, slaughtered and no one lifted a finger! The world abandoned an entire nation to mass murder. It turned its back and refused to see what was going on. The world fears responsibilities.

Since 1994, I have been speaking out about the genocide in Rwanda and the fact that the international community did nothing to stop it. My goal is that the world would not allow such a thing to happen again. A good teacher repeats his lesson over and over again until all his students have learned it. And so I have traveled the world speaking of the shame of the genocide in Rwanda. I knew I had to take this message to a wider audience, to try to convince the international community to help those who are suffering now. I do not speak out only on behalf of Rwandans. People in Africa are almost invisible outside Africa. How many people know—or care— what is happening to children in Northern Uganda? To civilians in the Congo? I realized that I have many more students to reach with my lesson.

Last year, I traveled to Darfur and eastern Chad with Don Cheadle, the actor who played me in the film *Hotel Rwanda*, to see with our own eyes what was happening there. What we saw in Darfur reminded me so much of what took place in Rwanda from 1990–1994: a militia armed by the government slaughtering with impunity; displaced people fleeing their destroyed villages; refugees sleeping in the wind and the rain, without food, water, shelter, education, and medical care. Several hundred thousand people have been killed, two million displaced and still the world allows it to continue. How many more must die, be raped, watch their homes burn, have their livestock stolen, be turned into refugees? What has the world learned from Rwanda? Rather than learning from history, we are allowing it to repeat itself. "Never Again" is an empty slogan as "Again and Again" unfolds.

The peace-keeping troops of the U.N. came to Rwanda in an attempt to maintain peace and to protect foreigners. They had no power to help the Rwandans. Their own regulations prevented them from taking up arms to protect civilians even when they were being butchered, mutilated, and raped. In Darfur, although there is a massive relief effort, there was no significant international pressure to end the genocide for far too long. Lands will continue to be confiscated, villages will still be destroyed, women and girls will be raped, more and more children will become orphans, and the number of dead will continue to grow.

Darfur Diaries is an important tool to raise awareness about the tragedies in Darfur. Let us use this book as a wake-up call, the way I had hoped the world would use Rwanda. After meeting the Darfurians in this book and learning of the horrors they endured and the bleak futures they face, let each of us go to our leaders and demand that they find solutions. Let us wake up and shake up governments worldwide to act responsibly—not just toward Darfurians, but also to all human beings.

In *Darfur Diaries*, you meet Darfurians who demonstrate their commitment to educating their children. You hear the pain they express about their destroyed schools and their strength and resilience as they build new schools in the refugee camps in Chad, not willing to wait around for the United Nations to educate their children. This struck me very forcefully, because it so matched what I myself found in those camps. What we saw there gave me no hope for the next generation. There are hundreds of thousands of Darfurian children who are not going to have an education. When the children in Chad saw us they staged a type of demonstration. About two thousand took a blackboard and wrote, "Welcome to our guests! But we need education."

I am often asked by people who come to hear me speak, "What can we do? Should we send money, or food, or clothing?" My answer goes back to an old Chinese proverb that I believe deeply: "Give a man a fish; you have fed him for today. Teach a man to fish; and you have fed him for a lifetime." Yes, the refugees of Darfur need food and shelter, but more than that they need schools to teach their children; they need the means to rebuild their lives and their homes with dignity and self-sufficiency. Listen carefully to the voices in this book. This is what they themselves tell you.

To the people of Darfur, I offer this message: Hold on and stay strong. Think about dialogue, of Africans and Arabs sitting together to solve their own problems and find their own solutions. Sooner or later you will have to sit together to heal your country.

To the international community, I offer this message: It is the duty and the obligation of adults to teach the children to heal. The international community would be wise to help provide jobs and education for the adults and children of Darfur. It must assist in enabling the refugees of Darfur to return home and rebuild their lives, their communities, their society. Children of genocide, left to be orphans, uneducated, and jobless, will grow to be adults who will repeat the atrocities they have witnessed.

TO THE READERS of this book, I offer this message: The stories in *Darfur Diaries* must not be forgotten. We must never stop trying to learn crucial lessons from human-made disasters. Though it is ultimately the responsibility of the citizens of Darfur to heal their children, as it was in Rwanda, the rest of the world must not stand silent in the midst of such pain and devastation. Genocide is happening today, in Darfur. Now that you know, what do you plan to do?

MY HOPE IS that these first-person accounts of the suffering endured by people in Darfur will bring all of us back to our duties, obligations, and responsibilities toward humankind.

PAUL RUSESABAGINA's real-life actions saved over twelve hundred people during the Rwandan genocide and inspired the critically acclaimed movie *Hotel Rwanda*. He now travels and speaks all around the world about the tragedy in Rwanda, connecting it to other crises, including the one in Darfur. His recently published book, *An Ordinary Man*, chronicles his story. He has set up the Hotel Rwanda Rusesabagina Foundation (www.hrrfoundation.org) to help the survivors of the Rwandan tragedy.

foreword

by Dr. Francis Mading Deng

IN SEPTEMBER, 2005, I first saw the documentary film *Darfur Diaries: Message from Home*. I found it very effective in revealing the human face of what is widely recognized as one of the worst tragedies in the world today. The book *Darfur Diaries: Stories of Survival* provides a deeper context for the film and gives insight into the characters that the film could only introduce at a quick moving pace. We also hear for the first time the story behind the story from the perspectives of the filmmakers, whose voices were deliberately absent from the film.

I was profoundly touched by the fact that three young persons, Aisha, Jen, and Adam, would place themselves in harm's way to document the Darfur crisis and let it be known to the world. The fact that they had been exposed to other tragedies around the world only meant that they were not naïve about the possible dangers. If there is any doubt about what human compassion behind such ventures means, the experience documented in this book should remove such doubt.

Apart from the dedication of these three young people, a number of things impressed me about the project. The first was the way the filmmakers allowed the victims in the documentary to speak for themselves, by themselves. As they explain in the final chapter of the book:

Our film would be a platform for Darfurians, those whose lives had been most deeply impacted by the crisis, to tell their stories for themselves, in their own words . . . We did not want any outside voices.

Another thing that impressed me in both the film and the book was the dignity of the people despite all the destruction, degradation and humiliation that they had suffered so profoundly. An aspect of that dignity was their magnanimity. Their struggle was for human dignity for all, including the Arabs themselves. Asked if he had a chance to talk to some of the Arab fighters face to face, what he would say to them, one Darfurian answered:

I would say to them that what they are doing is wrong. We can meet together and talk about what you need and what I need, about what is right, what is wrong. Arab tribes in Darfur are being used by the government . . . it's not because the government likes the Arabs in Darfur. No. If the government likes them, why are Arabs now suffering? Many of them have been killed in battles. Some of them are suffering like us. Because of that, if I had a chance to meet an Arab, I would say this is a wrong policy of government . . . all the tribes, we can live together in Darfur in peace, and solve our problems with meeting, with talking, not fighting.

Another said:

Everyone needs to have his rights. Even Omar Bashir!

There is a popular saying that when God created the Sudan, he laughed, marveling at the immense diversity he had created. In view of the tragic experiences the country has suffered throughout its recorded history, God should have cried over his creation. While diversity is potentially a source of enrichment, it has brought only conflict and extreme suffering for the Sudanese people. The conflict in Darfur is only the latest in a series of internecine wars that have been the lot of the country since 1955.

Almost everyone who has had close contact with the Sudanese is full of praise for the people's kindness, gentle nature, and hospitality, wherever they come from in the country. The paradoxical question is how a people who are so highly acclaimed for their humanistic virtues can be so inhuman in their treatment of each other? The answer to this question, I believe, goes back to what I have always referred to as the crisis of national identity in the country. Conflicts of identity tend to be zero-sum. The survival with dignity of one identity threatens to denigrate, diminish, and perhaps eliminate the other. This is the core of the genocidal conflicts that have proliferated in the country for half a century, initially in the South, and since the mid 1980s extended to the Nuba Mountains and Southern Blue Nile. The atrocities committed by the government and its Arab militias, the notorious Janjaweed, against the non-Arab groups in Darfur have drawn even greater international attention, and have been more authoritatively documented.

The country has widely been perceived as an African-Arab dualism, which is clearly an oversimplification. While there are those of mixed Arab-African descent who simplistically identify themselves as Arab, a sizeable percentage of the people of the North, especially in the Nuba Mountains, Southern Blue Nile, and Darfur, though Muslim, are Black Africans and indistinguishable from the people of the South. The Beja in the east are also indigenous. Even the Nubians in the far north have retained their indigenous languages and are reviving their pride in their Nubian identity and heritage.

With a land mass of nearly a million square miles, Sudan is geographically the largest country in Africa, with ten neighbors, Egypt and Libya to the north, Chad and the Central African Republic to the west, the Democratic Republic of the Congo, Uganda, and Kenya to the south, Ethiopia and Eritrea to the east, and Saudi Arabia on the other side of the Red Sea. The regional diversities represented by these neighbors are reflected in the internal configuration of the country.

Sudan's estimated population of over thirty-five million inhabitants are said to fall into fifty ethnic groups that are further divided into nearly six hundred distinct subgroups. This wide array can be grouped into three principal clusters: the so-called Arabs of the North, who are in fact an African-Arab hybrid; the non-Arab groups in the North, who, though Islamized and to a degree influenced by Arab culture, have retained their indigenous identity; and the Southern Sudanese, who are the most indigenously African in race and culture, the majority of whom adhere to traditional religious beliefs, but large numbers of whom have embraced or are increasingly embracing Christianity, almost as a counterforce against Islamization. None of these clusters are internally homogenous. The Arab and non-Arab groups in the North are divided into subgroups, while the peoples of the South are even more fragmented than those in the North, where Islam and the wide use of the Arabic language as the *lingua franca* are unifying factors. Conflicts have been raging between and within these various groups with varying degrees of intensity and devastation.

Of course, it is not mere differences that cause conflicts, but the implications for the shaping and sharing of power, wealth, services, development opportunities, and the overall enjoyment of the rights of citizenship. By this yardstick, the South clearly found itself at the eve of independence the most marginalized and discriminated region in the country. As a result, the first conflict, which pitted the North against the South, erupted in 1955, eight months before independence on January 1, 1956. The conflict was halted in 1972 by a peace agreement that granted the South regional autonomy, and was resumed in 1983, when the government unilaterally abrogated that agreement. While the first war was separatist, the declared objective of the second, championed by the Sudan People's Liberation Movement and Army (SPLM/A), was to restructure the country into a New Sudan that would be free from discrimination due to race, ethnicity, religion, culture, or gender.

This recasting of the issues in the conflict began to gain support in the non-Arab regions of the North. The Nuba of Southern Kordofan and the Ingassana or Funj of Southern Blue Nile, who border the Southern region, were the first to join the SPLM/A in the struggle for equality. In 1991, a group of Darfurians allied with the SPLM/A staged a rebellion that was ruthlessly crushed by the government armed forces. Elsewhere, the Beja in the eastern part of the country are engaged in a low-level conflict that threatens to escalate. The Nubians in the extreme north are reported to have organized two movements: the Kush Movement for Democracy and the Constitution and Sudan Liberation Movement (SLM) for South and North Dongola.

Sadly, Darfur is more the norm than the exception, both in the form and magnitude of genocidal conflicts that have at their roots the mismanagement of racial, ethnic, cultural, and religious diversities. Gabriel Meyer in his book *War and Faith in Sudan* correctly observed that "The Western media seems intent on viewing Darfur as an isolated atrocity; but, in fact, it's part of a much larger, and more complicated evil," which began in the South, spread northward to the Nuba Mountains and Southern Blue Nile, and then to Darfur."[1] *Darfur Diaries* introduces the link with the South in the comparative account of James, a Dinka from the South, living in Darfur:

All the people in the South are like the Darfurians. There's death, there's killing from the government forces . . . The situation in the

South and Darfur is the same. The problems are from the same starting point. They oppress people.

Another Darfurian, well versed in national politics, comments:

> The marginalization that created the war in the South is the same cause as the war in the West. If the government continues on the same track, there will be wars in other areas, as has already started in the Nuba Mountains. The Darfur war will not be the last for this government, if they remain in power.

The atrocities in Darfur recounted in this book are identical to what other war-ravished regions underwent: Kitir Congo, a fighter in the SLA, details abuses with the place and year and the number of people killed, demonstrating that the policy of intimidation, discrimination, and violence in Darfur extended back decades. The inhumanity of the atrocities committed against innocent civilians continues, as another Darfurian testifies:

> The government deployed its troops to outside areas (near El Fashir) and killed people. They captured some of them and dragged them through the streets of El Fashir and burned them in front of a crowd of spectators. In a town north of El Fashir, all of us saw a man who was captured by the government. They brought him in broad daylight. They tied his hands behind him, tied his legs, strung him in the tree, and burned a plastic tire on top of him. The plastic tire melted on his body. What is this?
>
> The Janjaweed and the government rape girls. They cut the woman's vagina with a knife. In Jebbel Marra, we saw a pregnant woman murdered by the Janjaweed. They cut her womb. There were twins, the babies were still alive. This is a horrible image.

Compare these with the accounts of atrocities from the South. Mansour Khalid, a prominent Northern intellectual and statesman, wrote:

> The anger of the military was directed against the Anyanya (separatist Southern Sudanese rebel army from the civil war which began in 1955) and the civilian population alike, in both rural and urban centers; villages were burnt down and centers for tortures were established.[2]

In Upper Nile Province, for example, Kodok was designed as a center for torture, and in August 1964, schools in the provinces were closed because most of the schoolteachers had been rounded up, taken there, and subjected to daily torture. The form of torture was especially inhumane:

> Chilies were put into their eyes and genitals, and each was given two hours' whipping every day tied to a tree with their heads down. The first to die in these tortures was the headmaster of Dolieb Hill center for girls, and several other casualties ensued.[3]

The magnitude of the war was more encompassing than can be demonstrated adequately by isolated incidents. Since 1983, two and a half million people have died, over four million have been displaced internally, and about half a million forced into refuge abroad. Much evidence was furnished by tribal leaders whom I interviewed shortly after the end of the seventeen-year war. In response to a question about what the war meant to the ordinary people in the South, Chief Thon Wai responded:

> Our brothers [the Northerners], in their anger with us, harassed all those people who remained at home, including

their chiefs. Even if the people of the forest [the rebels] had only passed near a camp, they would come and say, "They are here inside the camp." They would proceed to destroy the camp. Children would die and women would die. The chief would only stand holding his head. If you tried force, you fell a victim. Whatever you tried, you fell a victim. . . . You just sat mourning with hands folded like a woman.[4]

The account of Chief Stephen Thongkol Anyijong of Atwot is very descriptive of the perception associated with this genocidal conflict and the bitterness with which the war is remembered. Suspected for sympathy with the rebels because of information furnished by an Arab trader with whom he had a hostile encounter, he was arrested and tortured severely. When he was eventually released, Chief Thongkol escaped and joined the rebels. The consequences of his act on his family were devastating:

Because of my going to the forest, . . . they destroyed my things . . . in a way that never happens. If you were to know about them you would cry with tears. First of all, they took my small child who had only a common cold. When they heard he was the son of a rebel, they killed the child . . . They came and took twenty-eight goats and sheep from my place. Then they went looking for my other home. They took eighty sheep and goats and burned the village. Then they . . . went to my cattle camp and took one hundred cows and three girls . . . My wives went and built another home at a distant place . . . They came and broke down the home . . . They caught my little girl and took her away. The women they threw into . . . a big fire. You know those big Dinka huts that are raised on high platforms. They put fire under the hut. The hut was turned into an oven in which the women burned.[5]

The conflict continued to escalate, leading to abduction of women and children into slavery and the virtual depopulation of the area. Minyiel Row, a renowned Ngok Dinka poet and singer, commemorated the events with a song pleading for justice, in vain, from the central government:

> Fire continued to blaze [as houses burned],
> And our cattle were driven away;
> But we had no one to hear our case.
> We called and called,
> But no one asked what we were calling about;
> We cried and cried,
> But no one asked why we were crying.
> We talked and talked,
> But no one asked what we were saying.
> God, it was you who gave the Dinka the cow
> And you gave the Arabs their wealth in money,
> The Arabs have consumed their wealth,
> And they have gone to capture our herds,
> And there is no one to whom we can take our case:
> Our cattle have been captured,
> And our villages have been burnt down;
> We are now clustering under trees like birds.[6]

The symbolism of living under the trees like birds, prominent in the Ngok Dinka song of lamentation, is reflected in the accounts provided in *Darfur Diaries*:

> We are living under the trees, here, there, here, there. We are spread all over the area under the trees in more than twenty places. We just came under this tree today, but we are already moving . . . We are confused.

From the mid-1980s, as the war began to spread to the North, beginning with the Nuba, what had been viewed as a conflict confined to the South began to afflict the non-Arab North with identical degradation and dehumanization. The experience of the Nuba, as documented by Meyer, was similar to that of the South. The story of Agostino el-Nur Ibrahim, a Nuba, who was arrested, detained, and tortured for being a Christian, sounds very much like that of Chief Thongkol and numerous other Southerners:

> I was arrested there on April 14, 1985, and taken to Heiban. I spent one week there under torture. They tied me up with ropes and chains and beat me, there were lashings. "Quit being a Christian," they said, "and close your church." After that, I was transferred to Kadugli. The conditions there were worse. "Christianity is not the religion for Sudan," they said, "it's a religion for foreigners. What have you got to do with this religion of infidels?" . . . I was tortured there for four months, deprived of food and water for days, hoisted up, spat upon and beaten, my genitals pulled with pliers, my beard pulled out.[7]

Similar to accounts in *Darfur Diaries,* Meyer gives a graphic account of the bombing of Kauda school by a low-flying Antonov, dropping bombs several times on a scene of chaotic panic, some children falling flat on the ground for safety from the bombs and others conspicuously running away in the fruitless attempt to escape. When it was over, nineteen children and their woman teacher were dead. It is a horrific tale of inhumanity that can only be explained by the demonization associated with the national identity crisis in which the Arabs were motivated by vengeance against a people they had considered fellow Arab-Muslims, albeit subordinate, who had betrayed the cause.

As the tragedy spread to Darfur, the same themes of torture continued to be repeated. Abdel Wahid Mohammed Ahmed Nour, who was to become the leader of the Sudan Liberation Movement and Army, SLM/SLA, issued an appeal from prison on August 9, 2002:

> I am making this appeal from my cell in Zalingei Security Forces detention centre. The cell space is 16 square meters and is overcrowded: there are 12 of us in this small room without ventilation or windows . . . Food is very scarce . . . I have only one lung and I am diabetic. When I was arrested I was suffering from malaria. The security forces refused to allow me to see a doctor.
>
> I would also like to highlight the suffering of my people, the Fur . . . The security forces act with virtual immunity, terrorizing the Fur people, raiding randomly and arresting people including the elderly and children, detaining them without charge or trail. Many have been subjected to torture. Many Fur men have fled to the mountains to find a safe haven and have left their lands. The Arab tribes attack their lands, looting their properties and stealing their livestock. Many Fur villages have been completely deserted . . . [8]

The economic factors involved in the Darfur crisis mirror the situation in the South and the neighboring areas: the clash between Arab herders seeking to graze and water their animals further South, under the pressure of increasing desertification, and Black African farmers protecting their crops and land against this encroachment. Traditionally, these competing interests were regulated and conflicts were managed and resolved by traditional leaders in accordance with intertribal conventions and customs. With traditional leaders and normative principles for intertribal cooperation increasingly weakened, both by the adverse attitude of the initially leftist dictatorship of Jaafar Mohamed Nimeiri (1969–1985) toward native administration and by the pressures of the war, these methods have been fundamentally undermined and severely weakened.

Even more than the weakening of traditional administration and competition for scarce resources has been the divisive penetration of the central government that has repudiated traditional norms and practices of peaceful coexistence. Commenting on the way the relationship with the Arabs used to be, one elder in *Darfur Diaires* recalled:

> Previously, we and the Arabs exchanged marriage . . . It was a complete community life. In the past, in peace time, the Arab nomads moved from south to the north of Darfur after the rainy season. They would spend the whole winter in the north, with us, with Fur, Masalit, with any tribe. We would help each other. When someone lost some of his livestock, everyone came and helped seek the lost animals. We built good relations between us. Definitely, some conflicts happened between individuals, and then the tribal leaders and the elders sat together and solved the problem . . . After the livestock grew bigger, and the number of citizens themselves grew larger, the farmers needed a wider area of land to plant for their food, and the herders also needed a wider area for their livestock. The needs of the life for the herders and these farmers came into conflict, and the government found the chance to wedge between the two and keep them separate and push them towards war.

These proliferating conflicts are the result of a long historical process in which three factors—Arabization, Islamization, and slavery—played a pivotal role in shaping the identities now in conflict. The moral framework provided that a person who was a Muslim, Arabic-speaking, culturally Arabized, and could claim Arab descent was elevated to a position of respect and dignity, while, in sharp contrast, a non-Muslim Black African was deemed inferior, a heathen, and a legitimate target of enslavement. By the nineteenth century, this historical process had crystallized into a division between the North, two-thirds of the country in land and population, becoming identified as Arab-Islamic, and the Southern third considered indigenously African in racial, cultural, and religious terms, with Christianity as a novelty associated with colonial intervention. The British-dominated Anglo-Egyptian administration (1898–1956) governed the country as two distinct entities, with the North advancing politically and economically, while the South remained isolated and undeveloped. At independence, this dualistic administration was reversed into a unitary system in which the North dominated and began to implement a policy of Arabization, and Islamization in the South. By then, not only had the South consolidated a legacy of resistance to slavery, Arabization, and Islamization, but the separatist colonial policy and the influence of Christianity and elements of Western culture had reinforced a distinct Southern identity. This resulted in the formation of two antagonistic identities with two contrasting visions for the nation—an Arab-Islamic vision and a secular Black African vision.

While Islamic fundamentalism has now become the most divisive factor, it should be noted that originally, Islam in the Sudan was promoted by leading Sufi orders, whose distinguishing feature was the degree to which they accommodated pre-Islamic practices, allowing syncretism between traditional African religious beliefs and Islamic rituals. Islam became identified with the local community and adopted many uniquely Sudanese characteristics.

This tolerant and accommodating version of Islam contrasts sharply with today's politicized and intolerant use of Islam by Arabized Muslim leaders at the center. Even among today's Islamists, there are profound differences between the religious sects with roots in Sufism and the more contemporary Islamic movements that claim to represent a "rivalist" version of Islam. Nevertheless, until the recent developments that have begun to bridge the North-South divide, the "Southern Problem" unified the North under the banner of the Arab-Islamic vision, which they sought to impose on the South.

The irony is that regional conflicts were erupting in the North at a time when progress was being made to end the war in the South through a peace process brokered by the sub-regional organization, the Intergovernmental Authority on Development (IGAD), with strong backing from the international community, in particular the quartet of the United States, Norway, the United Kingdom, and Italy. A framework agreed upon by the parties in the Kenyan town of Machakos on July 20, 2002, followed by a series of protocols, negotiated in another Kenyan town, Naivasha, charted a path toward peace in the South, Abyei, the Nuba Mountains, and Southern Blue Nile. The protocols also stipulate principles for inclusively addressing the grievances of other marginalized areas, such as Darfur and the Beja region. The process culminated in a comprehensive peace agreement that was signed by the parties on January 9, 2005, in the Kenyan capital, Nairobi.

These conflicts are all interconnected and it was hoped that a peace agreement between the government and the SPLM/A over the South and the Northern regions of the Nuba Mountains and Southern Blue Nile would provide a constructive basis for resolving the other conflicts in the country, including in Darfur. But, as *Darfur Diaries* notes, the situation turned out to be paradoxically different:

> It's not a coincidence . . . that the heat began to turn up in Darfur just as peace talks began in earnest between the government and the southern rebel movement, the SPLA. Darfur rebels took up arms at the time they did, partly because Darfur had been excluded from the wealth and power sharing agreements hammered out between the government and the southern

Sudanese rebels ... The Sudanese government was facing serious pressure to accommodate power-sharing demands of the SPLA with some control of incredibly rich oil reserves. It was not about to give concessions to any other factions. The government's response in Darfur was a clear message to the rest of the marginalized people of the country to remain submissive or expect its wrath. In all likelihood, the brutality won't stop with Darfur.

There is ample evidence to support this discouraging appraisal and prediction. And yet, there is a silver lining in the tragedy of a country whose identity has been distorted and used as a basis for discriminating against a wide array of indigenous populations. These proliferating regional conflicts are symptomatic of a nation in painful search of itself.

What is unfolding in the Sudan today is challenging the prevailing myths of identity and revealing the complexities of the country's racial, ethnic, cultural, and religious configuration. With the South having resisted Arab domination, and asserted an African identity and demanded equality, other non-Arab groups are awakening to the call. This mounting pressure is challenging the Arab dominated center to respond creatively and constructively, or risk eventual overthrow by the convergence of rebellious regional forces, with even greater devastation to the country in the meantime.

It is, however, not easy to predict the ultimate outcome of these conflicts of identities. The more threatened the Arab-Islamic establishment, the more it entrenches itself in unscrupulous defensive-offensive measures and is widely supported politically and materially by the Arab-Islamic world, whose influence internationally is far greater than that of Black Africa that supports the cause of the non-Arab Sudanese.

On May 5, 2006, the government of the Sudan (GOS) concluded

the Darfur Peace Agreement (DPA) with the wing of the Sudan People's Liberation Movement and Army (SLM/A) led by Minni Minnawi, while the wing led by Abdel Wahid Mohammed Ahmed Nour and Justice and Equality Movement (JEM), led by Dr. Khalil Ibrahim refused to sign. Brokered by the African Union, in collaboration with other major actors from the international community, including the United States, the agreement offers the people of Darfur a measure of autonomy, security arrangements, wealth sharing, representation at the national level, and compensation for loss of lives and property incurred in the conflict.

It is debatable whether the DPA adequately addresses the root causes of the conflict and whether it is worth the sacrifice that has been made by the people of Darfur. Unlike the South, whose agenda was clearly defined with self-determination as the cornerstone and the New Sudan as an optimal vision, the objectives of the liberation struggle in Darfur were less defined. Therefore, the liberation movements in Darfur were less focused, coherent, and clear in their strategic vision and negotiating capacity and approach. Given these constraints, some believe that they have achieved the optimum possible under the circumstances, while others believe that the DPA falls short of addressing the national question of which Darfur is a part.

The Comprehensive Peace Agreement (CPA) between the GOS and the SPLM/A was supposed to create a framework and lay down principles that would guide the resolution of the other regional conflicts in the North. It was supposed to lead toward the transformation of the country into a New Sudan, in which traditional discrimination on the bases of race, ethnicity, religion, culture, and gender would be eliminated. While the late John Garang de Mabior, leader of the SPLM/A, was seen as a staunch advocate of this national vision, his successor, Salva Kiir Mayardit, though echoing the call for a New Sudan, is believed to be more focused on promoting the unity of the South and carefully steering the implementation of the CPA

toward the right of the South to decide whether to remain in the
united Sudan or become an independent state.

Will the CPA, the DPA, the prospective agreement in the East, and
other potential regional peace agreements prove to be building
blocks in the process of creating the New Sudan or part of a shrewd
strategy of containment that does not challenge the status quo?
Only time will tell.

Meanwhile, *Darfur Diaries* offers good insight into how Darfurians feel about the current situation. It presents their vision for the
country they hope to help create and be proud citizens of. It is a
documentation of tragedy, resilience, aspiration, and determination to
make a difference. It is also an engaging, albeit painful reading, well
written, and even with the tragic surrounding, reveals some estheti-
cally pleasant moments, as Jen recalls:

> As the night grew darker, we watched the rise of a full moon
> and the array of stars. It was so beautiful, peaceful. I had a sense
> of complete freedom. It was difficult to reconcile those feelings
> with the fact that we were in Darfur, Sudan, the place of recent
> and ongoing atrocities perpetrated against millions of innocent
> people.

The essence and value of *Darfur Diaries* could be summarized in
the words of the Darfurian who said to the filming team, appealing
to the UN and the international community:

> You came over here to find the truth and to understand our
> sorrow. Please take our message to all the other nations . . . I
> don't have anything more to say. Please give our message to the
> international community and let us know if human beings are
> supposed to live under these conditions.

The authors of *Darfur Diaries* correctly feel that they have accomplished what the Darfurians asked of them, which was indeed their mission: putting a face on the situation in Darfur so that people would care enough to want to act. To give a voice to those who nobody was hearing. Adam summed it up, addressing his two colleagues, Aisha and Jen:

> Both of you and this process have been great. We are going to put something out there that will help mobilize opinion, and hopefully action. At least people won't be able to claim ignorance because of lack of access.

They have done their part very effectively. What is left is for people to see the film and read the book, and when they do, the suffering of the people of Darfur will come across clear in sight and loud in voice, calling out for help. Encouragingly, the world appears to be seeing, hearing and helping, but much more is needed to bring an end to this human tragedy and to help the Sudan find itself in this turbulent, painful, and destructive search for an all-embracing national identity.

Washington, D.C.
June 2006

FRANCIS MADING DENG served as Sudan's Ambassador to the United States, Canada, Scandinavian countries, and as Minister of State for Foreign Affairs. He currently is a Research Professor at the School of Advanced International Studies of Johns Hopkins University and is Director of the Sudan Peace Support Project in Washington, D.C. He has written or edited over thirty books in the fields of law, conflict resolution, international displacement, human rights, anthropology, folklore, history, and politics, and has also written two novels on the theme of the national crisis of identity in the Sudan.

Notes

1 Gabriel Meyer, *War and Faith in the Sudan*, William B. Eerdmans Publishing Company, Grand Rapids, Michigan/Cambridge, UK, 2005, p. 182.

2 Monsour Khalid, *The Government They Deserve: The Role of the Elite in Sudan's Political Economy*, (London: Kegan Paul International, 1996, p. 192 .

3 Ibid.

4 Francis Mading Deng, *Africans of Two Worlds: The Dinka in Afro Arab Sudan* (Yale University Press, 1978), p. 167.

5 Francis Mading Deng, *Dinka Cosmology* (London: Ithaca Press, 1980), pp. 122-28.

6 Francis M. Deng, *War of Visions: Conflict of Identities in the Sudan*, Washington, D.C., The Brookings Institution, 1995, p. 90

7 Gabriel Meyer, *War and Faith in the Sudan*, William B. Eerdmans Publishing Company, Grand Rapids, Michigan/Cambridge, UK, 2005, pp 175-76.

8 The British journalist, Julie Flint, one of the individuals who was most instrumental in drawing attention to Darfur, published this appeal in the Parliamentary Brief of July 2004.

introduction

by Aisha Bain

FALL 2003: I had started a master's program in International
Peace and Conflict Resolution and was interning at a small
Nongovernmental Organization (NGO) called the Center for the
Prevention of Genocide. Within two days the director had dropped
a folder on my desk with the word Darfur handwritten in black
marker on the tab. "We're getting some strange reports coming out
of the region. Figure out what's going on."

Right, I thought. First thing's first—where's Darfur?

After reading the file and doing some preliminary research, I discovered that refugees had begun spilling into Chad in February
2003—the first the world learned of any crisis in the neighboring
western state of Sudan. Yet, I hadn't heard anything about any
refugees or any problems along the Chad/Sudan border. All the focus
on Sudan had been on the long awaited North–South agreement to
end Africa's longest running civil war spanning two decades since
1983. Many world powers were hungrily anticipating an agreement, waiting for safe and full access to the country's oil reserves that
lay in the middle of the battleground for the last few decades. It
seemed like nothing could interfere with such a high-stakes process,
not even thousands of refugees marooned on the Chadian border in
the Sahara desert.

The Center's file also held reports of attacks, killings, razed villages, but nothing was confirmed. My research continued to uncover more alarming information—the government of Sudan had closed all the borders of Darfur (it is uncertain exactly when), expelled international presence from the entire region, and had instituted a media blackout. I contacted Medecins Sans Frontieres (Doctors Without Borders) and learned that their staff had been made to leave the country, and a few doctors tried to remain behind to help. They had received some terrifying reports—bombings, militia attacks, people internally displaced—but asked that we keep everything confidential for the safety of their doctors. I began calling other organizations and found a Christian group that had been operating in the area that gave similar reports before their staff had to flee. I began to track down Sudanese people in Washington, D.C., trying to find some way to contact people in Darfur and get firsthand reports.

THEN WE GOT an unexpected visit. Dr. Tigani Sissi, a Darfurian who had worked as a former local governor in his home district, had fled Sudan fearing for his life. He continued to get horrifying reports from his people on the ground and was trying to obtain support from the international community. In exile in England, he had traveled to the United States, certain that once people were simply made aware of what was happening they would help his people.

He and his three Darfurian colleagues described what was happening on the ground. Arab militias, called the Janjaweed, were razing villages all over Darfur. Attacks included aerial bombings, villages burning to the ground, militias killing civilians, people fleeing, government soldiers involved—he painted a picture of total chaos. "The government?" I asked. "The Sudanese government is involved?"

"Yes," he assured me. Not only had civilians reported seeing government soldiers and vehicles, but there was no way that the militias had access to planes and could carry out such a massive bombing campaign, he insisted. He explained that when President Omar Bashir came to power in a coup in 1989, he struck an alliance with certain tribal groupings and the military to promote an Islamic agenda. While this consolidated support for the government among some people in Sudan, the government remained unpopular with the majority of the population.

Darfur—an impoverished area with little development or infrastructure—was one of the regions that opposed the government. Having fought lengthy wars in other parts of the country to gain such control, the ruling party had turned its attention to Darfur. Their plan was to remove opposing populations by exploiting the region's tense tribal relations. Their support for Arab nomads in growing conflict with settled farming populations began with the Arab–Fur war of the late 1980s but grew into an all-out war after the Sudan Liberation Army's (SLA) attack on Fasher in April 2003.

I brought out a map. "Where exactly is this happening?"

He pointed to his region in the central-westernmost part of Darfur, "This is where I am from. This area is devastated," he declared.

"Where else?" I asked.

"We have reports coming from the north and south of Darfur as well, it is happening all over."

"Do you have names, places, villages, numbers of people—any facts I can use?"

"You can talk to all of my people on the ground," he offered.

I gathered all of his contacts and tried to arrange as many meetings as possible for him during his few days in the country. We called other NGOs, people in the State Department, and congressmen and senators—anyone we could think of to meet with Tigani so he could inform our leaders of what was happening. Only a few organizations agreed to meet with him. Everyone else was too busy.

AFTER MEETING WITH Tigani I began connecting with his contacts. I soon established an intricate reporting network. I was talking to civilians, to rebel fighters, to family members, to anyone I could get ahold of. I talked to a doctor in Darfur who said that his hospital was overflowing with burn victims, stab victims, gunshot victims, rape victims, people who had been left for dead. He said he couldn't handle the load and had nowhere to put new patients. I reached a relative of Tigani who said they were housing displaced victims and were in fear for their own lives. I talked to another man who said that people were coming to the town by the thousands, maybe tens of thousands, he couldn't be sure, but all of a sudden there were people everywhere he looked, all of them had horrible stories of their villages being destroyed and people dying. I asked everyone I talked to for facts and figures, anything and everything I could gather.

MY LIFE BECAME surreal—going to class by day, calling a war zone by night. My schoolwork fell behind, I started missing classes, sleeping less—there was no way to justify any other action in my mind. The Darfurians in D.C. had asked me for my help, the people I talked to in Darfur had asked me for my help, and I had given them my word as I sat in my comfortable apartment in Washington, D.C., while a world of hell was beamed into my room by satellite phone.

We sent press releases to the local, national, international, and United Nations news wires. We called all of our contacts in the House, the Senate, the State Department, various other embassies, and human rights organizations.

I hunted down the *New York Times*, the *Washington Post*, NBC, ABC, CNN, *The Herald*—their foreign correspondent desks, the correspondents in Africa, the list went on and on. I left messages, kept calling back, and gave them all the information I was receiving. I offered them all the contacts I had—the reporters could talk to people in Darfur themselves. I urged them to go to Chad and see the refugees, or to go into Darfur and told them I had contacts set up to help and take them in and around the region.

"Thank you so much for the information; we'll be in touch," I was told.

"We're unable to cover this at this time," they said.

"We'll have to look into this and we'll get back to you," they responded.

"I'll connect you to our news desk; just go ahead and leave a message there," they said nicely.

"We've got no one heading to that region at the moment," they apologized.

"We just did a story on Uganda," they told me.

"Well, if it's not already in the news, it must not be a big enough story," they said.

If it's not already in the news it must not be a big enough story. It was January, almost a full year since the refugees began pouring out of Darfur, and yet "another conflict" in Africa was just not about to make the news—there was Iraq, Afghanistan, election year, and too many other top pressing stories according to the media outlets.

FEBRUARY 2004: WE managed to organize a briefing on the Hill for the Senate on Darfur with the help of Human Rights Watch. But still no media bites. We pushed on.

APRIL 2004: WE were certain that the ten-year anniversary of the genocide in Rwanda would force the world to act, if not out of responsibility, then out of embarrassment. We organized a march in Washington, D.C., to end in front of the Sudanese embassy and invited NGOs, students, other marginalized communities, and activist groups. Over a hundred of us, mostly Darfurians, walked three miles in a candlelight vigil to the Sudanese embassy on Massachusetts Avenue, where people gave speeches and accounts of the victims, the crimes, and cries for action. The NGO—Center for the Prevention of Genocide—that I was working for closed shortly afterward due to lack of funding.

Though I no longer had a center to operate out of, I couldn't let it go. A friend, Adam Shapiro, at my university was also interested in the region and had begun reading the releases put out by human rights groups. I filled him in on what I knew. He went and did some of his own research, and a few days later he came back and said, "Aisha, I want to go."

Adam had filmed his first documentary in Baghdad the summer before. I told him it was a total mess inside Darfur: the borders closed, the fighting intense, and there was a media blackout. He looked at me and nodded, and matter-of-factly said, "Aisha, there's always a way in."

I knew that people had been crossing the border of Chad frequently since the conflict started. I smiled, excitement filling my voice. "You are absolutely right!" I agreed. "I will help. I've been talking to people all over, in Chad and in Sudan. I've got contacts with rebels and people who will help you get in, places to stay. I'll help you any way I can."

"You wanna come?" he asked ever-so-casually.

We smiled at each other, and it all made perfect sense; we were going to go shoot a documentary in Darfur.

WE MET WITH my Darfurian colleagues and started approaching funders. It was May; we wanted to leave as soon as possible because once the rains came, travel in Darfur would become nearly impossible. I had worked for an alternative investment management firm who donated money to good causes every year as a tax write-off. We approached the investment company, sold them on the idea, and were guaranteed full funding for the project. We were in. I stumbled through school finals.

Adam contacted his friend, Jen Marlowe, in Jerusalem to see if she wanted to come help us. She did. We knew the Sudanese government was denying anyone trying to get a visa into Darfur, never mind people trying to document their abuses, so we would forego that process and sneak across the border through Chad. We would travel with the rebels for safety and because we had no other way of getting around in Darfur. We would leave the second week of June.

I ANNOUNCED OUR project to the human rights and humanitarian organizations concerned with the issue to an overwhelmingly positive response and encouragement. Some offered whatever assistance they could, all asked for reports when we returned. After months and months, we were going to record what was actually happening and expose it out for the world to witness, to understand, and to stop it.

Then I received a phone message from the investment company. They had talked to an academic who had worked on Sudanese issues for years but had never been to Darfur, to verify what was happening there, to check whether our project was feasible. He told them it was not, and that even if we could successfully film, thousands of people would still die. They pulled the funding. It was two weeks before we were supposed to leave.

I called Adam and left him a message. I bought a bottle of champagne and drowned the world out for a night. The next morning—Adam and I canceled the plane reservations, and began raising money from scratch.

JUNE 2004: DARFUR finally hit the mainstream media, almost a year and a half after the international community had noticed thousands of refugees in Chad.

By October, Adam had raised just enough money from

humanitarians, philanthropists, investors from his previous film, friends, family, money out of our pockets, my school loans—anyone and everyone. The sum of $23,000 was just enough to get the three of us to Darfur and back; we counted on raising the rest once we had the footage.

While we were finalizing the logistics, I met a man named Kolude Doherty, the mission director for the United Nations High Commissioner for Refugees (UNHCR), based in Washington, D.C. I told him what we were going to do. He looked at me suspiciously and bombarded me with questions. By the end of the onslaught, he had agreed to help me anyway he could. He contacted his people in Chad, gave us the latest security briefings, sent us with a letter to make sure we were aided by UNHCR staff in Chad, and promised to be on-call in case we needed anything, or got into trouble or worse. We were ready.

BY OCTOBER, THERE had been four months of media coverage on Darfur, spurred by the visits to the region by U.N. Secretary-General Kofi Annan and Secretary of State Colin Powell. Yet the reports were still missing the full accounts that wouldn't come out until months later. The sheer brutality of the attacks in Darfur by the Sudanese government troops and their allied militias were revealed in the coinciding reports of the survivors. Their campaigns were as follows: mass murder, summary executions, partially skinning victims, burning children and adults alive, impaling babies, severe beatings, fatal beatings, torture, dragging victims on the ground by horses and camels by a noose around the neck, gouging eyes out, tying victims up in the harsh exposure of the desert sun, systematic rape campaigns, gang rapes, gang rapes in public, abduction and detainment for sexual slavery, forcible transfer of populations, and massive air bombardment campaigns.

However, by the fall the focus had only been on the wide-scale rape of the women, the worsening humanitarian conditions for the refugees and internally displaced in Darfur, and the simplistic explanation of indigenous black versus Arab tribes warring with each other. Sudanese government officials were constantly in the media denying any involvement in the conflict, and the dominant voices of internationals were the only ones reporting and loosely analyzing the conflict.

Our project had changed now that the situation was exposed; we had specific goals in mind for the film. We decided to concentrate on children, as they are among the most marginalized population in any conflict, often suffer the most, and can be the most ignored in conflict resolutions. We wanted to capture this conflict through their eyes, hear it through their voices, see how they were being affected, and how this information could help in the future. Second, we wanted to find out from the Darfurians themselves about the complexities of the conflict and present a fuller picture of what was happening. Third, we wanted to show the real lives of these people, and that they had had a thriving life, society, and culture that preceded their appearance on the world stage as victims and refugees. Lastly, we wanted to privilege their right to be heard, and to give voice to the Darfurians. What we captured was their strength, their courage, their resilience, their dignity, and their hope.

THE FILM IS what we set out to do in its truest form. This book portrays our journey along the way.

A Northern Darfurian village

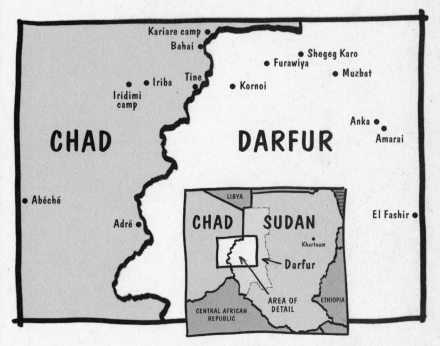

Map, drawn roughly to scale, of places visited or referenced in *Darfur Diaries*

darfur diaries

one

getting started

"THIS WILL HAVE TO BE A PRIORITY FOR THE
INTERNATIONAL COMMUNITY."

I **STOOD IN CHARLES** de Gaulle Airport in Paris, watching the passengers disembark, expecting Adam and Aisha to come through the door any minute. The Paris airport was our rendezvous point; in a few hours we would continue to N'djamena, the capital of Chad, then onto the refugee camps in eastern Chad, and ultimately into Darfur.

I was thrilled to have actually made it this far. Adam and I had been talking about the Darfur film for several months, but funding for the project was so precarious, I had resigned myself to not accompanying him and Aisha. Only two weeks before, Adam called me on my cell phone in Jerusalem.

"Some more funding came in. FedEx me your passport right away if you still want to come."

Of course I wanted to come. Once Adam had alerted me to what was happening in Darfur, I knew that I had to do something. Making a documentary seemed like a good, concrete place to start. I wasn't going to be intimidated by the fact that I had never done anything remotely similar to making a film.

Adam and Aisha finally showed up. Adam greeted me with a huge hug. "Jen, this is Aisha."

Aisha and I were complete strangers. Adam was my former colleague and close friend from the conflict resolution work we had done in Jerusalem, and he and Aisha were both pursuing graduate studies and leading student activism efforts at American University. It's possible that he liked the idea of going to Darfur with Aisha and me just for the visual humor. Aisha is six feet two inches tall. Measuring in at barely five feet myself, we must have looked quite comic together.

We had a few hours before our flight, enough time to sit at the airport café and get down the headlines. By the time we finished our M&Ms and Diet Cokes, I knew that Aisha's roots in activism started when, as a high school athlete herself, she volunteered with the Special Olympics. After university, she lived in Madagascar as a Peace Corps volunteer and had spent the past summer investigating child trafficking in Southeast Asia. I gave her my basic information as well, of conflict resolution work with Israeli, Palestinian, Cypriot, Indian, Pakistani, and Afghan youth, and of the theater education company I had been building before that in Seattle.

THE AIR FRANCE flight to N'djamena was four hours long. I used the time to review my notes about the history of Sudan and Darfur, trying to commit the information to the hard drive of my brain. *"Sudan, the largest country in Africa; population over forty million. Inhabited by dozens of tribal groups. About forty percent speak Arabic as their first language, and sixty percent speak indigenous languages, though Arabic is the 'lingua franca' in Sudan. Seventy percent are Muslim, twenty-five percent indigenous religions, five percent Christian. The non-Muslims live mostly in southern Sudan and Khartoum."*

I attempted to digest these bite-sized chunks of information about ethnicity and identity, knowing it was more nuanced and complex than my notes expressed. I plunged back into my notebook going over some important dates in Sudanese history, realizing I was only scratching the surface here, as well.

"1898—Britain conquered and colonized Sudan. Administered it in cooperation with Egypt. Darfur remained an independent Sultanate.

1916—Darfur conquered by Anglo-Egyptian forces, joining it with the rest of Sudan.

1956—Sudan gained independence from Britain.

North–South civil war broke out in 1955 over Islamization, Arabization, and control of resources. Ended in a fragile peace in 1973.

1983—War erupted again, when the Arab-dominated government in Khartoum tried to impose Islamic law on the non-Muslim South. John Garang started the southern rebel Sudan People's Liberation Army (SPLA). More than two and a half million southern Sudanese died, mainly from war-induced famine and disease, and at least twice as many fled their homes.

2002—Serious peace talks began, but only between the SPLA and the government; didn't include other marginalized groups in Sudan."

I turned my attention to my printouts about Darfur specifically.

"Darfur, western region of Sudan; population over six million people. Home to various 'African' tribes such as Fur, Zaghawa, Masalit, Berti, and many 'Arab' tribes, such as Riziegat and Baqqara. Almost all Muslim. Livliehood: farming for some tribes, cattle-raising for others, or a mixture of both."

As I pored over the statistics about the crisis and descriptions of the Janjaweed Arab militias on horse and camelback whom the articles I had printed painted as the culprits, numbers began floating in my head: two hundred thousand in refugee camps in Chad; 1.4 million displaced inside Darfur, or was it 1.6?; seventy thousand killed, as the media was then reporting (grossly underestimating, we later found out). I knew our experience on the ground would trump any preparation I could possibly do.

WE LANDED IN N'djamena at night. I grabbed the red Air France pillow and blanket and stuffed them under my arm.

"What do you want them for?" Adam asked.

"Could make it more comfortable, sleeping on the ground." Adam raised his eyebrow. I grinned.

"Hey, I'll give them back when we're on our way out!"

Adam laughed. "Now *that* I'd like to film."

The airport was bare, dusty, hot, and humid. We retrieved our backpacks and camera bags from the slow winding conveyor belts, and stepped into the musty night of N'djamena. Men in white turbans and *galabiyas* (traditional men's robes) squatted on the curb outside the airport doors, many of them jumping to their feet as soon as they saw foreigners emerging.

"Taxi? You need taxi?"

We saw a Novotel Hotel van. Aisha greeted the driver in French, and we climbed in.

"Did you study French in school, or do you know it from your time in Madagascar?" I asked Aisha as the van negotiated the pothole-riddled road, avoiding the deep gutters on either side.

"Actually it's my first language," she answered. "My mother is from Haiti. But I was a stubborn child and lost a lot of it."

It was late by the time we checked into our room, but none of us was tired. Adam, who had recently finished work on a documentary shot in Baghdad, had the clearest idea of what we needed to accomplish before heading to eastern Chad to film in the Darfurian refugee camps. Following his lead, we drew up a list of the prep work. We hoped to get it all accomplished the next day, Thursday, and to fly east on Friday.

FREE BREAKFAST WAS part of the deal at the Novotel.

"Gotta feed the machine," Aisha remarked as she and I filled up on crepes and sweet, sticky fruit juice, while Adam drank coffee. The hotel functioned as a kind of base camp for the United Nations (U.N.) staff, Nongovernmental Organizations (NGOs), and the few journalists who came to report on the Darfurian refugees. The United Nations High Commission for Refugees (UNHCR) had a table in the lobby, right underneath the hotel's portrait of Chadian President Idris Deby, covered with maps of the eleven refugee camps in eastern Chad, the numbers of refugees in each camp, and a time-line focusing on U.N. humanitarian intervention in the crisis.

WE TRIED TO absorb as much of N'djamena as possible as we ran our errands. Though the sky was clear, the city took on the tan color of

the dust that blanketed everything. The main street was lined with
run-down, dingy shops selling random goods from soda to tires.
There were billboards advertising Chad's only discotheque/casino
and *"Castel, the Queen of Beers."* Between storefronts, we caught
glimpses of a murky river that ran lazily behind the streets, and
women dotted along its bank washing clothes.

The first stops of the day were exchanging currency and pur-
chasing a Thuraya brand satellite phone. I had imagined a satphone
to be a large, bulky, high tech contraption, but in reality it looked like
an oversized, black cell phone from a decade ago. Adam negotiated
a deal with the salesman; if we returned the phone at the end of our
trip, we would get back one thousand dollars of the fifteen hundred
we paid.

NEXT WAS THE UNHCR headquarters. We were equipped with a
letter from Kolude, the UNHCR regional head in Washington,
D.C., asking that the United Nations help us in every way possible.
It was a two-day drive from N'djamena to eastern Chad. Kolude had
told us that we would be able to hitch a ride with the daily UNHCR
and World Food Program (WFP) flights that fly from N'djamena to
Abéché, the town that served as the base camp for the U.N. and
NGO field operations in eastern Chad.

We sat in the outer office of the UNHCR building, waiting to
talk to Ana Liria-Franch, head of the mission and a friend of Kolude.
As we waited, we took down the names and numbers of each others' families, in case something untoward happened.

"If you do end up calling my family for any reason," I told them,
"you probably should be aware that they don't exactly know I'm here."

"Are you kidding me? Where do they think you are?" Adam
looked at me incredulously.

"I don't know. In Jerusalem, I guess. No need for them to worry,"

I answered. Gauging by their reaction when I had first gone to Afghanistan and during times of extreme violence in Palestine and Israel, I was pretty sure my family wouldn't take the news of my traveling to Darfur very calmly. I thought it would be simpler to deal with the fallout after having gone and returned safely.

Her mother, Aisha told us, was horrified and angry when she had first learned about the trip. She had tried for months to persuade Aisha not to go. Aisha was the only child of a single mother; they were each other's only family. The night before the trip, her mother saw a TV program featuring the horror in Rwanda that had taken place ten years earlier. She called Aisha in tears to tell her that she was so proud of what she was doing and glad that somebody was going to try and tell this story.

"How did your family react?" Aisha asked Adam.

Adam shrugged. "They were more worried when I was filming in Baghdad last year. I think it helped that my mom went to Palestine this summer. She got a feel for what it's like to confront certain kinds of situations. It's different of course, but some of it is transferable."

Ana finally appeared. She was in her late forties or early fifties, regal, chipper, and clearly European. She welcomed us briskly in English. "Hello, hello, how can I help you?"

We introduced ourselves and Aisha handed her the letter that Kolude had given us. "Oh, Kolude sent you? Please, come right in!" She ushered us into her large, comfortable office and offered us seats. "Now, what can I do for you?"

Aisha explained that we chiefly needed logistical help getting from N'djamena to Abéché, and from Abéché to the refugee camps.

Ana promised us that the public information officer, Catherine-Lune Grayson, the liaison for journalists, would be helpful. A petite French-Canadian woman who spoke perfect English, Catherine-Lune briefed us on what was happening at the different refugee camps, who to talk to when we arrived in Abéché, and what challenges

UNHCR faced in their mission. Iridimi camp, close to Iriba, had only a few weeks of water supply remaining and was plummeting to a water crisis for its eighteen thousand residents. Oure Cassoni camp, outside Bahai, was too close to the border with Sudan, and the twenty-three thousand refugees seeking shelter there might need to be moved. I frantically tried to locate each camp and town Catherine-Lune mentioned on the U.N. maps we had picked up at the hotel.

"We just finished settling the last refugees from the border area into camps this week, so that's not something you will be able to witness. But, Bredjing camp is overcrowded; we're going to be trucking refugees who are there to Farchana camp over the next few weeks," she said encouragingly. "That might be interesting for you to film."

Adam thanked her for the tip. "So . . . can we get on a U.N. flight to Abéché tomorrow, then?"

"Tomorrow?" Catherine-Lune consulted a flight mandate attached to her clipboard. She shook her head. "That won't be possible. Both the UNHCR and the WFP flights tomorrow are completely full. There may be room on Saturday's WFP flight, but it's doubtful. No flights on Sunday, so, most likely, the earliest we're looking at is Monday. You already have your internal travel and filming permits, I assume?"

We stared at her blankly. "Internal travel and filming permits?" Aisha questioned.

"You won't be able to get to Abéché without them, much less be allowed to film."

"The Chadian embassy in D.C. assured us that we didn't need any other documentation . . ." Adam began to protest, but Catherine-Lune cut him off.

"Things change very quickly around here. It's a new regulation, but it is being enforced."

"So, can we take care of that now?" I asked hopefully.

Catherine-Lune smiled indulgently at our naïveté. "We can take you to the Chadian Ministry of Interior now. However, it's Thursday afternoon already, and we're in the middle of the Muslim holy month of Ramadan. Things shut down early around here on Ramadan, since everyone is home by sundown to break the fast with their families. There's not a chance they're going to issue the travel permits today and government offices are closed on Friday and Saturday. If you're lucky, you'll get the permit Sunday or Monday, but it's possible that it could take more than a week."

"We have just under a month for the entire trip. There's no way we can spend a week in N'djamena ..." Adam started to explain, but Catherine-Lune cut him off again.

"We'll do what we can to help you expedite this," she said, not unkindly. "But it's really out of our hands." She swung her chair around to her computer keyboard. "Now ... what's the spelling of your names and your passport numbers? We'll send you with a letter from UNHCR asking them to grant your request as quickly as possible. The filming permits shouldn't be a problem. Just leave me with two passport photos each, but make sure you take two more with you to the Ministry of Interior for the internal travel permit."

"Passport photos?" Aisha echoed weakly.

"You don't have passport photos with you? You'll need them before you go to the Ministry. We can take you to a photo shop just down the street, but it's going to mean you'll get to the Ministry even later. It's not going to help your chances with the permit."

Catherine-Lune sent us off with Mustafa, an N'djamena local working for UNHCR. He was more than willing to help us, if a bit baffled by our mission. We emerged from the photo shop ten minutes later and continued to the Ministry of Interior.

A woman at the front desk directed us to a dimly lit room with faded white paint. Shortly afterward, a man entered, examined our letter from UNHCR, collected our passports, and instructed us to sit in the plastic chairs lined up against the wall. Another gentleman, asserting himself as quite important, assumed his place in a wooden chair behind his metal desk and smiled at us, asking a slew of questions. Was he interviewing us for our credentials or just trying to chat? We weren't sure. Aisha tried her best to charm him in French, while Adam spoke with him in near-fluent Arabic. In addition to tribal languages, both French and Arabic were heavily used languages in Chad. French was due to the French occupation of Chad until 1960 (that Paris was the only European city with a direct flight to N'djamena hadn't escaped my attention). Arabic, because Chad was predominantly Muslim and neighbored Arabic-speaking countries Libya and Sudan. Having studied French until the end of high school and lived in Jerusalem for four years, I should have been proficient in both languages. I wasn't. I could understand quite a bit, but had trouble getting out a decipherable sentence. I was determined to try, however.

The administrator was talking to Adam about where he had worked and traveled, and inquired the same of Aisha and me. I gave it my best shot in Arabic. Adam gave me a strange look. Our host excused himself and left the room.

"Why did you tell him that you lived in Nazareth?" Adam asked.

"Is that what I said? I meant to say I had traveled to Egypt . . ."

"Don't worry—by the end of the trip we'll get you speaking Arabic fluently."

Our host returned minutes later. "We have your travel permits, but our copy machine is broken and we need to make copies. Your friend from UNHCR has gone back to his office to make the copies there, and when he returns you can take your permits."

Half an hour later, we were handing our passport photos to Catherine-Lune who was also amazed at our good fortune.

"The filming permits we can get for you tomorrow morning; those take just a matter of minutes to procure. I don't know how you convinced them to give you the internal travel permits right away."

Truth be told, neither did we.

"Still," Catherine-Lune continued, "I won't know about Saturday's flight until tomorrow, but you should plan on flying Monday."

We were not planning to fly on Monday. If seats were not available on Saturday's flight, our backup plan was to hire a driver to take us. If we left on Friday morning, we could be in Abéché by sundown Saturday.

"And make sure it is before dark," Catherine-Lune warned us when we ran this possibility by her. "Banditry is rampant between here and Abéché. Not to mention that there aren't really proper roads. It's difficult enough to drive by day. Nobody drives at night."

SUNDOWN WAS QUICKLY approaching. We had one more task to accomplish before everyone would be eating their *iftar* meal, breaking the day's Ramadan fast. This one didn't require running around to different offices; it only required using the newly purchased Thuraya satellite phone.

Aisha dialed the number that Omer Ismail, our main Darfurian contact in D.C., had given to her. "Hello? Ibrahim? This is Aisha."

"Hello!" I could hear Ibrahim bellow cheerfully from the other end of the satellite connection. "Aisha, Adam, Jen, you are here? I was expecting you months ago!" Ibrahim was expecting us months ago? Hadn't Omer been in touch with him in the meantime?

Ibrahim, though young, was a respected and relatively high-level member of the SLA, the Sudan Liberation Army, the largest of the rebel movements in Darfur resisting the Sudanese government. Omer had arranged for Ibrahim to meet us in Chad, take us across the border, and be our guide inside Darfur. We would spend our time in Darfur behind the rebel lines. It was the only way to get in and to get around.

"Yes, hello, Ibrahim, we arrived. Sorry about the delay, we had a problem with our funding. Are you in N'djamena?"

"N'djamena? No. I am in Abuja, Nigeria. I'm part of the negotiations."

Negotiations had begun again recently between the government of Sudan and the two main rebel groups, the SLA and JEM (the Justice and Equality Movement).

"How long will you be in N'djamena? Maybe I can meet you there in six or seven days?"

"Actually, either tomorrow or Saturday we're leaving for Abéché. We're going to spend some time in the refugee camps and then cross with you into Darfur, we hope?"

"Don't worry, I'll organize everything for you! Call me tomorrow, everything will be arranged!"

THAT NIGHT AT the hotel, Adam gave us our first tutorial on how to operate the camera: where to plug in the wireless microphone device, what controls to turn on for the mic to work, how to focus and zoom.

I manned the camera for practice, filming a fake interview with Adam. He used the opportunity to mock me:

"To Jen's family: I'm really sorry to have to tell you this, but we left Jen in Darfur. It wasn't our fault! She insisted on staying. You see . . ." Adam paused for dramatic effect. "She fell in love with someone from the Dinka tribe. And, as you surely know, the Dinka tribe is known for being incredibly tall. So the bad news is that your daughter is staying in Darfur. The good news is, despite your daughter's stature, your grandkids will have a shot at the NBA!"

Adam ducked as I threw the little red Air France pillow at him.

"There are Dinka in Darfur? I thought the Dinka tribe was from the south of Sudan?" I asked.

Aisha looked up from her book. "Yes, a small number migrated to the south of Darfur, after years of persecution and the North–South civil war. And there are rumors that some came to help fight in Darfur now that there's peace negotiations taking place between the government and the SPLA."

"Okay, let me show you how to use the small camera," Adam continued, tossing the Air France pillow back to me. "Where is it now?" He searched the room. "It should be in the tripod bag. Aisha, did I give it to you to carry?"

"No, sure didn't."

He slapped himself on the forehead. "I must have left it at the airport. I can't believe I did that."

There was no way we would be able to get the bag back at this time of night–it was well after midnight. We went to sleep, hoping that the bag would be there when we went to collect it. Not only did we need the second camera, but it would be difficult to gather usable testimonies and interviews without a steady tripod on which to place the camera.

OUR LUCK CONTINUED to hold. The bag was waiting for us at the airport in the morning, tripod and small camcorder still inside. A short explanation to the baggage folks at the airport and a quick laugh got us on our way. We hurried to the UNHCR compound to find Catherine-Lune at her desk, right where we had left her the evening before, talking to a photojournalist who introduced himself to us as Jehad.

"We've got your filming permits right here," Catherine-Lune informed us, pointing to a table in the corner of the office where our papers were stacked. And she had more good news. There was room for us on Saturday's WFP flight, with fifteen kilos of luggage each.

"WFP is really strict about their weight limit," Catherine-Lune warned us. "They will weigh your luggage and if it's one kilo over, you'll have to leave something behind."

It wasn't our personal belongings that we were worried about. It was the fact that our filming equipment took up most of the weight allotment.

Catherine-Lune and Jehad gave us some advice: where we could stay in Abéché, how to get on other UNHCR flights to go further into eastern Chad, whom to call on to give us good background scoops on what was happening in the camps. More than anyone else we had spoken to, Jehad knew what we would need and where to get it. He had been traveling with the SLA for twelve days and had just returned to N'djamena. He clearly had not shaved or washed in several days and he had something of a wild look in his eye. He continually tapped his fingers against his denim-clad thigh as he spoke.

"You'll want a tent," he told us firmly. "The ground is disgusting— animal shit all over the place, scorpions and mosquitoes. And camel spiders! You could probably sleep in the back of the truck you'll be riding on. We did that a few nights, but if you can get your hands on a tent, I highly advise it."

He had other advice—what we could expect in terms of food, what to bring with us. "Not much fighting going on in the north of Darfur," he told us. "The rebels in the north don't do much of anything but ride around. The SLA sent all the good fighters to the south."

"Where were you?" we asked him.

"We started in the north, but we worked our way down south. Saw some action there." His fingers continued to tap his thighs. He didn't get specific about exactly what he saw.

BACK AT THE hotel, we spent at least an hour going through every item in our packs in an effort to shed kilos: half our electrolyte packets to prevent dehydration, most of our reading material, extra flashlight batteries . . . if it wasn't essential, we would leave it at the hotel.

My cell phone from Jerusalem rang as I was trying to decide which two T-shirts I would take. I was startled. I hadn't realized that I could get reception here.

"Hello?"

It was my sister, calling from Connecticut. I stepped outside onto the room's balcony.

"So, what are you doing this weekend?" she asked.

"Uh, you know, traveling around." That was true enough, I justified to myself as I gazed over the well-manicured lawn and rose garden of the hotel. After all, we would be boarding a U.N. flight to Abéché in the morning.

"Where to?"

I felt backed into a corner. Either I had to tell a direct lie, which I had avoided doing so far, or I had to tell her where I was, something I wasn't eager to do. I took a deep breath.

"Um, Melissa, I'm not exactly in Israel and Palestine at the moment."

"Where are you?"

"I'm in N'djamena."

"Oh." There was a pause. "Where's that?"

"It's the capital of Chad."

"Oh." Another pause. "And Chad is . . . ?"

"In Africa."

"What are you doing there?"

"I'm working on a film project about Darfur," I said in a half-mumble.

"What's Darfur?" I was relieved. My sister, like the vast majority of Americans, including myself until four months ago, hadn't heard of Darfur. She didn't know enough to be concerned. "Wait a minute . . ." she said, a realization slowly dawning on her. "You must be doing something dangerous. Otherwise, why wouldn't you have told me you were going?" I didn't have a good response to offer her. Instead, I assured her not to worry and that I would contact her if I could during the course of the trip. She hung up, sounding unconvinced.

THE WFP PLANE was a tiny nine-seater, piloted by Airserv, a non-profit organization that provides air support services to humanitarian agencies working in remote areas. After a two-hour bumpy flight, the plane began its descent.

The airport in Abéché was only an asphalt landing strip that looked like a parking lot and a one-room building, next to a military base. A handful of folks were waiting on the tarmac to greet the flight. Two men stepped forward as we climbed down the folding metal staircase.

"Aisha, Adam, Jen? I am Muhammad Suleiman, and this is my friend. Omer called me from D.C. and asked me to meet you. I am prepared to help you in anyway I can." We all shook hands.

"You're from Darfur?" Aisha asked.

"Yes. But we have been in Abéché for more than a year now. We can assist you with anything you need," he replied in more than passable English.

His friend pointed to the room. "You go there to register. Do you have all your paperwork in order?" It was a good thing we did. The WFP in N'djamena hadn't looked at anything other than our passports, but the Chadian authorities checked it all, examining and stamping each piece of paper.

We got our first view of Abéché riding with the other passengers to the UNICEF office in the back of a U.N. pickup truck. Abéché was a hot, dry, dusty desert. Rising out of the sand were the occasional building and a few structures clustered together to form some kind of market. The NGO community added dramatically to the size of the town. A large pickup truck rumbled past us, filled with Chadian soldiers armed to the teeth.

Catherine-Lune had mentioned that we might be able to sleep at the UNICEF office. We inquired about that possibility after being introduced to Patrice Pagé, the head of the UNICEF mission in eastern Chad. Patrice was friendly, but clear: there was no place to stay there. A French-Canadian man, who introduced himself as Gaetan Duhamel, overheard the conversation. "You might want to try the Africare guest house," he suggested. He worked for CARE International in Abéché, overseeing the community service programs in the camps in eastern Chad. He was very willing to grant us an interview later that afternoon at the CARE compound. "Unless I'm taking a nap," he warned us. "I've got malaria—just got back from seeing a doctor in N'djamena."

Good thing I had brought plenty of malaria pills from Jerusalem. Adam and Aisha had taken care of nearly every other detail for the trip. My one responsibility had been medication.

THE GUARD AT the Africare guesthouse swung open the door of the gated complex. The guesthouse had the added advantage of being inhabited by a baby ibex, a gazelle-like creature, named Bambi. Bambi followed us from the gate to our rooms. The furnishings were scarce and beat-up, but quite adequate. Curious, I flipped a light switch. Nothing. The generator must not be on. I checked out the bathroom. There was running water, a nice luxury we hadn't expected.

We sat down with Muhammad Suleiman and his friend and pulled out our maps of Darfur. "So how long does it take to get from Kornoi to El Fashir?" Adam asked Muhammad Suleiman who was sitting on my right, while Aisha simultaneously asked the same question to his friend, sitting on my left. El Fashir is the capital of North Darfur state; Kornoi is a mid-sized village nearby.

"Four hours," Muhammad Suleiman answered Adam, while Aisha was told, "Two days."

I heard both responses, as if in stereo. "Which is it? Four hours or two days?"

Accurate estimates were hard to come by. Not having been inside Darfur for over a year, Muhammad Suleiman didn't know which roads were open, where the rebels had access, or what areas were depopulated.

"So, when we want to cross from Chad into Darfur, where do we go?" We consulted the map again. "It looks like the crossing at Adré is closest to Abéché. We can go there and maybe head north?"

"Do you have a visa to be in the government-held areas?" Muhammad Suleiman asked.

"No," we answered, explaining that even if we had been able to procure a visa, we didn't want to place the civilians in the government-run IDP (internally displaced persons) camps at risk. A U.S. congressional delegation had recently returned from such an investigative trip, obtaining all the proper permits and a government-provided "translator." The people they had spoken to in the camps were later detained and beaten.

"In that case, it is not good for you to cross at Adré. It is being watched." Muhammad Suleiman told us. He pointed on our map to a town much further north. "Here, Bahai, it's the best place to cross. No one is watching there."

We hammered out a rough plan to simultaneously make our way east toward the border and the refugee camps and further north toward Bahai, the crossing point into Darfur. We headed to the UNHCR compound to arrange our flights.

THE COMPOUND WAS a large, whitewashed structure with shady porches. Large, laminated maps of eastern Chad and photo displays including aerial shots of several camps hung on the walls of the screened-in dining area. I stared at them, trying to absorb the images of desolation and desperation they were portraying. We would be there soon.

The office arranging the flights was a one-room affair with charts and lists tacked to the wall and an assortment of walkie-talkies and Thuraya satellite phones charging off generator-powered electricity. A young, energetic French-Canadian named Benoit was in charge. He had come to Abéché to follow his girlfriend who was based here with an NGO. He had landed himself employment coordinating the U.N. flights in Chad. We put in our request to fly Monday morning to Iriba. Iriba was further east and north of Abéché and close to three of the large refugee camps, where we hoped to film for a few days before continuing on another flight to Bahai. Benoit wouldn't be able to confirm if there was room on the flight until the next day; three people were a lot to accommodate on a nine-seat plane.

WE HEADED TO the CARE office and Gaetan. "I'm not feeling great," he told us. "But I think we can go ahead with the interview." Gaetan seemed a bit nervous as he led us to a shady pagoda. "If I say anything stupid, don't use it. And I look terrible!"

We assured him that he looked fine, though we had no means to gauge whether he was more pale or gaunt than usual. We clipped the wireless microphone to his shirt, set up the tripod, and snapped the camera on, a routine we would repeat dozens of times over the next few weeks.

"Okay," said Adam, winking at Gaetan to help him to feel relaxed and comfortable. "Ready to be a movie star?"

Gaetan grinned and we began our first interview. He spoke about his role as a community service provider.

"Good community service extends to building community links again, reunification of families, as well as creating a sense of villages within the camp," he explained to us. "The challenge is enormous for the operation. There is no facility where we work, it's a plain field. There is nothing like a camp. It's like you start life anew. The large number of people coming in every day perpetuated the instability for the people living in the camp. The staff in the camps have only been able to attend to the basic needs of the people. They haven't had time to devote to more elaborate community service, like putting schools together or having social encounters, or time to play; so this has been very rare."

"Is there any psychological help for the children available or special care for rape victims?" Aisha asked, while Adam operated the lead camera and I filmed Gaetan's face from different angles with the smaller camera.

"We assessed the fact that there were children with special needs who require more protection. And there are women as well who need particular attention because of the question you raised about what happened in Darfur. For them, we are just now building a safety zone where they can participate in a community garden, take part in community meetings, learn a life skill, or a little vocational work, like tailoring. This engages a recovery process where these children and women can rely on their own capacity to adapt.

"The population of the camps is eighty percent female, either young girls or women. That leaves many women as the head of a household with a large number of children. She has to think about security of the family, in terms of food, health, living in this little tent with neighbors. The mother has very few resources to either cook or get water; water is not easily accessible. This is on top of having lost all her personal belongings, and not knowing if her husband was killed. It is very disruptive. Most of the women really need psychological and social support. Most of the time, the children are left to themselves. For example, the toilet is quite a distance from the tent. The children have to make their way to the toilet, so the mother cannot care for these children."

"What has been the psychological impact of the trauma and violence?" Aisha asked.

"As soon as an injustice or inequality appears in the camp, it sparks a fire. Any imbalance can bring out a lot of repressed feeling: anger, dissatisfaction, frustration, and grief. People start to fight with wood sticks over little incidents sometimes, and they hurt themselves for something that could be settled otherwise. It takes very little to reveal the hurt they've been through.

"The children are in the passive mode. It's like they know their parents are very sensitive to any irregular move. They know they have to be quiet. They obey by the finger; I don't know how to say it better. If there's fifty children coming at you, and just one adult says to them, 'Okay, go away,' they all disperse like a flock of birds. Because of how much the adults have suffered, they impose on the children a kind of silent and passive 'wait and see' future instead of being nurtured to develop skills or given opportunity to participate in the house life. The children need to play, to have recreational time built in a regular schedule. Every day of the week they need four, five hours together to play in a safe area with games. The priority is somewhere else for now, but I think that's what they're lacking."

WE WENT OUT to dinner that night with Muhammad Suleiman and his friend to a local Chadian joint. Muhammad Suleiman painted a pretty grim picture of Abéché. "Before the humanitarian agencies came, there was nothing here. Once, they tried to open a university in Abéché, but they couldn't find enough educated people in all the area to be professors."

His friend told us more about Idris Deby, the president of Chad. Deby was from the Bahai area, and of the Zaghawa tribe, which is also one of the largest tribes in Darfur. Tribal affiliations cut across the border between Darfur and Chad. Darfur, in fact, could have just as likely become the eastern province of Chad instead of the western region of Sudan. Another example, I thought, of how colonial powers carved up nations without taking into account the demographics of the population. Muhammad Suleiman told us that to become a Chadian citizen, one only needed to speak Zaghawa.

"Really?" Adam asked, a gleam in his eye. "You mean, if I learned fluent Zaghawa, I could get a Chadian passport?"

"Well . . . I'm not so sure about that," he backpeddled.

It was way too early to go to sleep. We lounged on the dilapidated sofa and armchairs in the Africare Guesthouse.

"The good thing about bringing Jen along," Adam said to Aisha, "is that she's a built-in entertainment system. She can quote word for word any movie you want."

"Really?" Aisha turned to me with a look of both amazement and expectation.

"Well, not any movie," I said, modestly. "Actually, just *The Breakfast Club.*"

"Well, show us, woman!"

I found myself acting out Molly Ringwald and Judd Nelson at the Africare Guesthouse in Abéché, Chad. The absurdity of it only enhanced the moment. We discovered that Aisha did a mean Eddie Murphy imitation, and we dove into old *Saturday Night Live* sketches and next, 80s sitcom theme songs, until we stumped ourselves with the collective inability to recall the theme song to *Who's the Boss?* We took our memory loss as a signal that it was finally late enough to go to sleep.

AS WE WALKED the next morning to the UNHCR compound, small children ran after us with arms outstretched and palms held up, shouting *"Cadeaux! Cadeaux!"* (Gifts!) Over breakfast we became engaged in a conversation with Mathijs le Rutte, the senior protection officer for UNHCR in eastern Chad. Mathijs's main concern initially had been trying to move refugees away from the insecure border area where cross-border raids on the refugees from Janjaweed had frequently occurred. His next concern was the continued security of the refugees among the host Chadian populations.

"At first, when the refugees came, they were assisted tremendously by the local population who shared what they had. When they moved to the refugee camps, the comprehension of the refugee situation by the local population was quite good. What we face today is not so much ethnic problems, but more a fight over resources. It's a very inhospitable region and has a long history of struggle over resources. There's very little water and firewood, the harvest has been really bad because of a short rainy season, and obviously the local population feels that its resources are being used up by refugees. This is one of the major security concerns."

What Mathijs was describing certainly matched information we had gathered about one source of tension in Darfur. Due to drought, the rate of desertification was increasing in Darfur at an alarming rate. Nomadic herders traditionally moved their animals through farmers' lands, grazing their cattle and fertilizing the land in exchange. What used to be a mutually beneficial arrangement was now a flashpoint for conflict, as the amount of arable land shrank. Mathijs's concerns suggested the problem was in Chad as well. The resources in Chad are so meager, he went on to tell us, that local Chadians had been coming to the camps demanding aid. It's quite common in refugee situations for locals to pose as refugees and get registered to receive aid, but here they are so desperate they don't even pretend.

He shared his concern that the competition over scarce resources could erupt into violence between the refugees and the host population, and then, with barely a pause to breathe, described the next pressing issue he was trying to address.

"A big worry from the very beginning has been our fear of recruitment of child soldiers. It's always hard to identify whether that's actually happening in the camps. It would occur under the cover of darkness, in secrecy. So far, we haven't had any confirmation of militarization of the camps, but it is always a concern."

I could understand why Mathijs was worried. Statistics about child soldiers were startling; three-hundred thousand children were estimated to be involved in armed conflict worldwide, one-third of these in Africa. I was aware that the SPLA, in southern Sudan, had trained and armed children. Abduction of children forced to perform horrific acts or serve as sex slaves was a regular tactic employed by the brutal Lord's Rebel Army (LRA) in Northern Uganda; thirty-thousand children were thought to have been kidnapped by the LRA. Members of the LRA often took shelter in southern Sudan, and were reportedly backed by the Sudanese government.

Mathijs also addressed the question of when the refugees would be able to return home. "Yes, villages have been burned and wells have been destroyed, but with a bit of goodwill that can be repaired. Security is the biggest obstacle for return. How long that's going to take is very hard to say. It's going to require a different attitude from the government. It entails a lot more dedication to securing the area. We're dealing with a highly traumatized population that has suffered violations from expulsion to much worse. I say traumatized, although I must also say that the population in general is extremely resilient. If you look at how people left and the kinds of crimes committed against them as a community, it will take a lot for them to feel confident enough to return. Usually the refugees themselves know when it's time. UNHCR doesn't have to tell them."

He described, as well, the rape of young girls, their subsequent pregnancies, and the rejection that they often face at the hands of their families. "It is important that these issues are dealt with quickly, but also true to the traditional way that it's handled in the community itself. It's not up to us to impose our Westernized ways of addressing these types of trauma."

Mathijs had been stationed in Abéché for six months, and he would be leaving in a few days for a new post. There seemed to be a high rate of turnover among the aid workers. I wondered how that affected the stability of the services provided.

Anette Haug had arrived in Abéché only a few weeks earlier to assume her post as the Education Officer for UNHCR in Abéché. Sitting erect in a metal chair on the porch of the UNHCR compound, with bright sparkling eyes behind round spectacles, Anette spoke with great enthusiasm about how the schools in the camps got off the ground.

"The refugees themselves started it. That's amazing to know. They started in the beginning, from scratch, to set up classes. They gathered all the children and they registered themselves as teachers. They didn't have any tents, but they began by having the children sit on the bare sand. It demonstrates the eagerness for children to learn, a sign that they feel that education is one of the most important things to achieve for their children and for themselves. We are supporting what they have started. But they are now waiting for us to come forward and really help them out. So if we are not responding, there might be a backlash, because they are really expecting and waiting."

I wondered what she meant by a backlash, but before I could ask, she had already continued.

"It's not just about the right to education; it's also protection for the children, having them in a safe place. And then they are not doing other things that we don't like children to do, so . . ." She lowered her glasses for a moment and peered over them, looking exactly like an old fashioned school teacher describing her naughty pupils.

"The students come at seven and are released at ten when the sun is too hot. It would be torture to have them under the sun for many more hours than that. One thing that prevents children from going to school is their families might need help from them. And they might not want to go themselves, of course. They might be trouble-makers. There is a gender question, having equal access for girls and boys. Not so much in primary school, but in the older classes you have the drop-out of girls. We have to go a little further into that question, find out why. It's also a cultural thing, of course. Girls are often looking after their younger siblings. So we might have to put care centers in place.

"Education in Darfur might have stopped in many places several years ago. So we have groups of children who have not had any schooling. One of our tasks will be to try to give the opportunity of education to older children who might not be ready for the higher grades.

"Unfortunately, as to the psychological side of treating the children in school, we have to admit that it's not in place yet. But we are working on it. We know that there is a great need for that. The signs of psychosocial stress go in both directions; some children are very silent, retracting into themselves, and others are too outgoing. Many of them have seen awful things in their lives: losing people, or losing their home, their friends. That needs to be tended to. But just being in school, a stable place for them, is one factor in that."

As Anette outlined the complexities inherent in a refugee crisis, Benoit delivered the status of our first flight requests. There were only seats for two of us on the UNHCR flight to Iriba the next morning. With the toss of a coin it was determined that Adam and I would go to Iriba in the morning. Aisha would stay an extra day in Abéché, gathering more information and supplies for our trip across the border and join us on the WFP flight the following day.

We wandered over to the CARE compound, just across the road from UNHCR. Gaetan greeted us warmly. He seemed to be feeling a great deal better than the day before.

"Will you be going to the French military base tonight then?" he asked us. We would need IDs to get in, Gaetan warned, which would require procuring more passport photos. But it was well worth it, he advised. It's the only place in town to get a cold drink.

We headed over shortly after sunset. Who knew that passport photos would be so useful in Chad? I made a mental note to bring extras in future travels to conflict zones. Aisha, using her skills *en français*, managed to sweet-talk the guards into letting us in without any proper documentation. The clientele was a combination of humanitarian workers, French soldiers, and Adam, Aisha, and me. We knew it was worth the effort when we saw the items being sold: frozen Snickers bars! Aisha and I washed ours down with cold beer. We had been in Chad only a few days, but we already realized that this was a meal to savor.

IN THE MORNING, we headed to the UNICEF compound to squeeze in a quick interview with Patrice, the head of the UNICEF mission we had met upon arrival, and his colleague, Ignacio Saez-Benito, before Adam and I had to catch our U.N. flight to Iriba.

Patrice went into more detail on the conditions that led the Darfurians to flee.

"This was a very well implemented campaign against the population of Darfur," he began. "The strategy to throw out populations from entire regions was very systematic."

I thought again about the tribal tension between largely Arab nomadic herders and predominantly African farmers. Real as that might be, it could not begin to explain the organized violence that Patrice was describing.

"In ethnic cleansing campaigns, as in Rwanda during the

genocide, or with the refugees from Darfur, the mortality rate will be very high among the adult male population, leaving behind the women to rebuild the family and social circle.

"The first refugees to arrive here in Chad were the most privileged because they left preemptively. But most of the people who fled Darfur were caught in the middle of fighting. The Janjaweed burned down the villages, took slaves, beat some of the leaders, abused many of the women . . . of course, for the children, to be a witness of all that . . ."

Patrice didn't finish his thought. He didn't need to.

"And then there is the very unsafe travel from their region to here. On the way, they were possibly abused as well. People might have stolen their cattle, their belongings. They arrived here in Chad in extremely harsh conditions. This is a desert region; it's very hot during the day, it can be very cold at night. It's a really tough place to live as a refugee. This is one of the worst crises since the genocide in Rwanda."

Patrice finished his interview as Adam and I began to gather our gear to head to the airport. "This will have to be a priority for the international community to address."

two

life as a refugee

"IT FELT LIKE I LOST ALL THE WORLD."

THE U.N. PLANE bounced to a landing on a patch of smooth, hard sand. The pilot unlatched the door and tossed down the folding metal stairs. Adam and I climbed down, squinting against the strong sun, and looked around. All that could be seen were small, scrubby growth protruding from the desert and a boy herding a few camels in the distance. A white Land Cruiser from CARE was parked on the side of the landing strip.

"Hi, we're Adam and Jen. Gaetan in Abéché told us we can stay at CARE . . ." We suggested tentatively to the CARE driver.

"Hello! I'm Yacoub!" Yacoub smiled and shook our hands, helped us hoist our stuff in to the back of the SUV, and signaled us to climb aboard.

YACOUB CHARMED US immediately during the drive to Iriba. He was quick to smile and laugh and even quicker, we learned, to offer his help when we needed it. He was in his early twenties, originally from N'djamena. He had been working for CARE in Iriba for four months. I remembered something Mathijs said at the UNHCR office. In many crisis zones where there is an influx of refugees, the local community benefits from employment with various U.N. agencies and humanitarian organizations that "open shop" and need drivers, cooks, etc. The local population in eastern Chad, however, has been so deprived of even basic education, that the agencies have been importing staff from N'djamena or southern Chad, where the population is largely Christian, for even "unskilled jobs." The locals, therefore, were paying the price of absorbing the refugees, sharing what they could of the incredibly limited resources in the area, and receiving none of the economic rewards. Mathijs had been concerned that this would lead to increased tension and possibly violence between the refugees and the local Chadians.

The path before us had no asphalt, only hardened, twisting tracks in the sand. That didn't stop Yacoub from guiding the vehicle at one hundred kilometers per hour, radio blasting. Adam and I grinned at each other—our former colleagues in Jerusalem, fearless transit drivers themselves, had met their match.

THE CARE FIELD office was simple but functional. Worn, dusty cots crowded the floor space in a tiny kitchen and sleeping area surrounded by high clay walls, the only local building material. A low hum could be detected from the generator providing electricity for a few hours each day. Hygiene needs were met by a hole in the ground in the guise of an outhouse. There was boiled/filtered water for international staff and guests.

Yacoub offered to drive us to Iridimi, the nearest camp. CARE was responsible for the administration of the schools there. Aside from the white NGO and U.N. Land Cruisers and a massive grinding Chad water truck, we scarcely saw any motorized vehicles on the dirt road running through the town. The homes were adobe style, mud walls with thatched straw roofs. Except for a few generators, there was no electricity and no government infrastructure to speak of. The town's refuse was blowing everywhere in the wind. Plastic bags were stuck to almost every tree, bush, or structure.

We passed through the center of Iriba in minutes. The road to the camp was also nothing but tire tracks in the sand. At times, the dirt tracks forked. Yacoub didn't hesitate, knowing where to bear left and right without ever lessening his impressive speed. I couldn't imagine navigating those tracks. After fifteen minutes of unbroken desert, scrubby bushes, and sun, an abandoned tank came into view, the only landmark I had seen thus far.

"A Libyan tank from the war," Yacoub explained, as he stopped the car for us to take a closer look.

In the 1980s, Libya's leader, Muammar Qadhafi, pushed his army south into Chad, seeking to capture the northern part of the country and annex it to Libya. Libyan opposition fighters had also used this territory to launch raids against the regime in Tripoli.

Yacoub blared a scratchy American pop-music tape as we drove. I was beginning to doze off. The endless desert heat and scenery made focusing hard. Just as the sleep waves started, Adam nudged me with his elbow.

"Look."

I glanced out the window and snapped awake. An obscured view of tents spread out over the horizon, hazy from the dust as much as from the distance. My breath caught for a moment. I had never seen anything like it. The sand-filled wind gave the scene a surreal feeling that was accented by the accompanying music on Yacoub's tape. 50 Cent was rapping out, *"It's your birthday . . . we gonna party like it's your birthday!"*

We slowly drew closer to the camp. The sprawl of tents was endless. Eighteen thousand refugees from Darfur were sheltered in this vast tent city. The scene sprang out of nowhere in the barren desert landscape. I felt overwhelmed, almost engulfed by it.

ADAM CLIMBED ONTO the top of the car with one camera. "Drive slowly, *ya habibi,* (my friend)" he cautioned Yacoub. Women in brightly colored robes and white-robed, turbaned men were lined up outside one large tent at a clearing.

"A distribution center," Yacoub said. "They're waiting to receive rations."

Under the blazing sun, women mixed sand with mud, shaping it into a four-foot wall, curving around their tent.

"They want more privacy," Yacoub explained.

Older men were digging holes, possibly for latrines.

Every child we passed stopped and stared at us. Many ran after the car, laughing and trying to keep up. They were used to seeing internationals riding in vehicles, but Adam's position on top of the car was something new. Standing barefoot in the hot sand, dressed in ripped clothing that hadn't, most likely, been washed in weeks, they chased our car to extend their glimpse of us, white strangers with cameras in their midst. Laughing and smiling brightly, they shouted out *"Salaam!* (Peace!)" and *"Ça va? Ça va?"* (How are you?)

I recalled a warning Gaetan had given us: "If there is a journalist coming in the camp, taking a photo of a child carrying water, half an hour later you have the reaction of the people coming to tell you 'They are picturing our children, why is that? We are not miserable people, why do they do that?' "

These beautiful, laughing, running kids, were certainly not miserable. They were vibrant with life. Still, knowing what I did, I wanted to find some way to protect them: from their pasts, which I could scarcely imagine when looking at their quick smiles, and from their futures, which were so precarious. I wanted to give them more than I possibly could.

LATE THAT NIGHT, nestled in my sleeping bag on the cot, I mulled over Gaetan's words and the car-chasing children. We were here to somehow try to help. We didn't want to present the same old images of African victims, but to give those who have suffered a means to address people all over the world. Would we be able to do our task, to make this documentary, without creating feelings of resentment or exploitation?

I WOKE UP in the morning to find Adam reaching over me for the satellite phone.

"Whatcha doing?"

"Trying to reach Omer in D.C. or Ibrahim in Abuja. See if they know anything more about getting inside Darfur."

Adam went outside to get reception and I closed my eyes again, enjoying the cool morning air. It wouldn't last for long.

He came back moments later and dropped himself back onto the cot.

"Damn satphone. Couldn't connect."

Half an hour later, we were in the back of the CARE car with Yacoub and the local CARE staff. Yacoub took Adam and me straight to the school and then headed to the landing strip to meet Aisha's flight.

Mahmoud, the headmaster, greeted us outside the small tent that served as the school's office. He wore a long white *galabiya*, a white turban, and sunglasses.

"I am sixty-five years old, an ancient man. I am from Kornoi. I worked in the Sudanese government forty-three years. I know this government. I worked in the south of Sudan, in the north, and I studied near Khartoum. I know the tribes and the situation in Sudan. In Darfur, there were slight problems between the tribes, between Fur and Zaghawa, for example, and between the Arabs and the other tribes in Darfur. The problems started in 1983 and every year it increased. 2004 came along, and they made us leave Sudan."

As Mahmoud continued, curious children gathered around us. A small boy, around four years old, settled into the sand next to me. He was wearing torn shorts and a ripped T-shirt, all a nondescript grayish color. He rested his hand on my arm. He wanted to make sure I knew he was there.

"If you govern the country, you have to govern it equally. You live in America. Is it possible to ignore one state and take care of another? The government in Sudan takes care of some states and ignores others. I know this; I worked everywhere. The policy followed in Khartoum is not the same in Darfur. The government ignored us. There is no development or education. For teachers, there are no salaries. That's why people demanded their needs. If using a pen and paper does not bring you equality, raising arms is the last resort. If they had given us our rights before we raised our weapons, we would still be in our country.

"I am speaking with you in the Arabic language. And my religion is Islam. We were expecting our Arab brothers to make some sort of intervention, that Arab organizations would come and help us. The African countries are working on solving the problems and I hope they can. But they did not send the troops to protect Darfur soon enough.

"The Sudan Liberation Army who represents us has certain conditions. Although the talks started in Abuja, we are still in the same place. We won't go back to Sudan, just to be killed by Janjaweed or attacked by the government with planes. No one is going to venture into a situation that is not stable."

The little boy tapped me on the arm. I turned to look at him. He held up his foot and pointed to it. There was a cut underneath his big toe. It was extremely dirty, though it didn't look deep. I patted his toe gently.

Mahmoud continued, explaining more about the circumstances of the camp and the current situation of the refugees. "We represent many regions. We are tribes from all over Darfur spread out in the camps. Our living here made us brothers. The relationships are very cohesive. There is no disagreement or problems between us.

"Every day, delegations come to check on us. It raises our spirits. You are one of those visitors. You come and see how we are doing, even if you're not bringing anything material. It's not mandatory that you take something out of your pocket to give us. But you do take our situation as important.

"There is security now in Chad, our health is acceptable, and we are no longer dying in the camp. The next priority is education. We have a lot of problems with the students. They are orphans, all of them. Their fathers died in the war. And those teachers that you see, they are old people, like me. There are no youth in between."

The little boy patted me again. He didn't want me to pay attention to the headmaster; he wanted me to focus on his cut toe.

"If we return to Sudan, uneducated, we would not have achieved anything. We had two years where we didn't study in our Sudan. We hope here that our children will be educated so when they go, they can cope with the people living in Sudan now. When we go back to our country, we must be on their level and progress forward. One of these days, we're going to return. We cannot remain here."

"Is it possible for us to meet with some of the teachers and students? To film in the classes?" Adam asked.

Mahmoud graciously waved his hand. "Yes, it's very possible. Spend the whole day with us. The students can tell you more than I can; talk to them. If you take our words with you to America, we will be very happy."

Mahmoud directed us to the nearest tent as the little boy scuttled away. We heard the voices of small people inside. We ducked into the opening flap. Moving from the glare of the sunlight to the stuffy semidarkness of the tent was an adjustment.

Speaking Arabic, Adam explained to the teacher who we were and what we were doing. I took the opportunity to look at the six-year-old children sitting on woven mats on the ground. The official UNHCR student-teacher ratio is fifty-to-one, but the agency was still operating in an emergency phase and there were many more students present. The supplies were minimal. A blackboard stood at the front of the tent. The students each had one small plastic bag marked with a large UNICEF logo, which contained a small notebook and something to write or draw with. Boys were on one side of the tent, girls on the other. The UNHCR tarps gave a greenish hue to the light that filtered through and washed over the children. They were quiet, staring at us intently, waiting for a cue from their teacher. I desperately wished I spoke Zaghawa or Arabic.

The teacher, a young woman wearing a pink wraparound shawl, clearly considered us guests of honor. It was impossible to ask her to go ahead with her regular routine and pretend we weren't there. We were expected to say some words to the students.

"*Salaam aleikum,*" (peace be upon you) we greeted the students.

The children answered in unison. "*Wa aleikum salaam!*" (and upon you!)

"How is the school? Okay?" Adam continued in Arabic.

"Yes!" they replied as a group.

"What are you studying? Arabic?"

Another resounding, "Yes!"

Adam held up his fingers: one, two, three, four, and the students enthusiastically called out the corresponding Arabic number, usually correctly.

Then it was their turn to perform for us. The teacher asked them to stand and began to lead them in song. A chorus of tiny voices rang out, repeating their teacher in a call-and-response chant. There were hand motions as well: clapping, hands-on-the-hips, and flapping-arms-like-wings. I had no idea what the words meant, nor how the movements corresponded to the lyrics. I fumbled for my camera and turned it on, trying to smoothly walk up and down the aisle to capture the presentation on film.

It was difficult to be behind the lens of the camera, establishing distance between the students and me. I wanted to be present with the kids, interact with them, appreciate their performance, but I realized my job was to record it.

Not all the students were fortunate enough to have the shelter of a tent. The next class we presented ourselves to was a kindergarten class studying outside on the ground. Wind was blowing constantly, and the children were huddled close to each other and to the teacher on a large blanket. The students duly stood up and sang for us. This time I simply watched. One little girl captured my attention. She was wearing a brown dress and her head was covered with a purple knitted scarf. A moment earlier, she had been singing and clapping. Now, performance over, she stood on the edge of the mat packed with her classmates. I was reminded of the "musical carpet" game I used to play while teaching drama in Seattle. All of the students would walk and dance around the room while the music was on, but as soon as the music was shut off, they had to immediately stand on a piece of carpet. As the game continued, the pieces of carpet would become fewer and fewer until, by the end, the students would squeeze all together on one small square of carpet. They would laugh and grab each other to keep from falling off the carpet piece. But this little girl was not laughing. She was biting her lip and squinting into the glaring sun as she maintained her place on the packed mat. This was not a game.

YACOUB RETURNED TO the camp, with Aisha in the seat beside him. She showed us a two-person tent she'd borrowed from a colleague of Jehad's she'd happened to meet, and told us about a translator named Dero he advised us to find once inside Darfur; though how and where to find him, she had no idea.

Meanwhile, there was someone whom Yacoub wanted us to meet. He drove to a different section of the camp and pulled the van next to a small, roofless, two-room, mud complex. A stocky, middle-aged man wearing a *galabiya* and white turban stood next to it, waving to Yacoub.

"Hello, how are you?" the man greeted us warmly in English as we descended from the back of the Land Cruiser, shaking hands with the three of us.

We followed him into the incomplete structure.

"My name is Kareem. I'm from Argot, a village in the Kornoi area. I was a teacher there."

Kareem was living proof of what Anette had told us in Abéché about the refugees refusing to wait for the U.N. to begin education for their children. The two rooms were, in fact, the school he had built. He proudly showed it to us. The mud walls had openings for windows and entrances, but no ceiling or roof to provide any shelter from wind, blowing sand, or blazing desert sun. Small, gawking faces and dirty hands filled the window nearest to us as Kareem spoke inside the half-finished mud room.

"This is the beginning of the school. All of this we refugees did ourselves in only fifteen days. Women made the walls, mixing water and mud together. And now we have three hundred and fifty pupils, girls and boys. We have seven teachers; five are male, two are female." There was much to be proud of, but Kareem didn't dwell on that. "The school needs many things. We don't have a blackboard. We made our blackboard by this patch." Kareem tapped his hand on a piece of dark siding that was attached to the mud wall with rope. "We haven't things to cover." He waved his hand to the open sky above. "We need exercises, books, and other tools. We want to build more rooms, because two classes still study on the ground. We are required as teachers to play our role, so that the young children won't miss education. We've been operating for a month with no real syllabus. Education is important. Any person without it . . ." Kareem paused, trying to find the words to finish his sentence. "There is no life without education."

Kareem had much more to say, but we wanted to meet some students now that class was ending for the morning. We made arrangements to talk with him more the next day.

THE STUDENTS STREAMED out of the tents. We sat in the central area of the school and quickly became the main attraction. The camps were full of international staff from the U.N. and the NGOs, but they didn't seem to walk around near the children. The kids swarmed around us, wanting to hold our hands, touch our hair. We turned the video cameras on with the viewing screen flipped around so they could see themselves being filmed. Surprise and delighted laughter erupted when they recognized their own image.

I noticed immediately how gentle the children were. More than seventy youngsters crowded in around us, forming a wall of humanity, each trying to make physical contact, get some attention, and see the equipment. I was nervous that they would get rough, or at least grabby, but they never did. Children took hold of our hands or arms with a surprisingly soft touch.

"Where are you from?" I asked the faces that surrounded me, utilizing my broken Arabic as best I could.

"Kornoi" "Sudan" "Darfur"—the answers came in unison.

"How long have you been in Iridimi?"

"Six months." "I don't know." "A long time."

"How is life in the camp?"

"It is good, but we want to go back home. But we are afraid."

"What are you afraid of?"

One girl in the sea of faces surrounding me took charge as the spokesperson for the group. She ticked off with her fingers. "One, the Antonov planes. Two, the government army. Three, the Janjaweed."

I wondered about how she had ordered her list. The media I had read labeled the Janjaweed as the real culprits. Yet this girl, surrounded by a sea of nodding, agreeing faces, listed planes and the Sudanese army as more frightening.

The kids were hungry for play and entertainment of any kind. Aisha ran in circles, mock "chasing" them. Howls of laughter erupted. Adam's "mouth-popping" led to enthusiastic imitations from dozens of little mouths. One bold girl actually hoisted Aisha on her back. Aisha tried to negotiate her release as crowds of children laughed loudly in encouragement.

I placed the camera bag on the ground and performed one of my "surefire kid-pleaser" gimmicks—finger magic tricks. I made sure the bag was still in my peripheral vision. I didn't want to take any chances with our equipment. A little girl, aged five or six, tiptoed over to the camera bag, lifted the top, and took a peek inside. Her older sister, aged eight or nine, dragged her away from the bag and slapped her hands, scolding her fiercely in Zaghawa.

I wanted to intervene on behalf of the hapless younger sister, but, in truth, I was impressed by the children's gentleness combined with their display of rule enforcement. The fabric of their society was so strong that it was holding up, even under the enormous strain of massive displacement.

We walked toward CARE's office tent as the afternoon grew late, the camera bag slung over my shoulder and my hands swinging by my side. It took a few moments to realize that two small children had crept up on either side of me and softly slipped their hands inside of mine. I felt the touch of their little hands long after they had scampered away.

WE SAW THE bold, laughing girl who had lifted Aisha when we returned to Iridimi the following morning. Would she want to talk to us about life in Darfur? She agreed eagerly. We tried to find a private place for the interview, but we quickly learned that it was nonexistent. Dozens of little ones followed us everywhere we went. Finally, we located a classroom tent that was not in use. Our young friend joined us in the tent, the others trailing behind.

"Sorry, we need to be alone with her . . ."

More kids entered the tent.

"Alone, alone," I tried to say in Arabic. They ignored me. Finally, using exaggerated hand gestures, Aisha and I managed to explain that they could not join us inside the tent. But there was no way to stop the dozens of little faces from peering in from the sides at every flap, fingers lifting the bottom of the tent, so that eyes could peek in to observe. Privacy was impossible in the midst of a refugee camp.

The girl sat down on a mat on the sand, while Adam checked the microphone and Aisha attached the camera to the tripod.

"Are you ready?" Adam asked her.

Aisha's friend, laughing and chatting seconds before, went silent.

"Can you tell us your name and where you are from?"

She was frozen for a long moment. Finally, she managed to whisper, "Serralad. From Darfur."

Adam, Aisha, and I had been to many areas of the world where we found children eager to talk. In Palestine, Thailand, Iraq, Afghanistan, Israel, and Cambodia, children wanted to tell us what they had experienced.

But Serralad could not speak about what had happened to her. Perhaps it was still too fresh, or maybe just so traumatic that it was impossible to retell. We found the same pattern with child after child. One moment laughing and playing with us, wanting us to film them clowning, even asking to be interviewed; but they immediately shut down when we turned the cameras on to talk about their lives. Their eyes went blank and their faces expressionless.

Then they showed us their drawings.

Ibrahim was ten years old and tiny for his age. He sat outside on a wooden, makeshift platform, showing us a notebook full of his sketches made with colored pencils: airplanes with bombs falling out of open hatches onto purple, blue, and pink straw-roofed circular houses; pastel colored tanks with soldiers astride, barrels blazing; camel and horseback riders shooting guns.

"Martyrs," Ibrahim said, when we asked what happened. "The planes hit and the Janjaweed burned the houses." He held up a page from his notebook.

"Can you tell me what that is?" Adam asked.

"Janjaweed riding a horse."

"What does the Janjaweed have?"

"A weapon."

"You saw the Janjaweed?"

"Yeah."

"Did you talk to them?"

"No! No. I'm afraid . . ."

"Why did the Janjaweed come to Kornoi?" Adam asked.

"To kill people."

"Why?"

"They come to kill people to take their stuff. And live there."

The wind flipped a page in his notebook, revealing a new picture.

"What's that?" Adam asked.

"Cars."

"Army cars?"

"Yes, army cars."

"What army?"

"Sudan government army."

Ibrahim turned to the next sheet. On it, he had drawn a village with huts of different colored straw. There was an airplane in the sky, raining bombs. One hut was on fire.

"What happened in this picture?" Aisha asked.

"They are bombing the village."

"Who are the people?"

"The people are Zaghawa. The plane killed them."

"What village is this?"

"Kornoi."

"Where is your house in the picture?" Ibrahim pointed to the hut with flames lapping from its roof.

"That's your house?"

"Yes," Ibrahim answered softly, averting our eyes.

"Who is in the house?" I asked, also quietly.

"I'm in it with my brothers."

"After the planes and the Janjaweed came to the village, where did you go?" Adam asked.

But Ibrahim had not finished telling us about the picture. "They died. My brothers all died and I ran away."

We were silent for a moment.

"All of them?" Adam managed to ask.

"Three were killed."

Ibrahim had been strong throughout, looking directly at the camera and answering our questions with certainty. But now, he bit his lip and his eyes rolled upward in an effort to prevent himself from crying.

"Older than you or younger than you?" Adam asked gently.

"Bigger than me. One was eleven. One was thirteen."

"Where are your mother and your father? Here?" we asked hesitantly.

"My father was killed and my mother is here."

He looked impossibly small and vulnerable, sitting alone on the wooden platform in his child-sized white *galabiya*, showing us the miniature drawings of an unimaginable experience.

Kareem arrived as we were finishing our interview with Ibrahim. "Hello!" he called out to us. "Shall we continue our conversation?"

I didn't know quite how to say good-bye to Ibrahim.

"Thank you, *habibi*."

He half-nodded and tried to smile.

"Maybe we can see you tomorrow?"

He attempted another smile and was more successful with his nod. He jumped off the platform and, within moments, blended back into the crowd of dozens of youngsters trudging their way through the hot sand from the school tents back to the home tents. I saw the little boy with the cut toe. His older brother was holding him firmly by the ear as they walked. He squirmed and ducked his way out of the ear grip, running on ahead, looking back every few seconds to make sure his brother wasn't going to try and catch up.

KAREEM LED US back to his self-constructed school. Children gathered around again, staring curiously. This time he spoke in Arabic,
which enabled him to express himself with more depth and complexity.

"Regarding security, *al-hamdulillah* (thank God), there are no air
strikes and there is no killing here in Iridimi. But from the perspec-
tive of losing one's country, family, and state . . . we live with much
anxiety. As if, upon becoming refugees, one does not know who he
is, or where he lives. As if he had no head.

"People look at a refugee as if he is not human. What is the difference between a citizen and a refugee? The citizen is free and has
ideas for development and work. But as refugees, our hands are
tied. We don't know where to go. If they were to cut off the food they
give, we would be totally helpless. We don't have independent sus-
tenance. The hardest thing is losing one's country; second, family;
next, losing destiny of life. Humans need a sense of destiny. This situation could last for years. Any hope we feel will be destroyed.

"The widows must gather firewood, and sell it in the market, and
try to bake bread for their children. There are a lot of problems for
the fatherless children. They lack clothing and life essentials. In the
winter it's very hard. The organizations don't have milk. There has
been no meat for a month. Some of the children really suffer, but they
have to be patient."

He described what had happened to the school in Kornoi as well
as to other schools in Darfur. "The government bombed and
destroyed our school, killing people."

"The airplane actually bombed the school?" We had all seen
enough in other places that we shouldn't have been shocked that a
government would attack a school. Nevertheless, I always was.

"Yes, inside the school. There are many schools that were bombed
by airplane. I was in the Jirbuk high school near Jirbukai village. Two

planes came and hit us. The students got scared when the missiles hit
and some of them ran away. We lost ten or eleven students. We still
can't find them. One of the missiles from the MiG that landed in the
school is still unexploded."

I wondered which of the children who had been playing with us
had directly experienced that particular assault. Meanwhile Kareem
continued recounting schools that had been attacked, giving all the
details that he knew. Clearly a strategy had been followed. It was not
random violence; it was coordinated and pointed.

"The government forces burned Abu Gamra and killed two
teachers there. The army entered as well, and killed three children,"
Kareem's voice cracked with emotion. "Those are the Arab Janjaweed! The government strikes and the Janjaweed burn and loot!
They killed the sheikh of the village. We ran. And we have not been
able to return."

I had read multiple articles stating that the Arab Janjaweed militias were an outgrowth of ethnic conflict. But a different picture was
beginning to emerge. The drawings, the lists of fears, it was all coming together inside my brain. Kareem clinched it.

"The problems that are happening in Darfur are caused by the
Sudanese government. It is a policy of divide and conquer. They target certain tribes, such as Zaghawa, Masalit, Fur, and the other black
tribes, so they can finish them off. They destroyed the Fur, in particular, because they had the best place to live. They dispersed the tribes
that were there as clusters. After removing those clusters, they armed
the Janjaweed and began the scorched earth policy of destroying and
burning land. When the organizations came to Khartoum to inquire
about what was going on, they were told that this is a normal civil war
between different tribes. The organizations aren't given permission to
enter and investigate. People have been killed and burnt. There are mass
graves that the organizations have not been able to reach until now.

"This war did not start in 2003. No. Arab Janjaweed militias were imported and armed by the government from neighboring countries since 1983. They would steal money. If you tried to chase them away, they killed you. If you went to the government to complain, you received no protection. Many places in Darfur were destroyed in this way. The Sudan Liberation Army was established out of obligation."

Kareem began pointing to the children gathered around.

"And so you have this kid, his father died. This small one, he's an orphan, this one too." He pointed to little one after little one. "This one is my brother's son. This one is my other brother's son. Their fathers died. The Janjaweed killed them."

Kareem pulled a barefoot five-year-old boy, dressed in shorts and a torn black T-shirt, in front of him. He gently placed his hands on the child's head.

"This is my sister's son. They killed his father, his grandfather, and his uncle in one group. The Arab Janjaweed took the money and killed them." Kareem's hands fondled the boy's head gently, softly patting his hair and pulling his ears. "He saw it all . . ."

The boy looked at his uncle curiously. He didn't yet know Arabic.

Kareem tenderly put his hand on his nephew's shoulder and said to him, gently, in Zaghawa, "I'm talking about your father and your grandfather."

The little boy looked down, half-smiled, and instantly made a face as if he wanted to cry.

"What do you fear for the children?" Adam asked.

"Fear?" repeated Kareem. "Until now, when the children in the camp hear the sound of a plane, they all lay down. Our greatest fear is that the Sudanese government in Khartoum won't change and won't disarm the Janjaweed or prosecute those who have committed these crimes. The international community stands witness that there are hundreds and thousands dying of killing, hunger, and disease. Kofi Annan has heard of it. He is the president of the world. It is essential that he come to witness this with his own eyes. Members of the international community have come and gone, and talked. But the situation is still the same. We want the United Nations to solve this problem rapidly. This is an indescribable international disaster.

"We are Muslims who speak Arabic, but where are the Arab and Muslim people around the world? Are they with the Sudanese government? Do they have no mercy for Muslims? The question begs itself. A Muslim is another Muslim's brother. We are one body. But there has been complete absence. We didn't find a Muslim reporter for months until finally, Amr Musa, the Secretary-General of the Arab League sent a fact-finding commission. We told them that the responsibility is yours; it is the responsibility of the Arab countries to solve this. They never came back again."

Kareem referred to the negotiations in Abuja between the rebels and the government.

"Those talks with the government are not serious. The government is not giving correct information. One thing is said there, another is said or done here. For example, in the first round of talks in Abuja, we were told that six thousand policemen were coming to protect the civilians. Instead, they came and killed us." Kareem was referring to the government's pledge to disarm the Janjaweed and send a protective police force to Darfur. Instead, members of the Janjaweed were absorbed into the police forces and dispatched to continue their brutality, under the guise of protection.

"Are you going to return?" Adam asked.

"If the international community is able to provide security, disarm the Janjaweed, stop the random air strikes, prosecute the war criminals, and remove the mines that are inside the country, we will return immediately. *Insha'allah* (God willing), this will happen soon, and we will create our own home with our hands. We hope that we will have more security in Sudan, with strong guarantees. When we return, we will educate those children so their future will be bright."

We walked with Kareem through the camp to his tent to meet his wife and new baby. Every few feet sat another tent, one after the other. Women and children milled about, some of whom would stare at us, others who would venture forward and say hello. The few men were ancient looking with weathered faces and missing teeth. We ducked into a makeshift entrance of what was an attempt at a small mud courtyard surrounding his tent.

Kareem and his wife had done what they could to make the tent comfortable. In the corner, there were stones and ashes with a cooking pot on top and a teapot to the side, and a woven mat in the middle with a blanket next to it. A bold, playful three-year-old girl dressed in a colorful smock and black bandana folded back the blanket, so we could properly admire the baby sleeping underneath. Flies swarmed all about us.

"How is the life in the camp?" we asked Kareem's wife.

"It is good," she answered. "We have everything we need. It is easier for me to feed my children here than it was in Darfur."

"How long do you think you will stay?" If conditions were actually better here, with U.N.-provided food, shelter, and basic medical services, it would make sense for her to want to remain as long as possible.

"We are going back as soon as we can. We are going back."

We left Kareem's tent. The CARE car was waiting for us outside. We were still being introduced to Kareem's neighbors, so I assured Yacoub that we would have no trouble walking back to the school. Yacoub drove off, and after speaking with several more of Kareem's friends, we said our good-byes and set off on foot.

NAVIGATING IN THE maze of indistinguishable tents was more challenging than I had anticipated. Everything looked the same; every tent the same drab color, every person looked like someone we had seen elsewhere. We stumbled through one block of tents after another, trying to find something we recognized. Were the water tanks on the hill the same ones we had seen near the CARE office? But then shouldn't the school be directly behind us? Behind us was only another endless stretch of tents. We were carrying equipment and we were all hot and tired. None of us was in the mood to get lost.

"You shouldn't have told Yacoub to leave," Adam grumbled to me. After a bit more stumbling, we found a sign: Iridimi School. We were in familiar territory.

A beautiful young woman wearing a pale pink wraparound flowered shawl was coming out of the "office" as we approached. We planned to duck into the privacy of the office to down some water, but there was something about the woman's delicate features and strong eyes that stopped us. She was holding a string of prayer beads.

She smiled at us with poise and grace. "Can I help you?"

We introduced ourselves and described our project to her. She readily agreed to an interview. We found an empty school tent and set up the camera.

"My name is Sou'ad," she said, in a voice both soft and rich. "I am from Kornoi. I'm married, *al-hamdulillah*, but my husband is in Sudan. I have four children. Safaa Ahmad is in second grade. Marwa Saleh is in the first grade. And I have Mohammed and Ahmad. They are little. I taught in a primary school in Kornoi. We were in Darfur comfortably, living in our country, with our people and our identity. But what happened, happened."

"What was it exactly that happened?" we asked her.

Sou'ad fingered the string of beads as she spoke. "Our houses were burned and we escaped without anything. At the end, the Janjaweed entered. I left my house with tears and four children. We ran. When the planes hit us from above, we lay down or hid under a tree. After they went far away, we would get up and run. We went a long distance on foot. My children became tired. We walked and walked until we finally found a car and it took us to Tine. We didn't have clothes or food. *Al-hamdulillah*, some people took us to their homes and they gave us food, and the organizations, *Allah* give them more wealth, did not shortchange us. They brought us to the camps. They fed us and gave us drink. They settled us."

Her voice grew tired as she recounted her journey.

"Are you afraid of anything here in the camp?" Adam asked.

"Sometimes of the Chadian locals."

"Why?" he persisted.

"They say, 'You are sitting and you don't have a country. You are not going to smell your soil.' Things like that. When people go out to do something or get wood, there are problems with the locals. But inside the camp itself, nothing happens."

We asked Sou'ad to tell us about the situation of the schools at Iridimi camp.

"To tell you the truth, there are a lot of problems with our school here in the camp. First of all, we have only a few books for some sections. We also don't have chairs. The teachers have been working as volunteers. We don't have anything. We're not even able to have lunch. But we bear this to educate our kids that are coming up after us.

"Before the problems, the children were fine. They were drinking milk and eating fresh meat from animals. Their condition was overall comfortable. But after the crisis started and we came here, there's no fresh yoghurt or meat for the kids. There are no vegetables or fruits. Due to diarrhea, many of the children are suffering from malnutrition. When someone comes to school late, and you ask him why, he'll tell you, 'I had to work in the market to get something to drink.' If I ask him, 'Why didn't you come from your home directly to school?' He'll tell me, 'I have to work to be able to buy some shoes to put on to come to school.' I understand them, I don't blame them. There are a lot of problems for our brothers.

"The men were used to moving from place to place. But the women and children stayed at home and did not have this change of scenery. Because of this, the greatest change has been for the children and the women. Three-quarters of the men in Darfur died and the rest are on the run because of the war. The children are left only with their mothers."

I wanted Sou'ad to explain what was happening with the children. Why, whenever we turned on our cameras, did they shut down?

"This is something in their eyes. You can ask any one of them to draw a Janjaweed or an Antonov plane or things like these and they will draw it all. I just have to give them a paper and a pencil and tell them to draw for me and they will sketch a plane striking or Janjaweed riding horses with a rifle in his hand, shooting people. They will draw you things like that, because they've seen it with their own eyes."

The pages of Ibrahim's notebook flashed through my mind like a flipbook.

Sou'ad continued, her voice and manner gently commanding our attention. "Specific to girls, there is rape of girls committed by the Janjaweed and the army. Old women, girls, and mothers, doesn't matter the age; this is something terrifying that has happened to girls."

"In the future, what do you hope for your kids?" Adam asked.

"I want to teach them so they become doctors and engineers and can grow in their country. Give them a good education so they can benefit."

"If you are here a year, two years, what will happen to the children?"

She shook her head no. She would not even entertain the question. "In Chad, they are living as refugees. They are alive, but they don't have freedom of opinion, they don't have the right to speak, they don't have anything."

"Do you have a particular message for women in the world?"

"The sorrow that happens in America, Sudan, England is all the same. I pray that whatever happened to us doesn't happen to them. The women in Arab countries, we are their sisters. We speak the same Arab tongue. We have problems we've never faced before. I wish that they feel our problems and take one stand with us together."

We began packing up our camera equipment, but Sou'ad had a message for us as well. "I also thank you very much for your effort, for the energies and troubles that you faced during your travels. You came and you stood with us. *Allah* rewards you and blesses you."

THAT NIGHT, I thought about Sou'ad's journey, walking on foot through the desert, lying low on the ground, trying to shelter her four small children whenever a plane flew overhead, dropping bombs on the columns of refugees. I compared that to the U.N. flight we had taken from Abéché to Iriba. I couldn't believe that she had thanked us for having endured hardship.

AISHA AND I headed to the camp with Yacoub at 5:30 in the morning. The emerging light of day made the desert seem softer. Even the tank from Libya looked gentler washed in the early sun. Camp life was in full swing when we arrived. Women and girls lined up at the pump, filling jerry cans of water to bring back to their tents. Women were constructing mud walls around their families' tents. Kids were everywhere, playing with makeshift toys or sticks and plain mud, and helping with morning chores. A tiny girl was happily wheeling around a pair of sticks tied to wooden wheels. Her hair was yellowish at the roots.

"Discolored hair, a sign of malnutrition," Aisha explained to me. The little girl wheeled her device with great concentration into people, jerry cans, anything that was around. She had a plastic band strapped around her wrist, indicating that she was receiving supplemental nutrition from the Doctors Without Borders feeding clinic.

I wasn't quite sure what to do with my camera. I wanted to capture the "normal" tasks of the start of the day. But turning on the camera and training it on whoever was nearby felt invasive.

I said hello in Arabic to an old woman who was squatting and washing her family's clothes in a small metal basin filled with very limited water. She smiled at me, by way of greeting. I lifted up the camera, raising my eyebrow in a gesture that said, "May I?" She stood up and came over, taking my gesture as an invitation to examine the camera. I showed her how it worked, pushing record and turning the screen so she could see herself. She gasped and laughed, her hand flying to her chest in surprise. I tried to exchange a few more pleasantries, but her Arabic was as limited as mine.

I called to Yacoub, who was standing nearby, yawning and stretching. "Can you help translate from Zaghawa into Arabic?"

"Why not?"

I asked Yacoub to politely inquire about her age.

"I am not sure how old I am, but I have enjoyed it for a long time," she answered his question.

"How old do you think you are?" asked Yacoub. "Seventy?"

"Maybe."

"Eighty?"

"Maybe." She made a facial expression that indicated that she didn't know and cared even less. "The truth is I exist for a long time."

It was impossible not to laugh. She talked with animation, surrounded by her grandchildren. Her hands rested on the head of her littlest grandson. She alternated between stroking his head and picking through his hair, removing, I suppose, dirt, bugs, or anything else she came across.

"In the past, we stayed in our place, working, eating from the farm. We were family. When there was a shortage of food, we shared together. This year, we prepared everything from the farm. But when the attacks came, we had to run and leave everything, and we had nothing to eat. They took all the animals. Three of our family were killed there. The rest ran away. We took our kids by the hands to come here on foot." She grabbed her grandson's hand to demonstrate. "The small ones were crying. A few people still had donkeys;

they put the children on them until we arrived. It took us ten days. We got so tired.

"We were among the first to come to this area. We had nothing to feed the children. The people in Chad had a little food. When we told them 'my children are hungry,' they gave a little bit to our kids. We survived like that until we came to Iridimi camp."

The old woman indicated the faces surrounding her. "All these are my grandchildren. Aid is given to a person depending on the number of children he has. Everything we have depends on the number in the family.

"Here we stay without work, without doing anything. If there is peace and security back home, we will happily return and dig holes, work the land and eat from it, but if there is no peace, then we cannot go back. The Janjaweed, they will never come here, *al-hamdulillah*. If it is safe, we will return. Otherwise, we must stay here."

Realizing I hadn't done so yet, I asked her name.

"My name? Hawa. My father's name was Gedeem." She paused. "I am. I was for a long time. That's it."

WE LEFT HAWA where we had found her, washing her grandchildren's clothes in a splash of water. She smiled and energetically waved good-bye to us. Adam, who had caught a later ride with the CARE staff, joined Aisha and me as we began to push through the sand toward the school. An old woman followed us.

"Hello . . ." I said.

She came right up to me and grabbed hold of my arm, squeezing tightly. My instinct was to pull away. I resisted it.

"They killed him. They killed him."

"Who? Your son? Your husband?"

"They killed him."

"Your brother?"

Her grip tightened for a moment, and then she released my arm and walked back in the direction she had come from, continuing to mutter to herself, "They killed him . . ."

I craned my head over my shoulder watching her, and almost tripped over another elderly woman crouched outside of her tent. I jumped back and apologized, but she beckoned us to come closer. "Do you have any news from my village? Is it safe? Can you take us there? Can you take me with you?"

There was nothing we could say. It would have been cruel to try to film. We found a way to disengage and walked silently for some minutes back to the school area. Adam spoke first.

"Should we try to find Ibrahim with the drawings?"

I agreed. It would be good for the film to get more "b-roll" (secondary footage) of him in his life. But there was another reason I hoped to find him. I wanted to make sure he was okay after yesterday. I was concerned that we had opened up something that he wouldn't have the inner resources to deal with. We scanned the streams of students leaving the class tents after morning session. We couldn't find him. We asked a few other children who had been with him the previous day. They shrugged their shoulders. We looked carefully at every boy who passed by. None of them was Ibrahim.

"Let's get some b-roll of Sou'ad teaching," Aisha suggested.

Sou'ad, however, wasn't teaching. She was in a training session. Mahmoud, the headmaster we had met the previous day, was leading the training with enthusiasm. I recalled Anette from UNHCR saying that teacher trainings were among the top priorities, as there was a shortage of skilled teachers among the refugee population.

Sou'ad and her colleagues were in a stuffy tent, overly warmed by the sun. They hadn't eaten or drunk anything yet that day. They were sitting on the hard ground writing in small UNICEF notebooks. They weren't getting paid to teach, much less to attend the training.

Her words from the day before echoed back to me: "We bear this to educate our kids that are coming up after us."

❧

AFTER THE TRAINING, Sou'ad introduced us to her neighbor, also a teacher, who invited us back to her tent. Her family gathered round to see the foreigners. Among them was her younger brother, Tajadin. He was seventeen years old. His eyes were filled with a deep intensity and silent rage. He sat rigidly on a woven mat. We asked if he had something he wanted to say to the camera. He did.

He spoke about what happened in Kornoi . . .

"I was a student in El Fashir High School. I came home to Kornoi because I had a vacation. The Antonovs had started bombing and the Janjaweed were killing people. I didn't find a way back to school."

. . . and about his brother who was killed.

"He was only twenty-one years. He was a student. He helped my mother and father and family. At holidays, he worked, brought food, and helped us go to school. He was responsible for us. He was bombed by Antonov and killed inside his home. His name was Muhammad. We took him to his grave."

His steady voice quivered for a moment, and then continued with determination. "It felt like I lost all the world."

He spoke about being a refugee, the light filtering into the tent from the outside and illuminating his face with a golden glow.

"We have been in the camp for nine months. In all that time, the toughest part was when we were forced out of our area to come here. The hardest day was when we became refugees. I think about my school and my relatives who were killed by the Janjaweed. I think about my possessions. I lost them. I remember too many things."

We drove away from Iridimi camp in typical Yacoub style. *"You got me going crazy . . . turn me on! Turn me on!"* his scratchy tape blared out

a popular Western dance song. We would be hitching a flight on a U.N.
plane from Iriba to Bahai in the morning. With a huge smile, Yacoub
presented us with a gift: three pieces of white cloth to wrap as turbans.
"You'll need this to keep out the dust and sand in Darfur," he told us.

Back at the office, we finally managed to connect to Omer in D.C.
He still hadn't reached Ibrahim in Abuja. "I will talk to him tonight
for sure. I will give you the contacts before you fly tomorrow," he
assured us. We were more determined than ever to get into Darfur
to film the places we had been hearing about.

I had trouble sleeping that night. It was hard to imagine the
intensity growing. We had spent only four days in Iridimi, but I felt
that I would "remember too many things."

Hawa, Iridimi Camp

three

crossing the border

"NOT POSSIBLE . . . VERY EASY."

THE **FLIGHT TO** Bahai lasted only twenty minutes, yet we felt as if we were heading toward the end of the earth. The small window revealed one of the harshest landscapes I had ever seen. There was no life. Occasional clusters of bushes managed to take root in the desert, yet they were dry and brittle. Sand spread in every direction beyond the horizon. Thousands of people had fled across land like this to escape brutalization, but watching the scenery from above, I found it hard to imagine how any of them had managed to stay alive.

We touched down on a patch of dirt that passed as a landing strip. Only a flag on a wooden pole signified this was anything other than more desert in the middle of nowhere. A car from the International Rescue Committee (IRC) happened to be on the strip. We were invited to squeeze in for the half-hour ride to town.

Bahai was even more barren and remote than Iriba had been. A few mud huts with thatched roofing could be seen in the distance, and a handful of old, small, mud and whitewashed buildings. Several majestic camels lazily walked to an unknown destination.

"Hi, cuties!" Aisha clucked at them. I gave her a strange look. "Soft spot for camels," she admitted.

The only splashes of color were found in the excessive trash littering the dusty town. As in Iriba, bottles, cans, labels, and a plethora of plastic bags were scattered across the sand.

T̲HE IRC CAR dropped us off at the UNHCR field site. A chain fence surrounded the compound, which was comprised of a low, flat, battered, white-plastered building that housed two offices, a kitchen, and a TV room. There were a few large, green, canvas tents to the side of the building where the UNHCR staff slept and where guests could also sleep for a reasonable fee.

The head of the mission, José Fischel, from Brazil, greeted us jovially and handed us information sheets about the compound.

"Refugee work get you down?" it read. Then it began to tout all the advantages of a stay at the UNHCR field site, the only possible option for internationals. He apparently liked to think of the compound as the Chadian contribution to the Club Med resort chain. *"An exciting feature of UNHCR's compound is a full range of wilderness workout material,"* his sheet informed us. *"You can lift concrete blocks and dead dry wood, jump rope and jog in the sand. All this will enhance your overall energy level and work attitude."*

The rules reflected a dark side to his sense of humor that I recognized from my own days in Jerusalem as a necessary coping skill when living and working in such difficult circumstances.

"Do not light up candles, cigarettes, and kerosene lamps inside the tents— there have been enough shelters already burned down in this area of the world."

"Please escort the empty bottles and cigarette boxes to the garbage cans— cultural relativity has its limits."

"Enjoy the night donkeys' love song & have a nice stay!" it encouraged us at the end.

We sat down at a picnic table outside the tents to formulate our plan. We still couldn't reach Omer or Ibrahim. As far as we knew, no one was expecting us, and no plans had been made on our behalf for entering Darfur or our time inside. We had a few names of SLA leaders, but no contact information for them. We had two choices. Either we could stay put until Omer contacted us from D.C., or we could try to find the rebels ourselves and make our own arrangements for getting inside Darfur. There was no need for discussion. We closed our notebooks and headed out of the compound.

Bahai, at the crossroads of Chad, Sudan, and Libya, has both the
"Sudanese market" and the "Libyan market." We were more likely
to find someone who could point the way to the SLA at the
Sudanese market, so we walked through the Libyan market without
stopping. Pieces of tin formed small stalls that were in the shadow of
two enormous trucks, sinking under the weight of goods piled
twenty feet high and masterfully strapped down with rope. It didn't
seem possible that those trucks could travel under the incredible load.

Three little boys were kicking a ragged soccer ball back and forth
on top of a small, litter-covered knoll.

"*Salaam aleikum!*" they greeted us. "*Ça va?*"

Adam returned the greeting and asked, "Do you know where we
can find the Liberation Army?"

The boys pointed in the general area of the Sudanese market in
a markedly unspecific manner and continued their game. I had
never imagined that we would be asking a bunch of kids where the
regional rebel movement was.

We reached the Sudanese market and wandered through the sandy
pathways and rows of tin and mud stalls layered with dust and a
mélange of goods for sale. We took a left at a stall stockpiled with Pepsi
and canned fruit drink, and ambled past mounds of peanuts and old,
crusty dates. We had no idea what to look for. Even if the rebel group
was in or near the market, it was highly unlikely we would find an SLA
sign tacked onto a stall. Everything was beginning to look the same.

"*Ça va?*" one shopkeeper after another called out to us in French,
as they had in Iriba and Abéché.

"*Ça va!*" we would reply.

"Hello, how are you?" a man's voice called from up ahead in English. Our heads simultaneously swiveled around in the direction of
the voice. Did we hear English?

Chad was colonized by the French.

Sudan had been under British rule.

Aisha, Adam, and I exchanged glances. This was our biggest lead yet. We headed toward the man's stall. He was in his late thirties, tall with dark skin and broad shoulders. He was folding clothes for sale in his stall. He introduced himself as Bashar. Guessing that his English was limited, Aisha used simple words to introduce us and explain our project. Bashar nodded cautiously. There didn't seem to be much use tenderfooting. Aisha asked if Bashar could tell us what we needed to know:

"Is there a way to contact the SLA here in Bahai?"

"No. No SLA."

Aisha continued, "We heard that the SLA is here and we are trying to coordinate with them to get into Darfur."

"There isn't anyone here. I do not know what you are talking about," he said firmly without looking up from his task.

We knew he did. Adam opened up his notebook to the page with the names we had from Omer. He held the paper up for Bashar to see. "Do you know any of these people? We were told we could find them here."

Bashar glanced at the names, half nodded, and finally answered dismissively, "No. I don't know them. They are not here. They don't exist."

We were getting discouraged.

He continued to fumble through some clothes, surveyed the area cautiously, and then sharply turned his head to look at us. Under his breath he said, "Come back at four o'clock."

We nodded, said our good-byes, and headed back toward the UNHCR compound, trying hard not to crack up until we were out of earshot.

"Maybe they'll exist by four?" I deadpanned.

WE SPENT THE rest of the afternoon watching BBC news, which José had managed to receive at the "resort." Yasser Arafat, the president of the Palestinian Authority, was ill and was being sent to Paris for medical treatment. Adam and I had both done extensive work in Palestine; we watched the segment with interest. Brewing unrest in the Ivory Coast was the other top story. Government warplanes had bombed a rebel-held town in the West African country to root out insurgents. As a result, nine French peacekeepers and a U.S. citizen were killed. The French military was launching air attacks in retaliation.

Finally, it was nearing four o'clock. We pulled our boots back on and crossed the litter-covered sand back toward the market.

A younger man was now tending Bashar's stall.

"Do you know where Bashar is?" Adam asked him.

"Not here."

"Do you know when he will be back?"

"Maybe 7:00 tonight."

"But he told us to come at 4:00," Adam insisted. We didn't yet realize that Chadian time was an hour behind Sudanese time.

"Maybe he'll be here soon. Why don't you sit? You can wait for him."

He directed us to a woven mat across from his stall. Canned fruit punch and biscuits materialized for our consumption. An older man with Ray-Ban sunglasses, white *galabiya*, and a white turban silently eased himself onto a corner of our mat. We smiled at him and he smiled back, returning our *"Salaam aleikum."*

The older man finally spoke to us in slow calculated English, "So . . . you want to go to Darfur?"

Adam communicated our needs.

The man let it "slip" that he was connected to the SLA.

"Is it possible for us to cross from Bahai into Darfur?" Adam asked.

"Not possible." he said. "Very easy," he mysteriously added.

"Can we get to Kornoi?"

"Very easy. Come back tomorrow at 10. We'll talk more then."

"Can we talk more now? We need to leave as soon as possible."

"No," he said firmly. "It is not safe to talk here." We looked around; except for a few camels and some tumbleweed, there was no one nearby. We thanked him and as quickly as he appeared, he slipped away.

We walked back to the UNHCR field office, past the Libyan market and giant trucks strapped down with goods reaching to heaven.

"I can see us wasting another whole day waiting to talk to people to take us inside," I grumbled to Aisha. "What, is he afraid that even the camels have ears?"

"Jen," Aisha pointed out to me. "Camels do have ears." Adam laughed at us.

I kicked an abandoned plastic bottle toward them both. I couldn't decide if I was amused or frustrated. Our immediate future rested on the cryptic and contradictory words of a shady character in a border town market in what felt like the last place on earth.

IN OUR TENT that night, Adam tried to teach Aisha and me Arabic words that we might find useful.

"I am an independent journalist," Adam instructed us. *"Ana sahafi mustakill."*

"Mustakill means independent?" I asked. "Can you use it in another sentence?"

"Sure," Adam responded as he switched off the single lightbulb hanging overhead, plugged into a power strip fueled by the compound's generator. "Here's your sentence: If you wake me up in the middle of the night to teach you more Arabic, well then, I *must-a-kill* you!"

We whispered and cracked jokes with each other until sleep got the best of us, the startling "donkey love noises" that José had warned us about accenting our dreams.

THE UNHCR STAFF was up and working by the time we emerged
from the tent. "Hey, there you lazybirds are!" José jibed at us as we
unzipped the door and stepped out. It was just after 8 A.M. I grabbed
a cup of instant coffee and sat on the ledge of the building, which
offered a view of the desert rolling out in front of the compound. I
noticed a white pickup truck in my peripheral vision. It was heading this way. As it grew closer, I could make out three men inside
wearing white *galabiya*s and turbans. They didn't look like the
UNHCR staff. And the vehicle was missing the special antennae
connected to a two-way radio found on all the U.N. and NGO cars.
The pickup truck pulled up outside the fence. One of the men got
out and began talking to the security guard posted at the gate. It
looked like Bashar from the market.

"Adam, Aisha!" I called over my shoulder to the kitchen area
where Adam was filling our water bottles and Aisha was brushing her
teeth. "I'm not sure, but . . . I think our ride is here."

Adam walked to the fence, raising his eyebrows at me as he
passed. He exchanged a few words with Bashar and returned to the
ledge, grinning. "We have ten minutes to grab our stuff and get ourselves on the truck. They're taking us inside Darfur right now."

We scrambled around, collecting our backpacks, equipment, and
cartons of water. José watched with interest, perhaps a bit of envy.
U.N. staff members have a great deal of restrictions, limitations we
certainly weren't burdened with. José would likely be fired if he had
tried to go into rebel-held Darfur to investigate the situation there.
"Hey, good luck and be safe," he told us as we climbed in. "See you
next week."

We each took a corner of the pickup truck, positioning ourselves
so we could see each other and the landscape around us. We had
been told that all that separates Bahai, Chad, from Sudan was an

unmonitored *wadi* (valley). We assumed we were heading there now. The truck bumped its way down the sandy track.

"Jehad in N'djamena told us the truck rides were horrible!" Aisha hollered over the wind. "This isn't so bad!" I pulled the little red Air France pillow out of my backpack and stretched out my legs.

The tire track path ended, but the pickup truck continued. A large *wadi* lay ahead and the truck slowed down.

Aisha nudged me. "Look at Adam."

Adam had pulled a newspaper he had taken from the UNHCR compound out of his bag and was reading it . . . pretending to read it, more likely.

"You're reading the paper? What, you have to show that you're so tough that sneaking across the border is no big deal to you?" Aisha and I teased him. Adam winked at us.

The nose of the truck slowly poked its way down into the *wadi*, bouncing us around a bit as we held on to the sides, crossed the bottom of the *wadi*, and climbed its way back up.

"Darfur!" one of our escorts confirmed for us, shouting out the side window of the cab.

Fifteen minutes later we were sitting on woven mats in the shade of scrubby trees, talking to Jabar, an SLA commander. We were offered sweet, thick, dark tea in metal cups. Jabar, a sinewy, wiry man with a small mustache, held his Kalashnikov gun across his lap. His Ray-Ban sunglasses made it impossible to see his eyes. Most surprising, however, were his socks. They were men's dress socks with small cartoon bears and the caption BABY BEAR stitched all over them. Not the footwear I was expecting from a commander of a rebel movement.

"So, where do you want to go?" he asked us in Arabic.

"Kornoi," Adam told him. "We've met dozens of refugees from Kornoi in Iridimi camp. We want to film what happened to their village."

Jabar nodded intently. "No problem."

He pulled out his satellite phone and made a few calls. More SLA fighters joined us, laying down rifles that looked as if they were left over from the time of the British. Our gear was removed from the back of the pickup truck, and Bashar and the other escorts returned to Chad. Another car would come along to pick us up, we were told, in three or four hours.

It turned out to be the first of many long waits. Adam and I made do with playing cards while Aisha read, as the afternoon drew on.

"I'm trying to fit everything we've been hearing into what I read before the trip," I said as I finished my final card, winning the game of Kings.

"OK," Adam replied.

I recapped what I knew about the history and governance of Sudan: the National Islamic Front government is presided over by President Omar Bashir, who took power in a military coup in 1989, overthrowing what had been the only democratically-elected government in Sudan's history. Aisha confirmed this was accurate, slightly amused at my recitation of Sudanese history. "The Darfurians we met in Iridimi say the government attacked them and created the Janjaweed proxy militia. According to the media, it's about ethnicity. Is the government trying to 'Arabize' Sudan?"

"I don't think it's that simple," Adam explained. "Look, the terms 'Arab' and 'African' are really imprecise. Ethnicity is very fluid in all of Sudan, especially in Darfur. How do you determine who is 'African' and who is 'Arab' in Darfur? Not by religion. Nearly everyone in Darfur is Muslim. Not by appearance. 'Arabs' and 'Africans' are equally dark. Liveliehood, intermarriage, political, and economic status—all of that influences who is called what, as much as anything else."

"So, what's the government's motivation, then?"

Adam gave his take on the situation as he dealt the cards again. Omar Bashir's government is drawn from a small number of elite tribes from the Khartoum area in northern Sudan. The regime is largely unpopular with the vast majority of Sudanese citizens, no matter the ethnicity. As with many governments resting on a small power base and trying to retain control, it relies on chaos in order to survive, certainly in order to justify its oppressive measures.

It's not a coincidence, Aisha further elaborated for me, that the heat began to turn up in Darfur just as peace talks began in earnest between the government and the southern rebel movement, the SPLA. Darfur rebels took up arms at the time they did, partly because Darfur had been excluded from the wealth and power sharing agreements hammered out between the government and the southern Sudanese rebels.

The vast majority of Sudan is underdeveloped, politically marginalized, and without access to resources or infrastructure at the same level as the elite tribes in the north. Rebel movements had been rearing up all over Sudan, such as the Beja in eastern Sudan and rebels in the Nuba in central Sudan. The Sudanese government was facing serious pressure to accommodate power-sharing demands of the SPLA with some control of incredibly rich oil reserves. It was not about to give concessions to any other factions. The government's response in Darfur was a clear message to the rest of the marginalized people of the country to remain submissive or expect its wrath. In all likelihood, the brutality won't stop with Darfur.

The pickup finally arrived. It was significantly more beat-up than the truck we had crossed the border in. SLA was written on the door in what might have been permanent marker, or possibly dried mud and a Kalashnikov gun was mounted on the top of the cab. The truck looked like it was held together with rubber bands. Thirteen young men were sitting on top of the pile of luggage that was tied down to the bed of the truck. It quickly became clear that the private ride we had enjoyed on the back of the truck from Bahai into Darfur was not going to be the norm. From now on, we would be riding with the rebels.

Aisha and I were told to sit in the cab with the driver. I climbed in the middle and Aisha squeezed in next to me uncomfortably. Adam climbed on top with the men, out in the open. The driver leaped in, turned on the engine, popped in a cassette of scratchy Zaghawa music, and we were off. The driver was from the Fur tribe, we learned, and couldn't have been more than seventeen or eighteen years old. He had curly hair, was wearing a yellow tank top, and drove with sharp, fast, sure movements. He wove the truck between trees, shrubs, and rocks, sometimes in tracks in the sand, other times next to tracks, and often where there were no tracks at all.

Gauging from the lake to our left, we seemed to be heading north, still close to the border with Chad. We stopped after an hour. The sun was setting and it was time to eat. The rebels stretched their legs, and lay down their weapons. I took my first good look at the group we were riding with. They were all relatively young, but two teenage boys were younger than the rest. They weren't, I noticed, carrying guns like the others. The truck was unloaded as the sky turned an array of colors—orange, purple, red. With the sunset, came *iftar*. The meal began with dried figs, followed by orange-colored water poured from a jerry can into a few available tin cups, which were passed around and refilled, and a slab of meat grilled over a small fire.

After the meal, many of the men walked away to pray. Adam grabbed the camera and climbed up some rocks, filming the scene. Aisha began clicking away with her still camera. I took my still camera as well, and framed a shot where I could photograph Adam on top of the rock and Aisha lying on her stomach below. I wanted to record us obtaining our first footage in Darfur. The truck was loaded once again in the last vestiges of light and, when darkness was complete, it was time to head out. I climbed on the back before anyone could stop me. I wasn't about to experience my first night in Darfur stuffed inside the truck. Aisha wasn't so lucky. Before she could join us on the top, she had been ushered back into the cab. I was on

Typical SLA truck

the middle of the truck bed with Adam directly behind me and one
of the teenaged boys in a plaid shirt and green turban squeezed in
next to me. He met my eye repeatedly, returning my smile each time.
I decided to see if my primitive Arabic was up to the task of speaking with him—not easy, especially given the noise level of the truck.
His name was Fadi, I was quite sure he told me, and he was fifteen
years old. He was originally from Darfur, but his family was in N'd-
jamena, Chad, where he had spent most of his childhood. I wanted
to know why he decided to join the SLA when he could be in school
in N'djamena and whether he had been coerced into joining the rebel
movement; but I knew not to attempt such a complex conversation.

   Stars slowly filled the sky. The truck drove on for hours, heading
east, deeper and deeper into Darfur. I looked over at my new young
friend Fadi. He had fallen asleep. Moments later, I felt something on
my leg. I looked down. Fadi's head had fallen against it. As the night
grew darker, we watched the rise of a full moon, and the array of stars.
It was so beautiful, peaceful. I had a sense of complete freedom. It was

difficult to reconcile those feelings with the fact that we were in Darfur, Sudan, the place of recent and ongoing atrocities perpetrated against millions of innocent people. I guessed that reality would register the next day, after we had seen more of Darfur than sunsets, stars, and moonrises, and had experienced more than the joy of riding on the top of a pickup truck through the beautiful desert night.

four

destruction of darfur

"BEFORE, THIS WAS IMPOSSIBLE."

WE WOKE UP COLD and crowded and unzipped the two-person nylon tent. In the soft early morning light, our surroundings were now visible. Jutting up out of the plain, directly next to us, was a towering reddish rock formation. We didn't say a word, not wanting to break the perfect silence. As soon as the SLA guys lifted themselves off their mats, they began to reload. We packed up the tent quickly and handed it up onto the truck as the baggage was covered with mats and a tarp and tied down with ropes.

The rebels climbed back onto the truck and we followed suit. Aisha found a place to sit on the side of the truck this time. Riding in the morning was as wonderful as it had been the night before. The crisp and clean air was still a bit chilly, though the sun had firmly risen. The moonscape began to give way to a desert spotted with thirsty shrubs, bunches of grass, and small, thorny trees.

I was leaning against Adam, trying to warm my face in the sun. He tapped me and pointed. We were driving past a pile of charred stone. I sat up and looked around. We passed another group of burnt stones, built as a tight circular wall. There were more up ahead. It took me a moment to register that we were passing our first signs of life in Darfur, or what used to be life: round stone and mud brick enclosures with charred conical thatched roofs, or no roofs at all; piles of rubble and stone; smashed or charred pots made of clay and mud.

"Furawiya," the young man sitting next to Aisha pointed, identifying the remains of the village.

The truck rambled up to a makeshift checkpoint. Two young men with old guns stared for a long moment and then smiled, exchanging repetitive greetings of *"al-hamdulillah"* with our escorts. We were waved through. The truck stopped after a few more yards. We dismounted and silently took our equipment from the back of the truck. The rebels drove off with an unspoken agreement to come back to get us shortly.

We walked toward the nearest destroyed home to take a closer look. The sun was bright and getting hot. It was quiet, eerie. A thin, tall man approached us. His head was wrapped tightly in a white turban, and his face was obscured by the covering. Only his eyes were revealed. They were intensely serious and somewhat jarring in a man so thin. His name was Musa.

Was he from Furawiya?

He was.

Would he mind taking us around and explaining what had happened to this once-village-now-ghost town?

He agreed.

He showed us around the village slowly. The destruction was remarkably thorough and systematic. We passed piles of stones that used to be people's homes. Everything inside—clay pots and tea kettles—were charred or smashed. Sheets of twisted aluminum siding were lying on top of a heap of charred wood: former market stalls. Musa took us to the remains of one particular stall. It was his, he explained, and went on to describe how armed men on horseback had stormed the village and smashed everything.

Perhaps most disconcerting was the emptiness. Adam, Aisha, and I had been to other scenes of large-scale devastation. In all those places, people seemed to spring up out of the remnants the way weeds stubbornly grow in cracks of a sidewalk. In Jenin, days after the refugee camp had been flattened, Palestinians had created makeshift tents with poles and blankets on top of the rubble of what used to be their home. New structures were built inside, on top of, or around the destruction in Afghanistan. I had even seen a little boy flying a kite perched atop a hill of rubble of what used to be the Kabul Hotel.

But here, it was different. It was almost entirely depopulated. Aside from Musa, and the young men at the checkpoint, there were no people in the village. Even the birds had left. The only sound was the wind and the hard sand crunching beneath our feet.

Musa wove through the rubble and led us into the school. Desks were smashed and broken. The floor was ankle deep in strewn paper. It was apparent that a school day had been brutally interrupted. There was still writing on the chalkboard.

"Who did this?"

"Janjaweed."

We exited the school and walked without speaking across a *wadi*. Musa silently pointed out a large crater. We peered over the edge. Remnants of a projectile were scattered inside.

"From Antonovs," he said quietly. "Government planes."

He led us to another missile, three feet in length. It lay unexploded.

"Also from Antonov," he said.

Aisha took a photo of the Russian lettering on the side of the ordinance. Russia was Sudan's largest arms supplier. Antonovs themselves were Russian-made bombers. It wasn't only Russia, however, who was engaged in a lucrative business with Sudan. China was Sudan's largest investor in its oil industry. No wonder the United Nations had been so lacking in political resolve regarding Darfur. China and Russia hold two of the five permanent seats in the fifteen-seat U.N. Security Council. I wondered more about my own government's response. The U.S. Congress had named the situation genocide several months ago. But nothing had been done since.

Musa described the bombing campaigns to us: Enormous missiles were rolled out of low-flying government planes, striking populated areas with little or no accuracy or control. The villagers fled, Musa told us, and just kept going.

Musa showed us his own home, scorched to the ground.

"Where is your family? Where are the rest of the people?"

"In Kariare." Kariare, we learned, was the name Darfurians used for the refugee camp near Bahai, Chad, that the United Nations labeled Oure Cassoni. "No one is left now . . . .they are all killed or had to run."

The SLA truck returned to get us. It was time to move on.

WE RODE FOR the rest of the morning over rocks, under trees, and on terrain that I don't think Toyota engineers had in mind when building their pickups. Jutting up out of the rocks and sand were scattered lone trees. The driver seemed to enjoy guiding the truck under them, no matter how low-leaning or sharp their branches. In the early afternoon, the truck stopped.

"Shegeg Karo," the same young man told Aisha. "A market village." We climbed down, stretched our legs, and looked around. Shegeg Karo now seemed to be a makeshift SLA command center. There was a small cache of weapons and one young man with a Thuraya satellite phone who identified himself as the commander. Fadi jumped off the top of the cab and began to inspect the arsenal. Everything looked archaic. I compared the rusty weapons lying on the ground in front of me to the enormous unexploded missile we had just seen in Furawiya.

We were talking to the commander when we noticed a young man shyly hovering near us. He seemed to be waiting for a good moment to approach. Aisha smiled widely, giving him confidence. He stepped up and greeted us in English.

"Hello. Where are you from?"

He was of medium height and build, with deep brown skin, warm, friendly eyes, a wispy moustache with a little bit of "peach-fuzz" on the sides, and two small vertical markings next to the corners of his eyes. His name, he told us, was Dero. The name was familiar.

"Dero . . . Dero . . . do you know the photographers Jehad and Ben who were just inside Darfur?" Aisha asked.

Dero's face lit up. "Yes, they are my good friends! I traveled with them for two weeks. I translated for them, I helped them in everything!"

"They told me about you. I wanted to contact you, but they said you didn't have a satphone; they didn't even know the name of the village where we could find you!" Aisha explained.

Dero shrugged. He didn't seem to find the coincidence as amazing as we did. "I am from here, from Shegeg Karo. It is easy to find me."

We told Dero about our project.

"Do you want me to come with you? I can translate, help in whatever you need."

"We would love to have you come with us, if you're able," Aisha answered for all of us.

"I am available. There is no work, so I have nothing to prevent me."

Dero led us down a small hill into the market and sat us down in a stall.

"Wait here for me, I'll be right back."

Dero returned minutes later with slightly chilled Pepsis. We had no idea how he had been able to procure them or keep them cool.

As we sipped, Dero told us a bit about himself. Having taken two English courses years ago in Libya, he was now translating for the handful of journalists and photographers trickling into the rebel-held area of northern Darfur. He haltingly mentioned that his brother had been killed but changed the subject almost immediately.

"Come, you can meet some people." We followed Dero through the market and the *wadi*, collecting more than a few stares on the way. The sand was filled with old, dried goat and ibex droppings. Dero led us up a small hill to a conical thatched straw roof supported by thin wooden beams. Sitting inside was a wizened old man with a white beard and a wooden walking stick. From his hut, we could see for miles around.

"The sheikh of Shegeg Karo," Dero told us. "He is very old. He knows everything about this area. You can ask him many questions." The sheikh seemed pleased to see us and happy to talk. "My name is Ali," he told us, as he invited us to sit.

Aisha snapped a photograph of the stately old man, the last on her role of film. She tried to muffle the sound of the automatic rewind as the sheikh launched into his history.

"The story of my home goes back a long time. Thirteen of my grandfathers were the leaders of this region. I am eighty-six years old. I know everything about the history. Whatever nation comes to my country, I remember. Whatever events happen in Sudan, I know about it."

He paused, his eyes gleaming, as Dero tried to translate. It was obvious that we weren't getting each and every word. No matter, we thought. We would get the footage translated fully after we arrived home. The sheikh pointed to a mountain in the distance.

"My ancestor came to settle here when he saw this mountain, in the eleventh century. After that the Turks came. Hussein came. After Hussein came Sultan Ali-Dinar, in the time of the Mahdi."

The Mahdi was considered a national hero because he had defeated General Gordon who the British had sent in 1885 to conquer him. The Mahdi, however, died shortly thereafter and was unable to prevent the eventual colonization of the country.

"After that the English came. Under the British, there was no country called Sudan, but, *insha'allah*, we became Sudan. After the English left, we were still okay, but at Bashir's time they came and separated Arab people and black people. He took the light-skinned people and he threw us away." He tapped his walking stick on the ground for emphasis. "Omar never liked black-skinned people."

I wondered about his assessment that everything was fine from Sudan's 1956 independence until Bashir's time. Bashir's military coup was not until 1989; oppression and violence both in Darfur and

South Sudan began long before that. The Bashir government took the brutality to a new level, perhaps, but power had been in the hands of a few elite tribes from the North since 1956. Regimes changed frequently, but always among the same privileged groups.

The sheikh began to tell us about the attacks his people had endured at the hands of the government and Janjaweed, giving detail that was becoming all too familiar.

"The government came first, shooting and bombing. The people ran away to the mountains to hide. The Janjaweed came after to finish. There has been nobody to protect us but *Allah*."

He spoke with great affection about the camels, goats, cows, and sheep the villagers used to own. "We rely totally on the animals."

He then described how the animals were taken by the Janjaweed, houses looted and burned, and how, on top of everything else, nature also seemed to be conspiring against them.

"The rains were short this season . . . and now the place has become like the desert. We are starving. We are just waiting for people from the international community to come and bring food. Only they and *Allah* can help us. The organizations tried to send food to us, but the government forced them to turn back. Since the government stopped everything, the people have to eat burrs."

The sheikh pointed to the burrs on the ground, which had been sticking to our socks, clothes, hiking boots.

"Now, mothers are suffering from hunger and don't have milk to feed their children. In the past, we were not hungry." He picked up a burr and rolled it between his fingers thoughtfully. "In Darfur, we were raised on milk." Dero explained that this meant that in the past, life in Darfur had been bountiful and the people were well fed.

The sheikh's hands were marvelous. Pointing, fluttering, gesturing, they illustrated each and every sentence.

"When I was young, the life was good. We were in our places. Arab people don't have land; they live on their camels as nomads. Arabs have been against the black people for a long time. In the past, they were afraid of us, but now the government is helping them, so they come to attack us. Before, this was impossible."

The sheikh was impatient and interrupted as Dero tried to accurately summarize his previous statement.

"The people who fled from here are now in Kariare camp in Chad. But I am strong. If there is peace or not, we will stay here. If they come to bomb us again, we will die here. We will never leave this area. We will defend ourselves." His hands fluttered with long, delicate fingers to accent his point. "We will die here. *Insha'allah*."

Why was it so important for him to be here until he died? The sheikh referred again to the thirteen generations of his family that had been leaders of the area.

"They are all buried on top of the mountain." He waved to the distance with his walking stick. "My ancestors' graves are still there."

"Can we go and see them?" we asked.

"No problem. This young man will take you." He tapped Dero lightly with his walking stick. "He knows where it is."

"Will you come with us?" Adam asked, but the sheikh smiled and shook his head.

"I can't climb because I have bad knees. I've had this condition for a long time, but no medicine."

"Your walking stick," Adam asked, pointing to it. "Does it have any special meaning?"

We wanted our documentary to show the culture and heritage of Darfur as a backdrop to the current tragedies. Perhaps people's personal items held cultural significance.

The old man laughed deep and hearty. "My stick? The only special thing about it is it helps me to walk!"

We thanked the sheikh and left him sitting in his hut, perched on a stool with his walking stick, presiding over a village that barely existed. Somehow, he maintained a sense of dignity and purpose.

"Can you lead us to the graves?" we asked Dero.

"It is very far to go there now," he said. "Too much walking."

It had become quite hot. We weren't overly disappointed to be told that we would not be hiking a few hours up a mountain with our equipment.

"The sheikh told us that organizations that tried to bring food to this area were turned away by the government. Why is that?" I asked. "NGOs are operating inside the government IDP camps. Why can't they come here?"

"Because this is area controlled by the SLA. If aid comes in, the government fears this will help the rebels."

"But there are thousands of civilians here who don't have any access to aid!"

Dero simply shrugged. "The people in Khartoum don't care about that."

"Can't the U.N. and agencies cross the border from Chad like we did?" I pressed.

Adam explained further. "They can't risk it. If the government found out, their visas would be revoked and they wouldn't be able to operate in the IDP camps in the government held areas anymore."

I listened in disbelief. In order to provide assistance to the victims, the U.N. and NGOs were essentially being held hostage by the victimizers. It was like being bound to an abusive parent in order to help a child who was being battered.

DERO BROUGHT US to an unscathed home on the outskirts of the village. A group of small children were standing outside the hut. They were very thin, covered in dust, and wearing rags with gaping holes. Several of them had yellowing hair. They stared at us in silence. We approached them, expecting them to be curious about us, wanting to play, as the children in Iridimi had. These children, however, retreated from us in fear. Only one little boy and his younger sister, bolder than the others, held their ground staring at us. We knelt down and smiled. There was no return smile.

"*Salaam, habibi,*" Adam attempted to greet them in Arabic. The little girl started to cry, and her brother dragged her by the hand back to where the other children had regrouped, watching us from a safer distance.

I tried to understand the difference in reaction. While the kids in the refugee camp at least had access to humanitarian aid these children still faced an extremely precarious existence. The children in Iridimi had also met or at least caught glimpses of aid workers from all over the world. We were likely the only foreigners the kids here had ever seen.

Dero took us inside the hut and introduced us to a woman named Hassaniya. She was wearing a blue shawl and cradled a three-year-old boy in her lap. The little boy was wearing only a brown, dirty T-shirt. His head lolled about on his mother's lap. It was immediately evident that there was something wrong with him.

"What's the little boy's name?" Adam inquired.

"Tugud," Dero told us.

Flies were settling around. We were sweating. Tugud's six-year-old brother sat nearby, eyeing us silently, protectively.

"What is . . . what happened . . . what happened to the child?" There was no easy way for Adam to ask.

"His body is hot. It started like a fever-sickness," his mother explained. "From the injury. When the missile was thrown, I was carrying him on my back. I was at the well, watering my cows."

"Were you able to take him to a doctor?" Aisha asked.

"We didn't find any treatment for him. We couldn't get him to a hospital. The wound still bleeds. He has a problem with his neck. It cannot stay upright. It drops this way and that way."

Hassaniya lifted the boy to a sitting position and demonstrated to us the instability of the little one's neck.

"He cries a lot and he doesn't sleep at night."

The boy struggled to look around as flies circled his face, feasting on his eyes and his drool. He was unable to brush them away.

"How old is he now?" Adam asked.

"Four years old," his mother replied.

"And can he speak?"

"No, he doesn't talk. Also, he doesn't walk. He cannot sit. He used to walk, crawl, and could hold water and stayed in the shadows of the tree, but he cannot move now. The injury is down his neck, here."

Hassaniya propped Tugud higher up on her lap and tried to gently lift up the boy's head, to enable us to get a better look at the deep puncture wound just under his chin. It had scarred up horribly. Tugud began to cry.

"That's okay," Aisha said. We didn't want Hassaniya to maneuver her son for our sake. We were concerned that she thought we could provide medical help.

"Was she hurt in the bombing?" Adam asked Dero to ask Hassaniya.

"No, I wasn't hit. We were carrying this baby, and my clothes were punctured, but *insha'allah*, I wasn't injured."

Adam made clucking noises to see if the child would respond. He didn't.

"I want to tell Doctors Without Borders about this kid. Maybe they would send someone out here," Aisha said. "If any NGO might be willing to take the risk, it would be them."

"No help ever comes to this part," Dero answered simply.

When we exited the hut, the other children were sitting on a woven mat under the shade of a tree. They seemed a little less afraid of us. When Hassaniya invited us to sit on the mat with them, they didn't run away or burst into tears. They merely all scooted to one side of the mat and continued to stare at us. Hassaniya brought us a tin bowl of flavored water. We were being treated as honored guests. Water was extremely scarce and whatever means she used to flavor the water must have been in short supply. Adam, Aisha, and I weren't sure what to do. We didn't want to drink the water, both because of its scarcity and because it was non-treated; yet, we didn't want to offend our host or waste the water. When Hassaniya went back into the hut, Aisha offered the bowl to the oldest child sitting on the mat opposite us, a girl of about eight years. She took it shyly and passed it on to a younger child. Once all the kids had drunk, the smallest ones needing her help, she drank her share as well. The empty metal bowl was replaced carefully on the center of the mat.

We spoke to Dero about going to Kornoi. We wanted to get footage of the destroyed village to match with the testimonies from the refugees we had met in Iridimi camp.

"It is difficult to get there," Dero told us. "And also, there are no people left, no one to talk to there. I think you should go first to see Suleiman. Yeah. Suleiman can help you."

Who was Suleiman? We checked in Adam's notebook. His name wasn't written on our list of contacts.

"Why is it so hard to get to Kornoi?"

"Kornoi is controlled by the government. We can't go near the government troops. We would need a convoy of three cars to take us anywhere near there. It's very difficult . . ."

We began to have a distinct feeling that the rebels and the Janjaweed and the army went to great lengths to avoid confronting each other.

WE RETURNED TO the SLA truck. Fadi was washing his feet with water from a jerry can. We asked if we could interview him. He nodded, carefully re-wrapped his green turban around his head, and followed us to a shady area, so that the blazing afternoon sun wouldn't wash him out on the camera. The view behind him was spectacular—yellow rolling hills spotted with patches of light green and clumps of bushes and trees.

"Why did you come to Darfur from N'djamena?" Adam asked.

"To be in the Movement. The Sudan Liberation Army. I've been a soldier for two years. I came here from N'djamena because of injustice. I want human rights only. I want to liberate Sudan." Fadi muttered his words almost inaudibly. We hoped the microphone was picking up his voice.

"Liberation for whom?" Adam pressed.

"All people. Zaghawa, Fur, and many people . . ."

Fadi described, mumbling with incomplete sentences, some of the atrocities he had witnessed in the last two years.

We wanted to know whether teenaged boys such as Fadi were forced to join the rebel movement. We wanted to know if children were being armed.

"I shot a gun once, during the training," Fadi told us.

"Have you fought the Janjaweed?" Aisha asked.

"No."

"The Sudanese government?"

Again, he shook his head.

"How do the older guys from the SLA treat you?" Adam questioned.

"They are good," Fadi answered simply.

"If you wanted to return to N'djamena, could you?" Aisha asked.

"Yes."

I told Adam to ask Fadi if there had been a time when he was frightened.

"No," Fadi said squarely. "I was never afraid." How many fifteen-year-old boys would want to ever admit feeling fear?

He told us more about his family whom he had left in N'djamena.

"What matters most to me are my parents and my brother and sister. I'm the oldest."

We asked if he wanted to film a message for us to bring back to them when we returned to the capital.

He smiled broadly. "Yes! Tell them hello, how are they doing? How are they living their life? My father, he is sick, and I want him to recover from his illness."

"And to your brother and sister?" Adam asked.

Fadi thought for a moment and then delivered his message.

"Their future is to continue to study, to be educated, and to be a teacher or director, minister, and president, too."

"Do you have anything to say to kids in America, the same age as you?"

"Yeah. Students, go to school. Study." Fadi flashed a big grin. "Greetings from Sudan Liberation Army."

He wrote down his parents' names and phone number in Aisha's notebook. Dero had disappeared while we interviewed Fadi, but without much warning, it was time to continue driving. Everyone clamored onto the truck again. Just as we were about to pull away, Dero ran up, carrying a tarp with his possessions tied inside, and jumped onto the truck. And then there were eighteen.

WE ACUTELY FELT every bump and rock as we bounced along. "Ugh," Adam groaned as the truck hit yet another bump at high speed, jarring him hard so his back landed squarely on the metal of the back of the cab. "I think I pulled a muscle in my shoulder that time."

We ended up in a sing-a-thon in the back of the pickup truck. Adam, Aisha, and I were given the chance to hear traditional Zaghawa songs and, in turn, we treated the rebels to Barry Manilow classics and *A Chorus Line.* They didn't know what to make of us, especially when Aisha, with her turban wrapped around her face the way Yacoub had showed her, deep throated a phenomenal solo of *"You say tomayto, I say tomahto . . ."* in her best Louis Armstrong impersonation. Gears grinding and exhaust pipe coughing out black smoke, getting slashed by thorn trees as we sped by, *"You say potayto, and I say potahto . . ."* the truck struggled its way up hills that were more rock than path as the late-afternoon sun bathed the barren landscape in a golden glow. *"Let's call the whole thing off . . ."*

AN HOUR BEFORE sunset, we arrived in the next village. "This is Muzbat!" Dero told us with excitement in his voice. "I studied here as a boy. I know this place well."

We leaped off the side of the truck and helped to unload, once again, the cargo.

"Really? You studied here? Your family was in Shegeg Karo, hours away. Where did you stay?" I asked.

"Yeah, I would sleep inside the school. I got food from my family. I would take some maize flour and some kind of a pot and stay a period of six months in school. During the holiday, I came to my family for two or three months. It was really hard to complete primary school. Sometimes I had problem in food because my family was far. I would have to cut the period of study to go home and get some food and return back to continue with my study. That was the problem. Yeah." Dero said.

"Were there any adults who helped take care of you?" I asked.

"No, but I had many friends. One day I would cook, tomorrow the other cook. We played together and we slept together. Most of them were my age. I remember that time as being very nice. Life was very simple and poor, but when I think about it, it was good." Dero smiled and chuckled a little bit at a memory. "One night, we were very hungry. We were looking for food to eat, but didn't succeed. There was a flock of camels at the well. Because my father used to have many camels, I had experience dealing with camels. We went to the well secretly. The owner didn't know but we got milk from his camels and returned back. That is very funny for me. I remember that night."

An abandoned police station had been converted into an SLA base, complete with a tattered handmade flag. A few of the rebels there offered to show us around. The village looked very similar to what we had seen that morning in Furawiya: clusters of burnt homes with charred and broken remnants of pottery, furniture, and household items. Unlike Furawiya, however, there were a few sections of homes that remained standing.

The mosque was the most notable building in Muzbat, perhaps the only structure not severely damaged or burnt, though there were a few bullet holes. Even when the village was standing, it probably looked out of place. It was built of stone and marble. The whole thing must have been imported.

"The money was donated by a man from Qatar who came to capture falcons," our guides told us. Walking to the mosque, we passed a water pump. "Ah, that was donated by Save the Children years ago," they continued. I lifted the handle to inspect it. "Don't bother. It doesn't work."

One man approached us as we completed our tour and neared the rebel base/former police station.

"How are you? How are you?"

They seemed to be the only words he knew in English and he repeated them to us with a strange smile, wide, unblinking eyes, and boundless enthusiasm. His name was Bashir. He walked with a severe limp, and as he came closer we noticed a massive wound to his head, a gash going from the front to the crown of his skull, over an inch in depth and width.

"Yes! Very good! How are you?"

He stroked the sides of his gash, speaking slowly with long pauses between or in the middle of his statements.

"This is from the soldiers of Omar Bashir."

He rolled up his sleeve and thrust his arm out. It was badly scarred from a knife.

"I was a civilian. I was injured last Ramadan . . . I was injured the seventh day of Ramadan last year . . . Today is the seventeenth day of Ramadan!" he said.

Ramadan begins ten days earlier each year. Was today the one-year anniversary of his injury?

"Still now I am in pain,"

"You are a soldier?" Adam asked.

"Yes, with the SLA," he responded.

"Why are you a soldier?" Adam continued.

"Because of tyranny and ignorance. We, as Darfurians . . . are oppressed in all the plans of Omar Hassan Ahmad Bashir . . . Our area is burned . . . Today I remain behind a tree."

His words were articulate, but his delivery made it clear that the wound he sustained to his skull had impacted his speech and thought process. He continually searched for words, his eyes darting around him, until he found what he wanted to say, and then punched the rest of his words out forcefully.

"Where are you from?"

"From Furawiya."

"Are you married?"

Bashir seemed excited by the question. "Yes, very good!"

"Do you have children?"

"Yes, I have children. Jihan and Yareeda. One is five years old; one is three years old. They are refugees in Kariare."

When he spoke about his children, his injury seemed less obvious.

"What do you want from the future? For the future of your children?"

Bashir took a long moment to think, punctuating his response with many pauses and a wild look in his eyes.

"We need freedom first." There was a long silence. "We need freedom first. Second . . ." Bashir gathered his thoughts. "Authority. Third . . ." He looked away for several moments and then turned back to face us again. "Only freedom."

"If you were face-to-face with the man who attacked you right now, what would you want from him?" Adam asked.

He paused again. "I won't do anything to him. I only need freedom. He wants colonization; that's the difference."

The sun had set and food preparation was taking place around us. We watched Bashir limp away with his walking stick to wash his hands and feet for prayer.

Bowls of food were placed on a large woven mat on the ground, which people began to gather around. The commander of the base invited us to join in. We didn't feel comfortable eating when people, obviously, didn't have enough for themselves. But they refused to let us push away their hospitality. It was *iftar*, they insisted, a meal to be shared. We accepted, guiltily but gratefully, determined to find some way to repay their kindness. It was our first traditional Darfurian meal. It was similar to Ethiopian food, where sauces and dips are served in the middle of a tray of spongy *injera* bread, but instead of injera, there was sticky cornmeal mush called *asida*. We watched how our hosts ate and tried to imitate, rolling the mush into a small flat surface on four fingers indented by the thumb and using it to scoop up the dip, in this case a spicy, lentil bean purée. The mashed lentils and cornmeal mush all got pushed into the mouth with the thumb. It was a surprisingly delicious meal.

WE SET UP the tent by flashlight and crawled inside. A fit of giggles overtook Aisha and me. Perhaps it was sunstroke, the malaria medication, or the electrolyte powder I insisted we stir into our bottled water, but the giggles grew louder. The harder we tried to suppress it, the more it burst out. The afternoon's sing-along on the truck revived, starting with the song "Pooh's Corner" and interrupted by louder peals of laughter that we desperately tried to muffle with clothing. Adam was reading by flashlight, glancing over at us every few minutes, as if he thought we had totally lost our minds.

"You know," he said, lifting himself on his elbow, working hard not to smile. "Friends asked me if I worried about whether you two would get along."

"We'd get along with you a lot better if you would help us remember the theme song to *Who's the Boss?*" I jabbed him.

He pointed his flashlight in my eyes. "Watch it. Those same friends made bets about how long it would take until I abandoned you in Darfur!"

Eventually, the sounds of the rebels talking outside the tent began to subside. Our joking did as well. A deep quiet took its place. The impact of the day began to take hold. Perhaps that's what the singing and giggling had been about—trying to avoid letting what we had seen and heard really sink in. We lay in our tent next to the destroyed buildings of Muzbat, lost in our thoughts long into the starlit night.

DERO GREETED US with a tin can of sweet, hot tea just as the sun was rising.

"Dero! You don't need to make us tea!" Aisha protested.

"It's my job to take care of you," he insisted.

"Have some," Aisha offered, but he refused politely, ducking his head.

"I can't. I am fasting because of the Ramadan."

Back on the truck, I managed to grab a seat on top of the cab, holding on to a rope with my left hand and the mounted Kalashnikov with my right. Our first stop of the day was Janed, a rain-fed oasis that appeared out of nowhere. It was crowded with hundreds of donkeys, cattle, and camels, evidence of the livestock trade that had served as the basis for north Darfur's economy.

Adam grabbed the camera and Aisha took the tripod bag. We trudged with Dero along the muddy edge of the lake, passing a woman in a bright red wrap herding a small group of cows. She threw a stone at one slow mover in the group who mooed her protests loudly. We climbed up a small hill and found a group of women sitting on the edge of a well under the shade of several trees. All of them were wrapped in brightly colored shawls and scarves, a stunning contrast to the largely dull-colored surroundings. With their permission, Aisha snapped a photo.

They were from a village south of El Fashir, a woman named Zahra told us, and had been forced to flee further north where they had remained for months, roaming with their surviving animals and hoping for safety. Some of their story was familiar: early morning attacks by Janjaweed militia on horseback, killing villagers and looting possessions and herds. A new detail emerged, however. Many of their relatives had been captured and they didn't know what their fate had been.

"They took so many people, some people from my family. Maybe they were killed, we don't know," Zahra told us.

Su'ad Mohammed, a ten-year-old girl with large eyes and wrapped in a white shawl, confirmed this with her own story. Her small frame was hunched over. In a very soft voice she said, "My mother is in a temporary shelter. My father is not here. He was captured from the village by Arabs. We don't know where they took him. We were with him when he was captured. And then we left. I don't know where he is."

Su'ad Mohammed smiled and giggled. But the way she looked down, averting any eye contact, told us that the smiling was a form of emotional defense, another sign of trauma.

"Yes, I'm worried about my father. I am crying for everything that

I think about," Su'ad Mohammed said, letting out a nervous laugh. She looked back down at her feet.

Zahra told us that they had experienced relative stability since arriving at the oasis. At least, they hadn't been subjected to attacks. But she never knew when their limited sense of security might reverse.

"Maybe they will come here, too."

Though she and her parents got separated while fleeing, she had managed to keep her five children together, ranging in age from seven months to ten years. They were healthy at the moment, she told us, but hungry. They had chopped down trees to make temporary shelters. But the situation was not sustainable. There was no lasting water source. Zahra pointed down the well that they were perched on.

"This well will be dry by the end of Ramadan. We might die from lack of water."

We glanced at the lake a half-dozen meters to our left. It looked like a substantial water source, albeit receding. Dero read our thoughts. "That water is dirty, no good for drinking," he said. "Many people have bad stomach problems after drinking there."

Two beautiful girls, both wrapped in brilliant blue shawls, had been staring at us. They were holding each other and giggling. They wanted to be interviewed, they said, but they didn't respond to our questions. We couldn't tell if they didn't understand Dero or if Dero was having a hard time understanding us.

"Are you in school?" Adam asked, trying one more question.

The two girls giggled again.

It was Su'ad Mohammed who spoke up. "I went to school. I was in the second grade."

"What did you study?"

"Everything! I liked it so much. I want to learn, but there is no education here. I will go to school if I find one. I will study until I die."

"Did you play games in your village?" Adam asked.

"Yes, we did before," she answered. "We don't anymore."

"Can you show us? Can you play one for us to see?" I asked her.

Dero translated, and Su'ad Mohammed laughed, ducked her head, and shook it.

"Why not?" I tried to coax her. "Can you be the teacher and teach us a game?"

"We played by ourselves," she stated.

Dero translated her resistance firmly. "This one said no. You can ask others to teach you."

Was it embarrassment at the idea of playing in front of others on cue? Or was play simply unimaginable for Su'ad Mohammed right now?

As we walked back to the truck, we saw two women filling plastic jerry cans with lake water. Perhaps it was to wash clothes. Or maybe dire thirst had won out over fear of disease from contaminated water sources.

It was time to re-load the truck and get on our way. "Do you know where we're going?" we asked Dero.

"Amarai," he said. "To see Suleiman."

Our driver was nowhere to be found. He had gone off with another truck, it was reported, thinking that we would be stationed here much longer. Someone else offered to drive our truck to locate him. We climbed back on, with the addition of another passenger, an old man with a deeply wrinkled face and an air of tranquility about him, clearly not a fighter. The truck banged along more violently than ever, rattling the teeth in our skulls. One of the rebels explained why. Our original driver was from the Fur tribe. The Fur, he told us, are known to be good drivers. Our substitute driver was a Masalit; apparently the Masalit tribe is not famous for its driving ability. I have never been one to buy into stereotypes, but as we slammed over a huge rock, our knuckle-white grip on the ropes the only thing that saved us from being thrown entirely off the truck, I found myself praying that we would locate our driver, or any other member of the Fur tribe, before our shoulders were dislocated.

*

WE FOUND OUR driver after an hour and began to head east, I gauged from the sun. We took another rest break an hour later. As this would be the break for *iftar*, it was our chance to reciprocate for the hospitality we had been experiencing. We contributed funds to purchase a goat.

The SLA guys jumped off the truck. "Janjaweed!" one yelled out loudly.

Adam instinctively reached for the camera, as the three of us simultaneously ducked down, our heads swiveling from side to side in desperate search of any sign of the militia. Were we about to witness a confrontation?

"Janjaweed!" another rebel called back playfully, tossing something off the truck for the first to catch.

We laughed at ourselves for having tensed up. It seemed that the rebels called each other Janjaweed in the same way that many oppressed peoples take up the terms of their oppressors and use them as nicknames.

I watched the old man who had joined us as he clambered easily down from the truck. We talked to him as he leaned against a gnarled old tree, thick branches twisting in every direction, waiting for the goat meat to be prepared. His white *galabiya* and turban reflected the soft glow of the setting sun and his words were slow and measured. His name, he told us, was Nurein, and he was seventy years old. He was from a village outside of El Fashir. He was getting a ride to Amarai, where the truck was heading after *iftar*, and from there would find another ride back to his village.

How did he hook up the ride with the SLA truck?

Nurein pointed out one of the rebels riding with us, a young man with a reckless smile and a large number of *hijabs* (leather pouches thought to bring good luck) around his neck.

"This tall one, he's my sister's son."

The SLA had recently taken control of his area. Nurein spoke about the differences since then.

"The area is with us. It used to be controlled by the government, but now, by the rebels. I don't know how they pushed out the government, but they did. The government used to dominate us. They always took our animals, our property. But there is no oppression now. The rebels brought justice and now things are good."

I wondered: would people in the rebel-held territory feel free to share complaints or criticisms about the SLA with us? Could we trust that the expressions of support for the SLA were genuine?

"It used to be good. We used to live together. *Wallahi* (I swear), the Arabs were our neighbors. They came to our territories, stayed for a time, and went back. But in the end, the government started injustices. The Arabs became our enemy, cooperating with the government and attacking and killing Zaghawa. I don't know why. I swear, we are innocent people. That's why our sons began the movement and the people started to fight."

"How can things become better?" Aisha wanted to know.

"I don't know how to improve the situation unless the government stops behaving unfairly. They need to stop the injustice."

He told us he had ten children, six boys and four girls, and grandchildren as well.

"What do you fear for the future for your children and grandchildren?" Aisha asked.

Nurein shook his head sadly. "*Wallahi*, if there is a future, I don't know. We'll put them in the schools, but I don't know what the outcome will be. I hope that times to come will be better."

"How many years ago did you and your wife marry?" I asked.

"We got married some time ago. Since I have grandchildren . . ." Nurein raised his eyebrows ". . . it's a really long time ago."

"Do you remember the day you got married? Can you tell us about your wedding?" I asked, hoping this could be an opportunity to learn about the celebration of life-cycle events.

"Of course I remember. Why shouldn't I?" But instead of elaborating, Nurein drove home a different point. "In the past, we were in better conditions. Now, our kids are growing up and fighting."

"Do you have any message for Omar Bashir?" I asked.

Nurein's voice hardened uncharacteristically. "I don't have anything to say to Omar Bashir."

"Most of the SLA is very young. What do you think of that?" Adam asked.

Perhaps Nurein took this as a challenge as to why he wasn't part of the resistance himself.

"Elderly people cannot run and cannot ride the vehicles. They don't have the strength. That's why the younger people are participating."

We asked about the *hijabs* his nephew had around his neck.

"He is fighting, that's why he needs these amulets." He indicated his own neck, bare of decoration. "But I am staying here. I don't need them."

There was a belief among many that the amulets held extraordinary power. Aisha had read reports of parents who spent what little money they had buying *hijabs* to protect their children. Nurein's explanation for the *hijabs* was simple, but struck a chord. I counted how many of the rebels were wearing them and remembered seeing them on many of the small children in Iridimi. They began to take on a significance for me that I couldn't quite articulate.

"Do you think that the Zaghawa and Arabs can live in peace again in this region?" Adam asked.

Nurein's answer echoed, I imagined, the concern of millions. "I don't know."

WE JOINED THE rest of the group in eating macaroni and goat meat, topped off with tiny, white, mealy watermelons. Then it was back on the pickup while the full moon, rising like a bright orange disk, served as a lantern as the truck pushed through the desert.

"Soon we will be in Amarai," Dero told us. "Suleiman will be able to help you."

I sat on top of the cab again, holding onto the Kalashnikov for balance with one hand and the rope strapping it down with the other. Even as the air got progressively colder, I loved riding up there. I pulled my flannel shirt from around my waist, putting it on when the truck stalled for a moment. The moon rose higher, morphing from orange to yellow to white. A few hours later, the truck stopped. Amarai. We had arrived.

In the black of the night, an elderly man greeted us jovially in English as we, tired, sore, and creaking, climbed off the truck.

Unexploded missile dropped by Antonov plane in Furawiya

"Hello, hello, I'm Suleiman!" He shook hands all around and began cracking jokes immediately. "Welcome to our multi-star hotel! You can sleep here." He indicated a small area covered by a tarp. "Or, if the ground is too hard, there is softer sand a short distance away, in the *wadi*."

"Oh, I can sleep on anything," Adam assured him. "My backside is plenty calloused from riding on your trucks."

"You? You can sleep with your backside on a pointy rock! I'm worried about the ladies!" From the light of the moon, we could tell he was smiling broadly. Aisha and I assured Suleiman that our backsides were equally tough and set ourselves up under the tarp.

We wondered who Suleiman was exactly, this wisecracking elderly man, and why he was the one we were sent to.

five

the SLA

"NOBODY TELLS THE ORPHAN HOW TO CRY."

YOUTHFUL VOICES WERE chanting and singing in the distance. We rolled over trying to ignore them. They got louder, closer. "What is that?" Adam muttered, covering his head with his sleeping bag. "Where is it coming from?"

Aisha unzipped the tent and we stumbled out groggily, trying to track the direction of the chanting.

"Good morning!" Suleiman walked over to greet us, as cheery as he had been the night before. He was tall and lanky, we noticed now that we could see him, with high cheekbones, graying facial hair, and a large smile with bright white teeth.

"Are those kids? Where is that coming from? Can we go there?" we peppered him with questions.

"They are training. Follow me."

Suleiman started making his way down toward a *wadi*. Throwing on our shoes and quickly grabbing the equipment, we tried to keep up with our spry host, as we scrambled over wide, flat rocks and pushed through soft sand. The air was still cool in the *wadi*, but we could already feel the heat starting to rise. The sky was brilliant blue and cloudless.

Suleiman walked serenely, but purposefully, in his white *galabiya* and turban, with his hands folded behind his back, chatting with Adam and Aisha. I couldn't hear what they were talking about—I was struggling just to keep up. In the distance, through a cloud of dust, I could see a cluster of boys chanting as they jogged.

"There!" Suleiman pointed.

Aisha and Adam took off running with the cameras, leaving the empty camera bag behind. I stood with Suleiman for a moment and watched Adam sprint to catch up with the group of boys, Aisha on his tail. They didn't appear to be getting any closer.

"So, you can find the place back again? The multi-star hotel?" Suleiman asked. I assured him we could. "Okay, then I will leave you here. When you return, we can make my interview."

I hoisted the empty camera bag over my shoulder and continued walking toward the boys. Adam had somehow caught up and was now running backwards ahead of them, filming as they jogged to the camera. I reached them as the boys eventually stopped to practice drills. They were marching in place, practicing turns, and call-and-response chants. Dust kicked up and swirled as many feet, some in shoes, some in flip-flops, some bare, pounded down into the hard desert sand. They were teenagers, dressed in an odd assortment of clothes ranging from sweatpants to dress pants, tank tops, basketball jerseys, T-shirts, and button-down shirts, most of them stained and torn. Some boys wore turbans, most were without. The twenty-year-old leader was the only one with a gun. Though not much older than the boys, he had their respect as he called out words that they repeated and barked commands that they followed, sloppy as the formation and rhythm was. Aisha moved in and out of their lines, filming.

"*The Darfur revolution is written,*" they repeated after the commander in a sing-song voice. "*The Darfur revolution is of the youth!*"

"I bet Fadi is in the group," Adam said to me. "See if you can find him so we can film him training."

I circled around the group of boys, trying to stay out of Aisha's camera shot angle and locate Fadi. Green turban, green turban . . . what color was his shirt? I couldn't remember. The boys were lined up three rows deep and with all the kicked-up dust it was hard to see, let alone to breathe. The boys tried to ignore our presence, focusing straight ahead, but it was evident by the occasional stolen glance that they were acutely aware of being watched. One was bolder than the rest. When the commander wasn't looking, he stared straight at me, made a face, and hooted. Was this normal teenager clowning for the strangers, or an expression of resentment at our presence?

I couldn't find Fadi. The boys jogged away from us, continuing to chant and peek over their shoulders to see if we were following. We began to walk back to the base camp. Just as we approached, we saw Fadi running to catch up with the other boys.

"Hey, Fadi!" we called out to him. "How's it going?"

He smiled and waved, but kept on running, late for his drills.

Suleiman wasn't at base camp when we returned; instead we found a tall, thin young man in tan pants, flip-flops, and a dark blue T-shirt. We asked him if he knew where our host was.

"He will be back soon," he told us.

He had straight-line scars across his forehead, more prominent than any other facial markings we had seen. His eyes were small, squinty, and serious. His skin was taut around his cheekbones and he had a large gap in between his front teeth. He wasn't from Darfur. He was a Dinka from southern Sudan, the same tribe as John Garang, head of the SPLA. He had been fighting for eight years with the SPLA and only recently came to Darfur.

"My name is James," he told us when we sat down to chat with him. "I've been here for six months. In the past, I was a fighter with the SPLA. I was a teenager when I joined. I fight because of oppression. The South is not like the North. There are more possibilities in northern Sudan. There is nothing in the South. The country is burned and everything is completely destroyed. There is no food. There's no education or educated people. The people are farmers. They grow maize and okra and vegetables, simple things. In the past when I was just a boy, I lived in the countryside. There was nothing there, no school, and you didn't have other work. You went to the fields and that's it.

"All the people in the South are like the Darfurians. There's death, there's killing from the government forces. Why did they kill the

Dinka? I have four brothers. All of them were killed in battles. I was about twelve years old. I was still young. People came in the night behind them and opened fire. Two died like this and the other two joined the SPLA. Many people fled in fear and those who remained defended the area. The situation in the South and Darfur is the same. The problems are from the same starting point. They oppress people.

"I am fighting in Darfur now. I will see it to the end, whether they kill for twenty years, thirty years, seven years, five, one. The people here are black like us. They are my brothers, I live among them. We all are one people. We eat together. When it is time to pray, I pray over here, they pray over there. The difference is only in name."

I wondered how wide was the solidarity that James expressed. Many Darfurians had been a part of the government army during the years of war with the South. The government had used religion to justify the attacks against the tribes of southern Sudan, such as Dinka and Nuer, who practiced traditional religions or Christianity. As Muslims, many Darfurians fought on behalf of the government. Now Darfurians were facing the same tactics that had been used against the southern Sudanese, but with the smokescreen of ethnicity masking the true motivation for the violations.

We asked him if there was anything he wished he could tell his parents.

"I would send greetings. Maybe I would inform them about my health, but I will say that I am staying. I don't need anything, and I am fine. There are no problems for me. If the situation improves, maybe I will come to them.

"Honestly, I wish the negotiations would succeed. Everything in Sudan would be better. Every poor person will be free. However, the problems come when the policy is bad. The people are tired and fleeing in the forests. Still we don't arrive at power, we don't rule. I want the armed conflict to end in order for there to be peace. We want to sleep."

We talked to James for forty-five minutes about Sudanese politics, the situation in southern Sudan, and his experiences in Darfur.
There was still no sign of Suleiman. The sun was getting more
intense. We lay down in the shade provided by the tarp overhang.
Dero was dutifully poring over a small notebook.

"What's that?" I asked him.

"Words I don't know," he answered. "This is how I improve my
English."

Motivated by Dero, I took out my notebook where I had been
jotting down Arabic words and phrases that we often encountered.
When was your village destroyed? How many people were killed? My Arabic vocabulary was expanding in very specific—and troubling—
ways.

"What does this mean?" Dero pointed to a line in his notebook.
"Po–li–ti–cal a–sy–lum."

We explained. Dero sounded it out, practicing its pronunciation
until he got it right. Then he blurted out, "You think I can get political asylum in the United States?" We didn't know how to respond.
We weren't quite sure if he was serious, practicing using the phrase
in a sentence, or if he really understood what he was asking for. He
smiled and winked.

Suleiman finally appeared, charming as ever, and full of apologies.
He sat down gracefully under the shade of the tarp, crossed his legs,
and stroked his closely clipped salt and pepper beard. "Shall we
begin?"

Suleiman began by stating his name, including his family name.
It sounded familiar. Adam grabbed his notebook and flipped open
to our contacts page. Sure enough, Suleiman's last name was written and noted as a key contact for us, the humanitarian coordinator
of the SLA.

"I was born here in North Darfur, in a place called Anka, in the
year 1947. I went to Khartoum for technical secondary school in

1964. I spent fourteen years working for the government, in the Ministry of Industry. I worked in a factory specialized in making paper bags, and cartons such as this."

He held up a bit of a torn cardboard carton that had blown over to where we were sitting.

"I was about eight years old when the British left. I don't remember the faces and the activities, but so many of our elder people say that the British period was better than the national period. At least the colonials oppressed us all equally and no Sudanese had power to dominate the others. The people who have been governing Sudan since 1956 until now are only from a few tribes. Since independence, the government of Khartoum has been trying to marginalize the bigger tribes of African origin in Darfur. Until now, we are missing power and participation in the government in ruling Sudan. We are missing education. We are missing health. We are missing any kind of development for the area. Since you crossed the border until you came here, what kind of civil life have you found? Nothing, except what was created by nature.

"In the south of Sudan, they were fighting since 1955 to claim their rights, the same exact rights as we are fighting for. From 1972 until 1983 they stopped the war, and then they started again. For thirty-eight years, they struggled for their rights and they did not find them. And the international community was deceived by our government of Sudan who prolonged the period of talk. We started this fight in Darfur in 2000 to claim our rights. The marginalization that created the war in the south is the same cause as the war in the west. If the government continues on the same track, there will be wars in other areas, as has already started in the Nuba Mountains. The Darfur war will not be the last for this government, if they remain in power. I have known some of the political leaders since they were students . . . if this government does not change, Sudan will not be settled."

I asked him about the relationship between the different tribes in Darfur.

"Previously, we and the Arabs exchanged marriage. Some of the Zaghawa are married from the Arabs. Some of the Arabs are married from Zaghawa, from the Fur, from the Masalit. It was a complete community life. In the past, in peacetime, the Arab nomads moved from south Darfur to the north of Darfur after the rainy season. They would spend the whole winter in the north with us, with Fur, Masalit, with any tribe. We would help each other. When someone lost some of his livestock, everyone came and helped seek the lost animals. We built good relations between us. Definitely, some conflicts happened between individuals, and then the tribal leaders and the elders sat together and solved the problem. Someone gave some money, cattle, or camels from someone to the other, and the thing was resolved. After the livestock grew bigger and the number of citizens themselves grew larger, the farmers needed a wider area of land to plant for their food, and the herders also needed a wider area for their livestock. The needs of the life for the herders and farmers came into conflict, and the government found the chance to wedge between the two, keep them separate, and push them to war. The war is taking place on behalf of the government.

"For the Arab tribes, the idea of this war is to get land. Not all the Arabs. I'm only speaking about the Janjaweed. Janjaweed is the combination of *jeen*, which is evil, *jawad*, horse, *jeed*, a kind of weapon. The Arab nomads tried to frighten the farmers off their land in order to feed their cows. The government joined their efforts. The government called for other nomadic Arabs from neighboring countries, mainly from Chad, Mali, Central Africa Republic, Cameroon, and sometimes from Niger, a collection of nomads moving from the west to the east. The government told them there is a good life and easy to find unowned livestock. Please, come and take. They came in heaps and big numbers, and they found themselves in the middle of some kind of war. So they participated in it.

"The government itself, why she is coming to our area and what is she seeking? If she left us with the Janjaweed, either of two options would happen. Either we would defeat them and they would flee back to their countries, or we would come to negotiations and agree to live with each other. But the government is trying to prolong the war. We don't deserve for this conflict to be extended. But what can we do? If the government wants to cleanse the area and replace us with the Arabs, we have two options: Either fight to survive, or grab our hands and sit until we are killed. So, we are fighting for survival, to defend our lives. We have nothing else to do. They cannot defeat us. They cannot clean us.

"We and the Arabs are compelled to this war on behalf of the government. You passed Muzbat yesterday, I think. Have you seen the holes made by the bombs? Do Janjaweed have fighter planes? The government is backing the Janjaweed and the Janjaweed are fighting on behalf of the government. Our true enemy is the government of Sudan. We are not fighting the Arabs. We are fighting against the government who is using the Arabs to clean us out of the area and pressing them to replace us in our lands.

"The Arabs are not using their minds because they feel that the government is backing them. If the government stops supporting them or giving them ammunition and guns, I think they would come to their senses and we would seek a way with each other to make peace and to continue to live peacefully, as it was before they started this conflict. We spoke to Arabs and we need to speak more, but they did not come to the realization that they are fighting on behalf of the people in power in Khartoum."

"Most of the SLA we have seen so far is young men. You are . . ." I hesitated, not wanting to offend.

"Yes, I am a very old man." Suleiman laughed.

"What led you to join the rebel movement?"

"In February 2000, the government started to detain and imprison me. I spent about four months in jail in Port Sudan. Then I was released. I had two months out of jail; then I was arrested again the same year in September. I sat about five months in jail and was released again. In 2001, I was again detained for about six months. When I was released the third time, I tried to come out and join the SLA. But I didn't find the chance. I was detained for the fourth time in 2003 and spent another six months in jail.

"Instead of giving us food three times a day, they fed us once or twice, to make us complain. But we didn't. Even if we would die of starvation, we refused to complain. They tried to beat me. I called their people and they were afraid to repeat it again. I was left just to sit in prison. The last three times I was not asked anything. No one interrogated me, no one accused me, no one told me why I was in jail. They said they feared I may be killed by some enemies whom I don't know. They said, 'The people of Darfur may harm you, so we are trying to keep you safe.' I know the real reason. They thought that I had relations with the SLA in Darfur, but they hadn't the evidence.

"When the thing became bigger and the government participated as a partner in this war, we elders felt compelled to go back. I spent forty years of my life in Khartoum, living an easy civilian life there, with my house and my family and my children. Nothing to be compared to the harsh life we are living now, these hard rocks."

I recalled his concern about our backsides on the rocky ground last night. He was twice our age and sleeping on those same stones by choice.

"Nothing could attract me to come here except the feeling that if I stayed there and did nothing while my tribe is being cleaned from the area, I will lose some of . . ." The muscles in Suleiman's face twitched almost imperceptibly as he struggled to find the right word. "I will feel ashamed. Finally, I escaped prison. I came to stand beside my tribe, the Zaghawa, and help.

"Now I am the humanitarian affairs coordinator with the

Movement. It is the window, the link, through which the NGOs and the agencies can pass to provide assistance for the people who are internally displaced and affected by war, the civilians who are in the area controlled by SLA. In the territory controlled by SLA, there's complete security. From last February until now, nothing happened in any region controlled by SLA. All the government violations are in areas controlled by the government. Even if the government succeeds in sending some spies through the NGOs, no one can move without being seen or known."

"You say that the civilians in the SLA domain are safe then?" I questioned.

"Perfectly safe," he responded with confidence.

"But everyone we have seen and spoken to say they are still very scared. What are the people afraid of?"

"They fear the bombing of the Antonov airplanes only. Nothing else."

"What kind of effect do you think the conflict is having on the women and children? Is it fair for the SLA to continue to fight if they know that civilians are suffering as a result?"

Suleiman took a moment before he answered my question, measuring his words. "Any kind of war affects children and women, definitely very badly, but if it is our fate and there is no other choice, what should we do? We just try to minimize the effect of the war on our citizens and continue fighting, until we come to our rights or at least to secure our lives. Our choice is to fight so that they may survive."

"The boys we saw this morning. Who are they? Does the SLA have a policy about children?" I inquired. I was almost afraid to ask. Would Fadi be sent to fight?

"When I started my job in humanitarian affairs, I took eighty of these children you have seen to Bahai, asking the agencies, who can take care of these boys? Most of their parents and families are killed, their villages are burned. Some of them fled, and they don't know where their parents are. I spent about a month asking all the NGOs and the refugee camps. No one accepted them. I left them there, and asked them to wait for me until I got back. When I returned, some of them were still there, waiting. Others did not bear the life of the refugees in the camps and came back to our SLA camps. They are practicing activities inside the camps and helping in the civil side of our Movement. They are not fighting. We are still asking, who is the agency that can take any kind of care of these children? At least, how to feed them? How to teach them? How to grow them up? We have so many problems among them. And we need an agency which can take care of them, to help them get back to their civilian life. But we still didn't find one. We are keeping them because they have nowhere else to go. But we are not taking them to participate in the war. Definitely! We have enough fighters. Those joining in the fighting are age twenty and above. The younger ones participate in humanitarian activities only, until they become fit for our rules, or to go back to their parents, if they found them still alive."

"Are we able to meet some of the kids we saw training? Talk to them?" I requested.

"Absolutely. This afternoon or tomorrow we will bring you to them."

"The media says that the conflict started when the SLA attacked the airport in El Fashir."

"The airport wasn't attacked until 2003. Ten years before that, a team of government police and military soldiers went into two villages. They detained four from each village. En route to Nyala, they were killed and buried. No one can say that the conflict started in 2003. We have so much evidence that illustrates that the conflict started when the government thought to clean out the African origin tribes and then replace the Arabs on the ground," he said. "We did not think about the government. We did not think about power.

We did not think, previously, to defeat the government or to take the government out of her power. But now, if we did not do this, we will not be left to live. So we are compelled to either fight against the government for our survival or wait to die.

"We do not want to secede from Sudan. If we make a country within the borders of Darfur, we will make a small country, without prospects. Sudan, as its borders are now, can be ruled by small, federal governments with a central base of power. We can make a federation. Sudan cannot be governed by only one central government."

"Do you have any hopes that the peace talks happening now in Abuja can lead anywhere?" Aisha asked.

"The door to the peace is to disarm the Janjaweed. But the government delegation includes the ministers who created and backed the Janjaweed. If those militias are not disarmed, peace will not ever come to Darfur. The government of Sudan is fooling the world. It is not acting toward resolution. They are trying to gain time, to prolong their rule. And we in the SLA will not put down our guns unless we are sure that the Janjaweed are disarmed and the government stops secretly giving them guns and ammunition. If the same man who created the Janjaweed and is their hero is the one sent to disarm his body, I don't think this will lead to any kind of peace. Our fate is to fight until we throw out this government. This is the only way. We have no choice. We believe that they have the same right that we have, to live in Sudan, but not to marginalize others. We will not finish them and they can't finish us. We should seek some kind of agreement to live with each other. This is better for them and for us."

"Thank you so much. Hope we didn't tire you out with too many questions," I said, unclipping the microphone.

Suleiman simply shrugged. "I am here to speak only. I have no gun."

We began chatting more informally. The conversation turned to U.S. politics.

"And this national security advisor, this Condoleezza Rice, is one of our grandfather's daughters."

He directed his comment at Aisha, clearly indicating that he didn't believe his grandfather shared ancestry with Adam or me.

"She's not as wonderful or strong as many people seem to think," Aisha muttered.

"So our relatives there are not happy with their daughter then? Since they are not pleased, then we are not pleased."

We were interrupted by the arrival of two rebel fighters, fierce looking men dressed in camouflage and wrapped in ammunition and *hijabs*. Suleiman gave them a noticeable amount of attention. They looked at us sitting on the ground, cameras by our side. They were interested in who we were.

"I'm Commander Salih Bob." Salih Bob had on a mustard-yellow turban, sleeves rolled up past the elbows, and what looked like a week's worth of beard and moustache growth. He was tall, thick, and broad shouldered. His face was chiseled and tough. He looked mean. "Bob," he repeated when we didn't respond. "You know Bob? Marley?"

"He is also one of our grandfathers," Suleiman added.

"Yes," Aisha laughed, and stopped abruptly, not sure if it was okay.

"We are all sons of Bob Marley." Salih Bob laughed himself.

"And what is your name?" Aisha asked the other man, dressed also in a mustard-colored turban. Large, dark Ray-Ban sunglasses covered half of his round, smooth face. He was draped in more ammunition than it seemed possible to carry and still walk straight.

"Commander Kitir Congo," he responded bluntly, without any emotion.

"These are two of the men who started the SLA," Suleiman explained further. "You can interview them."

The men sat down and laid their Kalashnikov guns at their feet. It took a few minutes for them to unwrap their rolls of bullets and lay them down as well. Salih Bob stared Aisha straight in the face. She naively asked how old he was, thinking this was an easy opener.

"I don't know my age. I was born under a tree, and lived under a tree, and I am struggling from under a tree," he muttered bitterly out of the side of his mouth in a low, deep voice, staring hard at her. "Look into my eyes and you will see my pain."

I was a little nervous to look into this man's eyes.

"What about Kitir Congo?" Aisha asked after a pause. The answer was no more straightforward.

"The person who knows his age is one who is settled in a good place and with peace and can think about these things and know when he was born. But we never saw this, so how can we know our ages?"

We weren't sure how to proceed.

"Go on, ask them anything you want," Suleiman encouraged us. "They are ready to tell you everything!"

Aisha's next question, she hoped, was less open for interpretation: why and how the SLA was originally formed.

"We didn't start as SLA . . ." Salih Bob began.

Suleiman interrupted him, prodding him for more detail. "When did you begin?"

"August 1, 2001," Salih Bob said.

"August 1, 2001," Kitir Congo confirmed from behind his dark glasses.

"We began when we were going to Jebel Marra," Salih Bob continued. "We called ourselves DLA, Darfur Liberation Army. After that, things progressed to who we are now."

We must have looked confused, because Suleiman clarified.

"When they started, they thought that the conflict was in Darfur only. They fought for a year and some months under the name of DLA. After this year, they realized their true aim. So they changed their name to SLA, Sudan Liberation Army. Instead of keeping themselves in Darfur, they raised their aims to throw down the central government for all Sudanese citizens. They realized if they didn't take down the government in power now, the conflict in Darfur would not be solved."

"The revolution is not just for Darfurian people only," Salih Bob added. "This is for all the Sudanese and marginalized places. Everyone needs to have their rights. Even Omar Bashir!"

Suleiman continued as he began to neatly arrange the long rolls of ammunition into tight coils. I hoped the microphone wouldn't pick up the sound of the bullets jarring against each other. "They called all the marginalized people anywhere in Sudan to join them, and they are. So many tribes are with us in our camps. You will see some Arabs and other tribes in our camps. You will find Southerners even."

James, our new Dinka friend, was a testament to these words.

Suleiman explained the growth of the SLA. "The fault of the government: in place of trying to punish the guilty, they terrorized the innocent, the civilians. The government burned the villages and sent the janjaweed to kill harmless women and children. Many people were angry and they joined the SLA to defend their villages and families."

Suleiman had summarized what seemed to me to be the crux of the affair. When the rebellion began, the government responded by intentionally targeting the civilians from whom the rebels drew their base.

Kitir Congo sat silently behind dark glasses.

Aisha questioned again whether the attack the SLA launched on the El Fashir airport was the starting point of the conflict. Salih Bob lit a cigarette for himself and one for Kitir Congo. He dragged on it deeply, looked at the lit end and then at each of us with a slight grin.

"Me, Kitir Congo, and Zayedan, we were responsible for the airport during the El Fashir attack. We freed the airport and burned eight airplanes, fighter planes, and Antonovs, which were loaded and ready to go to bomb our people. The Americans will investigate these truths."

Kitir Congo nodded silently behind his dark glasses.

Suleiman had something to add. "This was just a step on the road, one stop between many stations. The war was not started on this occasion."

The attack on the El Fashir airport may not have been the starting point, I thought, but it seemed accurate to mark it as the juncture at which the government of Sudan began to take the threat of the SLA seriously and ramped up their response.

"What would have to happen for the SLA to disarm?" Aisha asked.

Salih Bob answered, "We will stop fighting and put down our weapons if we receive our rights, for all the fighters and all the Sudanese." Salih Bob started to go global and historical. He looked straight at Aisha. "You were marginalized and enslaved and were taken all the way to America. We are fighting for those roots now. We help all people as much as we can. Not only the ones here in this area, even up to Rwanda ..."

"No, no, don't go away, talk about this area," Suleiman interrupted.

Kitir Congo crushed the end of his cigarette into the ground.

Salih Bob brought his point back home. "We will help any human being, Arab or Zaghawa, Masalit, Fur, no matter who."

"A big focus of our film is children," Aisha told Salih Bob. "Is there a message for the children of Darfur?"

"My message is: I am going to protect them. I protect women and children and the elderly. That's the only message I have."

"We spoke to many children in Chad who want to come home right away. Any words for them?" Aisha persisted.

"I myself want to go back to Kornoi, the area where I was born. But there is still danger from janjaweed and government. We hope to free our areas and bring our families back. I have no further message. I cannot tell them whether or not to come. Everything is written in the book."

Aisha looked at us. "Jen? Adam? Anything you want to add?"

Startled, Adam looked up from the lead camera, where he was adjusting the focus. Suleiman laughed.

"Adam slept! He slept with his camera."

Adam grinned and asked Salih Bob a question. "If the conflict finished tomorrow, what would you do?"

"Me, personally, I am a freedom fighter. I will go anywhere to stand up for others' rights. You can find me in Rwanda, Liberia, Congo, Somalia."

"Have you fought anywhere else besides Darfur?"

"No, just in Darfur. But I find the ways of resistance . . ." Commander Bob's face twisted, as he tried to explain what he wanted to say. "I understand fighting. I'm willing to go anywhere."

I couldn't help but ask myself how much of this was idealism and how much careerism. I had read a lot about mercenaries in Africa and elsewhere, jumping from one conflict to the next, to capitalize on and profit from the training they had received in their home conflict.

Aisha asked Salih Bob if he had anything more he wanted to say. He did.

"We don't want Americans to think we are just fighting. We are not killers. We are not bloodsuckers. We hope that everybody gets their rights and goes back to live in his place. In the end, we are Sudanese. The war is not by our choice, but circumstances force us to carry weapons and defend."

He patted his Kalashnikov on the ground in front of him for emphasis.

"I'm quite sure if this happened in Los Angeles from your own government or in Newcastle from the British government . . . all the world will hear you and help would come. But our case is different. Nobody is listening."

The afternoon was beginning to grow late.

"Thanks so much for talking to us," Aisha said, extending her hand to shake theirs as Adam and I switched off our cameras.

Kitir Congo, who had not uttered a syllable since confirming the SLA's starting date, suddenly cleared his throat.

"I have a few words I want to say."

He took off his dark sunglasses and wiped them down with a dirty yellow cloth before returning them to his face. We got a brief glimpse at his eye. It was severely damaged.

"Of course, of course!" We hastily turned the cameras back on. Kitir Congo had more than a few words to say. The anger and pain in his voice was barely concealed as he spat out his thoughts in rapid-fire Zaghawa.

"I, myself, the person who is sitting here, I have no one left. They were all killed. I am from Kreker village. It was burned by the government of Sudan and janjaweed in 1981. In this village was a combination of all tribes: Fur, Masalit, and Zaghawa. From the eighty families who lived together there, forty-five people were killed. All of us who had grown up together became displaced. We came to Ma'oon area and we reestablished Kreker village. And then, Kreker again was burned by the government in 1987. Fifty or sixty people were killed. At that time, we were young."

He pointed over his right shoulder with his chin as if to suggest that his youth was a long ago memory. The rage in his voice, however, indicated that the experience of his youth motivated him on a daily basis.

"The government is ruling all the country. It supports some citizens to murder others and burn their villages. It's not fair. If we are also Sudanese citizens, why didn't the government ever support us to kill other tribes?"

Kitir Congo's question was an interesting yardstick with which to measure equal treatment. I was reminded of Suleiman's earlier comment about the equality all the Sudanese had felt in being colonized by an outside force. It seemed that the very notion of equality in Sudan was skewed by the historical injustices people had endured.

"This village, where my great-great-grandfather was born, has no schools and no security for the people. Years ago, eighty camels were escorted by the government with four or five cars with heavy guns. They moved the camels through our farms, and if you tried to say anything to protect your farm, you would be executed. Since that time, they've been murdering one of our people every single day, our brothers, our cousins, our uncles, our mothers. They keep killing, killing, killing us.

"In 1991, there were fourteen people captured in a mosque during Friday prayers in a town in south Darfur. They were slaughtered. In 1993, the government surrounded a different area and captured seventeen herders. They dug holes with bulldozers, buried them alive, and ran over them, crushing them." Kitir Congo continued with his list, detailing each place, year and the number of people killed, the pitch of his voice growing higher. "If you protested to the government, they just put your grievance as ink on paper, whether they stole your camels, burned your village, or killed your people. As far as I can remember, why are we living this way since that time? We cry. Our homes are full of tears.

"Some Sudanese get easy lives from modern tools. They eat imported food, they live in villas and they have water pumps, televisions, and air conditioners. They are sitting inside the high-rise buildings and watching TV. We are sitting under these huts. Our mothers have to travel for miles to bring water from the wells in jerry cans."

The Sudanese Kitir Congo was speaking of didn't get their easy life merely from modern tools. I was aware that taxes paid by Darfurians were used for the benefit of the ruling elite in Khartoum.

"We're not concerned about our own lives, but the rights of our people," Kitir Congo continued. "Even one camel is part of the wealth of this country and should receive protection. Why do the citizens have no protection?

"We are tired of fighting. You are in Sudan. You came over here to find the truth and to understand our sorrow. Please take our message to all the other nations. If the media will take our problem to the United Nations, they will recognize that we have rights. The United Nations is the father of all countries, not just America. I don't have anything more to say. Please give our message to the international community and let us know if human beings are supposed to live under these conditions."

Kitir Congo retreated back into his silence.

Salih Bob had another final message. "The people who died, they told us to fight, to keep our message until we win. This responsibility is in our hands." He nodded significantly, looking right at me, and muttered from a half-opened mouth: "Nobody tells the orphan how to cry."

I was still considering Salih Bob's closing statement when I realized that someone else, also wearing the trademark mustard turban, had joined us. I didn't know who he was or how long he had been there, but he asked us to turn our cameras back on. We hesitated, knowing how limited our battery supply was. But Salih Bob was already passing him the microphone. We pressed *record*, sending up a quick prayer that we could recharge off a car battery that evening.

"My name is Mohammad Ismail," he introduced himself, and then launched right in without further pleasantries. "The revolution started because since we were born we've been looking for freedom. We have been victimized for a long time—our grandfathers, our fathers, and right now, us.

"I am from El Fashir, capital of North Darfur state. The government deployed its troops to outside areas and killed people. They captured some of them, dragged them through the streets of El Fashir, and burned them in front of a crowd of spectators. In a town north of El Fashir, all of us saw a man who was captured by the government.

They brought him in broad daylight. They tied his hands behind him, tied his legs, strung him in the tree, and burned a plastic tire on top of him. The plastic melted on his body. What is this?

"The Janjaweed and the government rape girls. They cut the woman's vagina with a knife. In Jebbel Marra, we saw a pregnant woman murdered by the Janjaweed. They cut her womb. There were twins, the babies were still alive. This is a horrible image.

"We realized that freedom will only come by force. It cannot be bought. We have to respect each other. We have to live freely. No one is allowed to burn our villages; no one is permitted to rape our sisters. No one has the right to rape us. Sudan got her independence in 1956, yet we are still under colonization. We want to live in peace. No one can oppress us and nobody else should be dominated."

The cameras were shut off. Salih Bob turned the intensity of his gaze on the three of us, but this time with a smile on his face. "You are Arab," he announced to Adam. Adam shook his head. "And you are from Bulgaria," he informed me. "And you are our sister," he said to Aisha. "From . . ." he paused, waiting for her to fill in the blank.

"Kiev," I corrected Salih Bob. "My ancestors are Ukranian Jews."

Aisha's story was too bizarre for Salih Bob to even comprehend. "Mother from Haiti. Father an Israeli Jew."

"But your name is a Muslim one," he protested to Aisha. "And you speak Arabic!" He jabbed his finger at Adam.

"Yeah, well, it's hard to pin us down."

Salih Bob understood the complexities of identity. "People claim that Sudan is divided into Arabs and Africans. But we are all black here. Even the name, Sudan, means Land of the Black!"

As night began to fall, the commanders left with our camera batteries, promising to return them charged. Another man who introduced himself as Musa arrived, wearing crisp, dark blue jeans and a plaid button-down shirt. He and Suleiman exchanged long greetings, saying *"al-hamdulillah"* many times and stroking each other on the shoulder. I had seen several people welcome each other that way over the last few days. A traditional Sudanese greeting, I surmised. Musa was energetic and cheerful, laughing loudly. He spoke some English that he enjoyed practicing on us.

James made a small fire in the corner of the hut. I offered to cook a meal for everyone. We had a pot we had purchased in Iriba, bags of pasta, and a can of something with a picture of a tomato on the label. I began my task with great gusto, but quickly discovered how inept I was. How to get the pot off the fire without a dishtowel or something to wrap around the handles? James handed me a few bits of cardboard, solving that problem. Where to put the pasta once it was done so that the same pot could be used to heat up the sauce? James suggested I place the can directly on the fire. I did, and promptly knocked it over, spilling out half its contents.

I finally strode back to the woven mat under the stars where Suleiman, Adam, Aisha, and Musa sat. Suleiman was in the middle of offering one hundred camels for me to marry James.

"You can live right here, in the multi-star hotel," Suleiman told me as I placed the pot down in the middle of the mat. "And you can have your pick of the one hundred camels," he said to Adam.

So Adam was my agent in this negotiation? From the smile on his face, I suspected that he had probably instigated it. After all, hadn't he predicted this very match in the message to my family he filmed in N'djamena?

Everyone tried to swallow a few bites of my horrible pasta-tomato mess. I appreciated their politeness.

"So, one hundred camels, huh?"

"I get to keep five of them," Dero intoned.

"Five of my camels? Why?"

"For agreeing to the marriage!"

We roared with laughter. Even mild, quiet, earnest Dero was cracking jokes with us. We loved it.

We lay on our backs looking at the darkening sky in silence as the starscape grew more and more brilliant. I was trying to remember everything we had heard that day from Suleiman, Salih Bob, Kitir Congo, and Mohammad Ismail. They sounded so committed and humane. But they also spoke to us with the hope that we would convey their story to the world, and that something would result from it. I was quite sure that the rebel groups in Darfur had committed some of their own unsavory acts and egregious human rights violations, though they might not admit it to us. Where was the fine line between believing in someone's cause and being naïve and romanticizing them?

"You were talking about Condoleezza Rice today," Dero broke the silence. "I want to meet her. I want . . ." he giggled, "to marry her."

"Dero!" Aisha sat up like a bolt. "You have a crush on Condoleezza Rice?"

"Maybe she can give me—what was that word again? When a country lets you come because you are not safe in your own country?"

I remembered his word list from that afternoon. "Political asylum?"

"That's it. Pol-i-ti-cal as-y-lum." Dero laughed and we all joined in. "How many camels you think I need to marry her?"

"Dero, man." Adam clapped him on the back. "You've got a whole different personality after sunset. We're gonna start a talk show for you or something. We'll call it . . . Dero After Dark! You are our mac-daddy."

We lay on the mats for a long time, trying to explain the word mac-daddy and talking, laughing, and singing Bob Marley songs. Well after I began to drop off to sleep, I heard Dero's voice, as he quietly sounded out his new words over and over again, trying to commit them to memory.

"Mac-dad-dy" and "Pol-i-ti-cal- as-y-lum."

Musa called to us before we were awake the next morning, dropping off partially charged camera batteries and breaking the news. "It
looks like your new president will be Mr. Bush again."

"What?!"

"The vote is not finished being counted yet. But Mr. Bush is ahead."

No matter how unlikely the source, the news wasn't any sweeter.

Dero dutifully brought over a cup of tea and handed it to Aisha
as we were wiping our faces and arms with baby wipes.

"Dero! I told you the other day, you don't need to bring us tea!
We can do that ourselves!"

"I must take care of you," he said simply as he went to refill the
tin can with the tomato picture for Adam and then again for me.

Suleiman was already gone, but he had instructed Musa to help
us. We asked Musa if we could meet some of the boys we had seen
training with the SLA yesterday.

"I don't know if I can find a car," Musa said doubtfully.

"How far away are they?"

"It's at least four kilometers."

Did he think we were wimps? We grabbed our equipment.

"We can walk, no problem. Let's go."

We pushed through the sand, littered with goat droppings, for
nearly an hour until we arrived at a cluster of trees with blankets and
mats spread out under the branches, tea kettles on small piles of coals
and strings of *hijabs* nailed onto the trees.

A group of boys was hanging around, sitting or lying, talking. Musa
lined them up.

"These journalists want to speak with some of you. You." He
selected one of the boys. "You. You. And you."

The four boys stepped forward and sat with us under one of the trees while we set up the camera. They were very quiet with empty and vacant eyes. They didn't show any reaction when I smiled at them and introduced the project and us.

Musa volunteered Ibrahim to go first. He was wearing a fatigues shirt, khaki pants, and had a string of wooden beads around his neck. He stared straight ahead into the camera as he spoke to us. Though he showed no expression, there was somehow an openness and vulnerability in his face.

"I'm sixteen years old, from Furawiya. My area was burned by the Arab people. That's why I'm here. I'm under training. They told me to stay here. They didn't tell me to go fight."

"Did they ask you to stay because you are young?" Musa asked (or prompted) Ibrahim with his question.

"Yes. 'War, war, don't go to war.' I'm learning and doing military training."

"You're from Furawiya?" I asked him. He nodded somberly. "We were there two days ago. We saw it is destroyed. Can you tell us your story?"

"I saw Arab people. They were riding horses. I don't know if they were with the army or not. They burned the houses and killed people and took all the stuff. Many people were killed and many ran away. I fled alone with nobody but later found my friend. My friend and I slept inside a cave that night and left in the morning. We got so thirsty and hungry. A village on the way gave us some food to eat and ground corn from their supply to take with us. We filled jerry cans with water and put the ground corn inside the water and ate and drank that the entire time. After four days in the mountains and caves, we found the SLA. It's been a month since joining the army."

Aisha asked him about how his life has changed since he fled.

"I had more friends in the village than I do now. I have just two friends here. In autumn, I went to plant on our farm sometimes.

When I was in the village, I went to school. My best subject was read-ing Qur'an. I can't go to classes again, but I don't need to study more anyhow. Our instructors didn't teach us anything. I only need to grow up and do what the people are doing."

"What news have you heard from home?" I asked him.

Ibrahim shook his head. "I didn't hear any news. I don't know if the Janjaweed are out or are still inside. My family, they are still around the area someplace. I have one older brother, but I don't know where he is. My mom, she is somewhere around the *wadi*."

"You know, Ibrahim, we were in Furawiya a few days ago. We can tell you what we saw if you want to know," I said.

Ibrahim seemed confused. "I didn't hear any news," He repeated again.

I asked him how he felt as he was living through all of this.

"I wasn't scared. I'm very sad. I'm going to kill Arab people."

It was interesting that the response toward Arabs from a child was so markedly different from the response of the rebel leaders we had talked to the day before.

"Why do you want to kill Arabs?" Adam asked.

Ibrahim's face didn't change. "Well, Arabs killed so many people. Killed my goats." His voice cracked, but I didn't detect hostility. "They burned the village and my area. That's why I'm angry and that's why I'm here."

We moved on to Adin, the next boy. We would have much pre-ferred to spend time with these boys, forming a relationship with them before clipping on the microphone and asking questions. But we were short of time and battery, so Aisha clipped while I asked and Adam filmed. Adin was wearing a turquoise turban and had beauti-ful black eyes and full lips. He was thirteen years old, from Kornoi, and had been with the SLA for one month. The details of his story brought back to my mind the pictures drawn by the children from Kornoi, we had met in Iridimi; warplanes attacking, Janjaweed killing and looting, eventually burning the village. His older brother, a twenty-two-year-old cattle herder named Atayeb, was murdered along with other family members. His story of arriving to the SLA echoed Ibrahim's before him: running from the burning village, sleeping in a cave, finding food and water from villages until arriving to the encampment. No one took him here, he insisted. He came by himself. His voice started shaking as he talked about his relatives giving him the news of his brother's murder.

"Is this hard for you to speak about?" I wasn't sure what else to ask.

"Yes, really, I feel bad."

"Do you and your friends ever talk about these things together or do you prefer not to speak about them?"

Adin shrugged, barely opening his mouth as he answered. "We mention him."

"In Iridimi camp we met people from Kornoi. Why didn't you go to Chad?"

"We ran a lot, but we didn't find someone to take us there. We moved very far. I don't know where my parents are. They moved in this direction, but I don't know how to find them. It's very hard."

"If you could tell your parents anything, what would you say to them?"

Adin chewed his lip for a moment. "If I could, I would tell them I am here. I am with the revolution."

"When the war ends, what do you want to do?"

Adin knew exactly. "I want to go to school to study."

Abdullah, the next boy, sat with his legs drawn up to his chest. His cheek was pressed against his knee. As he got further into his story, he buried his face deeper into his knee until it was difficult to even hear him.

"My brother and I were together and the Janjaweed came to the farm. We didn't say anything to each other. He was sitting there, and I was here. They entered from my brother's side on camels. My brother said to them, 'Don't bring the camels in the farm.' They said to him, 'Slave! Why shouldn't we enter?!?' And they shot him on the spot with a gun. Then they left. I ran to the village. Some people brought the dead body and buried it. The next morning, the Janjaweed returned. They torched the village and then left. We were humiliated. That's the reason we came to the revolution. *Wallah*, we were degraded."

"Who are you angry at: the government or the Janjaweed?" Adam asked.

"All of them are the same," Abdullah answered.

"Do you think you can you change the situation here?"

"No, I can't do anything."

Dero had a question of his own. "What do you want to do for your brother?"

"I pray for him, I give charity for him. I do everything for him. At the beginning I felt very sad. Now, I feel humiliated. I may be young, but nobody will humiliate me."

The last boy was from the Masalit tribe and had come to the training camp from south Darfur. He looked terrified as we began to speak to him.

"My name is Ali. I am sixteen years old. *Wallahi, wallahi,* they came and attacked us in the village. I ran until I got to Nyala [the capital of south Darfur] with my brothers and my mom. The government said to us, 'Don't stay here!' They wanted to send us back to our village. My mom and my brothers went back, but I came to the revolution because I know if I returned, they won't leave us alone."

"Nyala is very far in the south; how did you get here?" Adam asked.

"I became a member of the revolution and they took me here by car."

"Did you study?"

"I did. My favorite subject was mathematics."

He still looked terrified. I tried to lighten things up a bit. "Is there one special girl that you think about?" I teased him.

"Yes, there is."

"How do you know her?" I asked.

"I know her from school."

"Is she your girlfriend?"

"Yes."

"What is her name?"

"Her name is Aisha."

"Hey, that's her name," Adam piped in, pointing to Aisha.

"Maybe she's your girlfriend," Musa added to the joking.

Ali tried to smile. But he couldn't pull it off.

"What would you like to tell her, if you could give her a message?"

"My message to her: *salaam*."

"Do you know where she is? Do you hear any news about her?" Adam inquired gently.

"No. I wish I could see her," he answered softly.

"If in the future you and Aisha are married, and you have a child your age, what will you tell him about these times?"

"I will tell him the situation I'm in now. I will say, when I was your age, when I was sixteen years old, in 2004, Janjaweed burned our village and we ran out. I joined the Movement, *insha'allah*, to liberate Sudan."

"If you could give a message to the kids in America your age, what would it be?"

"I will wish them peace and I will tell them we are here in Darfur. Our villages were burned, we are in a very bad situation. We ran to the Sudan Liberation Army." He paused, trying to think of what else he could ask his peers in America. "How are you guys doing?"

WE WALKED BACK to Amarai in silence. "I may be young," Abdullah had said, "but nobody will humiliate me." Acts of vengeance have almost always been precipitated by words or sentiments such as these. But who could blame him or Ibrahim for wanting revenge? Salih Bob's words from the day before rang through my head: "Nobody tells the orphan how to cry."

SLA Commander Salih Bob

anka

"I DON'T KNOW WHAT THEY HAD AGAINST THIS VILLAGE."

I, **SLEPT OUTSIDE THAT** night under the stars. Suleiman's native village, Anka, was only a few kilometers from Amarai. He said he would arrange for us to go there in the morning. I wondered: did it really make sense to go to his village? We had already seen Furawiya and Muzbat. The entire territory of north Darfur seemed to be nothing but village after destroyed village, piles of burnt rubble, and round bases of houses. I expected Anka to be more of the same.

BUT WHEN WE arrived Anka felt different. It had been built on a hill, so we could view the expanse of the scorched remains. Every remnant was suffocated in black and gray ash. Wooden fences had been cremated, leaving gray-black lines in the sand. Our SLA guides told us the story of the village as we picked our way through the rubble. Anka had been a vibrant community famous for its bread. They pointed to what had once been large kilns that were now indiscernible from black debris. I tried to imagine the morning of the attack: women baking bread with little ones playing around them, older children off to school, teenage boys going to herd, men sitting outside having a casual conversation. They told us the bombs came in the early morning. As the people fled to the nearest *wadi* under the trees, the planes followed them and continued to strafe them.

There were possessions strewn everywhere. I zoomed in with the camera on a teapot sitting outside the debris and on a lantern lying in the middle of the neighboring ruins. There were abandoned shoes and sandals pointing in every direction poking their way out of the rubble, some broken, some burned. And I realized then what felt different. The abundance of these visible traces of the life that used to be here made its absence stand out all the more acutely. The silence was pregnant with the noises we should have been hearing. Instead, what remained was the howling of the wind as it traveled softly through the skeleton of the village.

I wandered down the hill, trying to balance my desire to capture as much as possible on film with the need to preserve the half-charged battery. At the bottom of the hill was a small, pink, white-washed building. The metal door was stuck. I leaned my shoulder against it and pressed as hard as I could to thrust it open. When I finally succeeded, I had to allow a moment for my eyes to adjust to the darkness. The cracked chalkboard and twisted, smashed, metal benches told me that I was inside a school. I needed more light in order to film this. The windows wouldn't open easily, either; I had to climb on the sill to force them open and let in small squares of light. It was probably too dark for the footage to be useable. Back in Iridimi camp, the camera often put an unwanted distance between me and the children. But now, standing in this abandoned, destroyed classroom that should have been filled with those same kids, I needed that barrier in order not to break down. Bad light and battery short-age regardless, I filmed.

MUSA OFFERED TO introduce us to the *omdah* (leader) and other dis-placed people from Anka who were hiding not far away. After a fifteen-minute truck drive, he led us into a small enclosure. There was one older woman, sixty-five or seventy years old, wrapped in a light blue cloth, and a few younger women, all sitting in the shade on the ground.

"The *omdah* is not here at the moment, but he should be back soon," Musa informed us after consulting in Zaghawa with the older woman, who, though petite, was clearly in charge. Her eyes were bright white and sharp, her lips were thin and pursed together, and her black pupils fixed on us through her wrinkled face. "This is the wife of his father. She is happy to speak to you. Her name is Hassaniya."

We asked Dero to explain to Hassaniya that we had just come from seeing the remains of Anka, and would like to hear more about her home. Hassaniya nodded mournfully at the mention of her village.

"I am from Anka, this village which is burned. My husband was the *omdah*, Adam Ali. He passed away almost forty years ago. He is the father of the current *omdah*, Abu Ummu. Anka was wonderful when I was a child. The time was good. The people had livestock, they engaged in trading. They were living very well before this man displaced us."

We knew which man she was referring to without having to ask. Instead, we asked her about the rest of her family.

"I have only a few children: two girls and one boy. I educated my children successfully. Right now all ten of my grandchildren are going to school." There was a note of pride in Hassaniya's voice, then a pause as she recalculated. "Actually, I have twelve or thirteen grandchildren."

The young women sitting behind her smiled and whispered. I wasn't sure if it was because they were the daughters whom Hassaniya had mentioned, or if it was simply the presence of foreigners with cameras.

Hassaniya described the attack on Anka. After every few sentences Dero tried to work in a summary translation, but once Hassaniya got started, she didn't want to pause. Her voice was in the upper registry, squeaky, almost birdlike.

"I was in the village when I heard a sound like a thunderstorm. I ran out and then just ran away. At least fifty of my goats were killed by machine guns from the ground, airplanes from above, and from Janjaweed who slaughtered them by slitting their throats. Their stomachs were opened and their organs were taken. Janjaweed jumped to the pens where we kept the animals and killed all the animals from pen to pen until sunset. They stayed until after midnight, killing people.

"We ran and ran and hid under the trees. The village which was behind us was also burned. I'm not sure how many people were killed. The men know. My husband's son is coming now. He can tell you the exact number."

We had been so absorbed in her story that we hadn't even noticed the approach of the *omdah*, Abu Ummu. He entered, shook hands all around, and seated himself next to his father's wife. He looked only a few years younger than she. His eyes, despite all they had seen, were always ready to crinkle into an easy smile. Without missing a beat, he continued Hassaniya's story, filling in specific details.

"We heard information on the evening of February 11 that the government troops and Janjaweed were moving toward Anka. We told the children and people to go out from the village because we didn't know what would happen. On February 12, they reached Anka. They started firing shells from the west of the village. Then, they entered the village and stole every single thing. They killed forty-six people."

"Were any of your relatives hurt?" Adam asked.

"From my family, my son Shatta was killed, and my son Faisel was injured, and Mohammed Hassan and Issa Mohammed were killed. From my family alone, not to mention the other families, six people were killed."

"How many people lived in the village?" I asked, wondering what percentage of the village the slain victims represented.

"If we consider children, there were around two hundred people, and in this village alone, around two hundred bombs," Abu Ummu told us. "The plane flew around overhead and came back and kept bombing." He shook his head. "I don't know what they had against this village."

There was a moment of silence while this information sank in.

Two hundred people living in the village; two hundred bombs dropped—one for each person.

Hassaniya broke the silence. "Then they burned the village down."

Abu Ummu continued with further details. "All the institutions, the hospital too. The school was burned by soldiers and Janjaweed, but the hospital was burned by Antonov. We went down to the *wadi* and made temporary shelter for ourselves."

"We are living under the trees: here, there, here, there." Hassaniya demonstrated with her hands how dispersed the community had become. "We are spread all over the area in more than twenty places. We just came under this tree today, but we are already moving. We have nothing to eat, no way to bring water, nothing to wear. We have no life. We are wandering, moving from here to there. We are confused."

"Has any help come to you?" Aisha wanted to know. "The U.N. or NGOs?"

"The foreigners didn't deliver to us here," Hassaniya said simply.

Aisha turned to Dero for translation help. "Please tell her that we will do our best to make a memory of her home that will survive. What would she like to tell the world about her home?"

Dero translated dutifully, but it was Abu Ummu who responded. He wasn't concerned about sharing a memory of his destroyed home. He wanted the outside world to know whom he held responsible and why.

"This is not a wise government who burns villages and kills civilians. This is not a government that anyone can elect or support. In war, soldiers fight soldiers, but we never heard about soldiers fighting civilians. We didn't carry guns against the government. Everything here—schools, courts, police station, hospital—did they protect these, or burn them? If the government did all these things, is this a legitimate government?" He turned to Hassaniya for backing. "What do you think about this government?"

Hassaniya nearly snorted in reply. "There is no government! It's truly bad! Our kids almost die of hunger and cold. We are exhausted. We go here, we go there. Today is under this tree, tomorrow under that tree. That's our situation."

"Do you have a message for Omar Bashir?" Aisha asked.

Abu Ummu showed surprise at the question. "Me? To Omar Bashir? What are we going to say to him? We don't want to talk to him at all. If there is any message to him, it's this: he is the president of the country and he kills his own citizens, pushed them off their land, and burned property and government institutions. What kind of president are you? This would be the message if we were to send one—but we don't have any desire to send him a message," he hastened to add.

"There hasn't been an attack in this area for a while," Aisha pointed out, drawing on what Suleiman had told us previously. "Do you and your family feel safe? Do you think you may be able to go back to Anka and rebuild?"

Abu Ummu's assessment was different from the SLA leadership. "There is no safety. Where is the safety? And come back again, you ask, to our village? It is very difficult. If there is security, we will come back; if there is no security, everyone will stay under a tree or in the mountain."

"What responsibilities did you have as *omdah* of Anka?" I asked him.

"An *omdah* always has a lot of people he is responsible for," Abu Ummu explained. "Now, I have more than five hundred people and thirty or so sheikhs under my responsibility. If the government needs to do anything, such as collect taxes, build schools, or make roads and fire lines, I am responsible. The government comes to me and I tell the sheikhs and the sheikhs tell the people and people do what needs to be done. I also have a court and the government gave me the authority to judge problems."

He spoke in present tense, as if the life he was describing still existed.

"My father and my grandfather and my grandfather's father . . . all of them were *omdah*. I am the fifth one from the family. That far back I know, before that I don't know."

There was something about Abu Ummu's eyes that let us know he would enjoy a bit of teasing.

"Who was the best *omdah*?" Adam asked. "If there was an election between you and your father, who would win?"

Abu Ummu laughed at Adam's question, but delivered a straight-forward response. "I only knew my father, I didn't see the others. My father was strong, stronger than me. He was famous. In El Fashir, if I said his name, everybody knew him. Even if I went to Khartoum and said my family name, they would respect me. My father served well during the British colonial period and after it became a pure Sudanese government, during Parties time and Nimeiri time. He was a recognized person, well known to the president. He even received an honorary uniform, given to those who served with excellence. It was burned in the fire."

Abu Ummu was referring to the unarmed civilian protests in 1964 that led to unprecedented political party dominance of the political scene in Sudan. This came to an abrupt end, however, in 1969 when Colonel Jaafar Al-Nimeiri seized power in a coup against the civil-ian leadership. Nimeiri survived at least twenty-four coup plots until his government was overthrown in 1985.

"We don't have elections for *omdah*. The family and the sheikhs appoint you and give approval. They wrap a string around your wrist when you become the *omdah*. There are also family swords, heirlooms that the Sultan gave to my grandfather which get passed down from grandfather to father to son. The family will give you these swords."

"Do you still have the swords?"

Abu Ummu turned to one of the young women sitting behind Hassaniya. "The metal that was a gift from the General Governor. Is it here?" he asked her.

"Yes."

"Go bring it." She rose to comply.

"As the *omdah*, did you ever negotiate with Arab tribes because of problems in the past?" Adam asked.

"Yes! Many times!"

Abu Ummu began to talk about the peace agreements between tribes he had personally attended, accompanying his father as far back as 1964. Conflicts over territorial issues were negotiated directly between the tribes. Differences were preemptively solved, or if violence had erupted, the affair was settled with blood money for the ones killed, thus ensuring that the conflict be contained.

The young woman who had gone to fetch the sword returned and handed it to Abu Ummu. He handled it reverently, lifting it up in all its angles. It was a dull silver sword, long and thick with a broad square handle. He held the base to the ground and the point rose high above his head. He looked up at it.

"There were three of these," he told us in a voice that had become strangely soft. "From Sultan Ali and from Sultan Hussein. The fire burned two. Only the metal part remains of this one; the cover, strap, and handle were destroyed by the fire."

"You're lucky that it survived the fire . . ." Adam started to say, but before he could continue, Abu Ummu broke out in deep, hearty laughter.

"If I were lucky, the fire would not have burned the other swords and the government would not have burned this area!"

"Is anything written on the swords?" Adam wanted to know.

"There is nothing written. *Belonging to Sultan* was written on the ones that were burned, but this one, no."

There were small half-moons carved into the blade.

"Do the symbols mean anything?" Adam pressed, in another attempt to connect carvings and engravings to Darfurian culture.

Abu Ummu turned the symbols to his face, examining them, and then stared at Adam as if he had asked a bizarre question. "They are just for decoration, nothing else." He handed the sword back to the young woman and stood up. "I'm going down to the pumping area. That's where we are building new shelters. Come with me and you can see."

Abu Ummu led us to an area with more trees than we had yet seen. There was a buzz of activity. A tall, stately woman walked with branches and sticks loaded on her head. A squat middle-aged man chopped a small tree with a tiny hatchet. I wondered about the long-term effect of using the scarce wood available. The desert in the Sahel was expanding possibly at a faster rate than anywhere else in the world. The barren landscape of north Darfur was testimony to that fact. And now, with homes and villages burned to the ground, people were forced to use what little wood growth remained to build shelters.

Abu Ummu strode up to a group of women who were pounding wooden logs with stake-like ends into the ground. Apparently, they were constructing a shelter for him.

"Where did I put the bathroom?" he asked a thin, wiry woman named Gash.

Gash stopped pounding for a moment and wiped the sweat from her forehead with the back of her hand. "The bathroom we are putting on this side. It's better to come out of the door of the house and not see the bathroom."

Abu Ummu smiled, satisfied with the architectural decision, and began to get involved in the building. "Give me that one," he said to the man who had been chopping the tree and had now brought his fresh spoil to the site of rebuilding.

Gash took hold of another stick, possibly a better implement for the task. "Let me make the hole deeper." The structures were large and round, with thick branches thrust into holes in the sand and smaller branches woven in-between the stakes. The circular houses were always under the cover of a tree to protect them from planes flying overhead, we were told. Though planes hadn't flown in this area for months, the fear was still very real.

The women gave us permission to film. They were holding back smiles, trying as hard as they could to talk and act normally. A group of small boys who had wandered over made no such pretences—they took one look at us and began to run away.

"Come here!" the man who had been chopping called out to the kids.

"They're scared," Gash told him.

"Scaredy cats!" Abu Ummu called after them with a good-natured laugh. "Where are you running to?"

The boys cautiously approached again, eyes shifting back and forth from the construction to the strangers with the video cameras. The women began laying stones down, for what exact purpose, I could-n't yet envision.

"Take that one off, bring this one. If you have a stone, bring it here. Uncle," she turned to Abu Ummu. "This is for the door."

Gash stood back to survey her masonry work and made an executive decision. "Let's take all of them off."

One woman, with two small girls at her side, wove sticks into the circular structure. She saw us watching her with interest and stood up, brushing off her clothes.

"My name is Nasra," she told us proudly.

It took us a moment to realize that she was speaking English.

"I am teacher," spoken slowly, each word emphasized.

She switched to Zaghawa, pausing for Dero to translate. She wasn't able to express what she wanted to tell us in English.

"I was at the school when the Janjaweed came."

"What happened?" Aisha asked.

"First, the airplane attacked. After that, Janjaweed and government and cars came. They destroyed everything at the school."

"What happened to the children?"

"When they heard the sounds of the Janjaweed coming, the students ran away. Anybody who hears those sounds and movements cannot stay."

"Were any of the children hurt?"

"About twenty-five of them were injured, but not too seriously. They were treated and are okay."

The two little girls had taken up refuge behind Nasra's skirt. The younger one peered out at us from time to time, made funny faces and ducked back behind her mother's skirts. The bigger one let her face emerge from the folds of the bright fabric only enough to gaze at us silently and shyly.

"How many children do you have?" I asked.

"Three. This is Amira." She placed her hand gently on the older girl's head.

"And the little one?" I asked.

"Limya." At the mention of her name, Limya popped out with her nose wrinkled and her tongue stuck out and then disappeared in the fabric again. It was hard not to laugh. "These are two of them; the third one is somewhere else."

"How old are they?"

"This one," Nasra reached behind her to tickle Limya, who giggled, "is three and a half years. Amira is five years."

I knelt down to make eye contact with Amira. "Do you want to say anything?" I asked her.

Amira met my gaze straight on, but stayed silent.

Her mother wanted her to talk. "Amira, were you there when the school was bombed?"

Pause, then a soft, "Yes."

"How was the sound of the airplane and the bombing? The sound that killed the people?" her mother coaxed her.

Amira said nothing, keeping her gaze from behind the skirt strong and steady.

"Can you say how the situation affected your children?" Aisha asked Nasra, shifting the focus away from the little girls so they wouldn't feel pressured into talking or led into giving certain answers.

"It affects the kids to take them outside the village. They become hungry, thirsty, and tired. It is wintertime and they are cold. This is a real humanitarian crisis for the children. The kids have bad dreams. During the night some of them run away and we try to bring them back. Even some of the kids became crazy and we take them to healers. Still, some of them are sick. Me, I am ill from the effects of the bombing. They shock us and it has made all of us sick. It is a kind of poisoning, is it not? And we are sick from the poison. Most of the women are ill." Amira didn't take her eyes off us for a moment.

"Were any of your family injured or killed in the attack?" Aisha asked.

"Three quarters of my family are buried," Nasra said, matter of factly.

Limya poked her head from behind the skirt again. Adam had crouched down to get an upward shot of Nasra with the camera. Limya, nose-to-nose with Adam for a moment, was obviously startled. He smiled at her and she disappeared again.

The little boys who had bolted at first sight of us grew less bashful over time. They inched closer, checking us out. We smiled at them. One of the bolder ones smiled back. One boy was thinner than the others, much too thin. He had pus caked to the corners of his eyes, and there was a chalky whiteness overlaying his black skin. His name, he told me in a whisper, was Muhammad. Without any further introduction or conversation, the boys ran a few meters to a nearby clearing and started playing, jumping up and down, hopping first on one foot, next on both feet. They indicated with hand motions that we should do the same. We joined them, jumping up and down until we couldn't jump anymore. The children nearly doubled over in laughter watching us. Muhammad was too weak to play. He sat on the side, watching.

AFTER THE JUMPING, we returned to where we had met Hassaniya. Musa assured us that the SLA truck would be back momentarily to fetch us. We leaned against the trees and waited. Dero must have been thinking about all the painful stories and political analysis that he had been translating for us.

"I told you my brother was killed, yes?"

Dero hadn't spoken about his brother since a halting mention in the market in Shegeg Karo. He looked troubled and serious as he brought him up now. This was a different Dero than the "Dero After Dark" we were getting to know. We all straightened up to listen.

"My brother is one example, but many, many people like my brother were killed all over Darfur. Some families that I know, all completely killed. There are more and more crimes in Darfur. We need more pressure from the international community, economic pressure, for example. All the money from oil is used to get weapons to fight the civilians in Darfur and in southern Sudan. Those weapons are purchased from other countries. The situation is getting better because of the African Union force, but we still need the United Nations and the USA and all the world to pressure the government to yield to what we are demanding. Yeah."

Dero was referring to the African Union troops that were being deployed to Darfur and would hopefully ensure calm in the region. We did not yet know how inadequate the troops would be in terms of numbers or logistical support, nor that their mandate would be to monitor cease-fire violations and would not include the protection of civilians.

"What is it that you are demanding?" I asked.

Dero explained, "In Sudan, there are hundreds of tribes, but the government is ruled by only two or three tribes from the center of Sudan, in Khartoum area. Because of that, we are demanding to share in the government, all people in Sudan: Darfur, North, East, everywhere in Sudan. We don't know what is happening in the center of the country. We only open our eyes to find airplanes attacking us, and troops shooting. We don't know why. If we share in the government, we can know what's going on. Because of that, I demand the international community to press our government to be a democracy, for all the people to share in government. That will be some kind of protection from the crimes that happen when only a few tribes in power like now."

"What do you think about Arab people?" Aisha asked.

"In Muzbat, there were no Arabs when I was in school, but in East Sudan when I studied in high school, I knew some Arab students with me. They were good with me. Yeah. We were playing, talking, eating together. We haven't any problem with Arabs. We have a problem with the policy of the government. Arabs are being used by the government to fight us. They equip them with modern guns and they promise to give them land to look after their animals. Arabs are being used by the government . . ." he struggled to find an appropriate analogy. ". . . like a gun. You use a gun to kill something. The government uses Arabs like his gun to kill us."

"But the difference is that a gun does not agree or disagree. A gun cannot choose. In this case, the Janjaweed agreed," I argued.

"They agreed because they're looking for land. They haven't land. All the area of Darfur is divided into tribal lands: Dar Zaghawa, Dar Fur, Dar Masalit. There is no Dar Arab in Darfur. Because of that, they were promised by the government, 'If you fight with me against the African ethnic groups, I give to you the land of Africans.' In addition to that, they give them money, military equipment, food, and many villages. They built them schools, and they give them higher degrees in government."

"If the situation were opposite and the government said to you, 'Dero, we want you to fight the Arabs. We will give you the weapons and in exchange you will get all of your rights. You will have good schools and more livestock and we will protect you, give you roads, give you everything, but we need you to fight the Arabs,' what would you do?"

Dero shook his head firmly. "No. I would not agree, because I am suffering now from this policy. They would be feeling like I am feeling now. Because of that, I need equality, all the people, not Arabs, not Africans, all the same citizens of Sudan, working together for their country. But fight Arab-African, African-Arab—no. I don't agree with this policy. Now, people who are not educated, they say their enemy is the Arabs, we must fight Arabs. But I know that this policy is from the government to the people of Darfur, both Arab and African."

"If you had a chance to talk to some of the Arab fighters face to face, what would you say?" I wanted to know.

"I would say to them that what they are doing is wrong. We can meet together and talk about what you need and what I need, about what is right, what is wrong. Arab tribes in Darfur are being used by the government. It's not because the government likes the Arabs in Darfur. No. If the government likes them, why are Arabs now suffering? Many of them have been killed in battles. Some of them are suffering like us. Because of that, if I have the chance to meet an Arab, I would tell him this is a wrong policy of government to hold in Darfur. All the tribes, we can live together in Darfur in peace and solve our problems with meeting, with talking, not fighting."

He paused for a moment letting his words settle with us as well as inside himself. Then he nodded and added a final, "Yeah."

We lay there for a while, enjoying being with each other and with Dero and Musa, mulling over the conversation. Two hours later, and Musa continued to insist that the truck would be along at any moment.

"How far exactly is it back to Amarai?" we asked.

"Oh, very far," Musa said. "Much too far to walk."

"How far?" we pressed.

Musa did a quick mental calculation. "Around . . . three kilometers."

Adam stood up and hoisted the camera bag over his shoulder. "Let's walk."

We arrived in the small marketplace of Amarai. Adam nudged Aisha and pointed out a camel strolling nearby, contentedly chewing some grass.

"Hey, gorgeous!" Aisha called out to the camel.

"You want to ride the camel?" Musa asked Aisha. "Go right ahead!"

Aisha hesitated only momentarily. "Will it be okay with the owner?"

"All the camels in the area belong to me!"

The camel, responding to Musa's clucking, knelt down in a rocking fashion, double-kneed as the creature was. Aisha climbed on and the camel rocked its way back and forth back into a standing position. I snapped a few photos of the camel walking in a circle, Aisha triumphantly on its back, and wondered about Musa's statement. Did he actually own all the camels? Or did he mean it figuratively, as an indication of who held the power in these parts?

We found Suleiman in the market shortly afterward.

"Ah, you have come back from my native village!" he greeted us warmly. "What did you find there?"

We didn't need to describe it in detail. Suleiman had surely seen it, and much more, with his own eyes.

"Tomorrow I have many places for you to go to," he said. "There

is a camp of displaced people that we are running, not like the
camps in the government-held areas of Darfur. There is one clinic in
this area that functions. And I want you to see a true Darfurian celebration, so we will arrange one, with music and dancing."

I wondered how genuine the celebration could possibly be if it
was going to be organized on our behalf.

"Actually, I'm worried about making our U.N. flight from Bahai
back to N'djamena in enough time to catch our flight from there,"
Adam said. "It's going to take a few more days still to get from here
to Chad. Maybe we need to start heading in that direction tomorrow?"

Suleiman was gracious as always. "As you like, as you like! Tomorrow morning, then, we will take you in a car directly; we will go to
the border and we will throw you back into Chad!" He made a
sweeping motion with his hand and beamed at us through his
clipped white-and-gray beard.

Later that night, after the sun had set and the Ramadan fast broken, Suleiman received a call on his satphone. "Change of plans, my
friends," he said to us. "You will leave to go back toward Chad
tonight. A car is coming soon."

We wanted to make use of our last hours with Suleiman. He was
the humanitarian coordinator of the SLA and we hoped to facilitate
a connection between him and the U.N. agencies and NGOs doing
humanitarian work in Chad. We set up the camera and, using a flashlight to get some light on Suleiman's face, began to record.

"We need the help of the whole world to stop this ethnic cleansing and genocide taking place in Darfur by the government of Sudan
and its Janjaweed. It is very hard for our people to bear. We are ready
to accept visitors from anywhere to become eye witnesses to help us
and to take our problem to the world to be known. To the U.S. Congress, the British Parliament, the U.N., I call on them very sincerely

that we need their help. We can't take the whole picture to them. We are asking them to visit us and to see the situation by themselves."

As we began to pack up our equipment, Suleiman asked a favor of us. "My daughter lives in Indiana," he told us. "I haven't seen her in a long time, too long. I want to go and visit the United States, but I have no passport. I can't exactly go to the Ministry of Interior in Sudan to get one. Maybe I can get a Chadian passport, but that will take time." Suleiman paused for a moment, smoothing his white robes with his long fingers. "Can you tape a message from me to my daughter and send it to her when you get back to the United States?"

We didn't give our battery situation a second thought. We snapped the camera back into the tripod and began to film.

Shortly after the taping, the car showed up. It was a rusted station wagon, with no rear window. It had been painted with thick red-brown mud with the letters "SLA" scratched out, revealing the white car underneath. The luggage was tied down securely on the luggage rack on top of the station wagon. I climbed up on top of the luggage on top of the rack, in between two teenaged SLA members.

It was from on top of the car that I said good-bye to Suleiman. In a period of a few days, he had assumed a grandfatherly-like role in our lives. I wished he could have come with us.

If our first truck had been held together with rubber bands, this one was even worse. It made loud rattling noises and spewed exhaust fumes every inch of the way. The driver clearly wasn't from the Fur tribe. Every half hour or so, the car got stuck in the sandy tracks and needed to be pushed out. After one such episode, the two boys who had been riding on top with me moved inside the station wagon, and Adam joined me on the luggage on the roof.

We were discussing thoughts on what to do with the footage when the car skidded out of the tracks, sliding wildly to the left, to the right, and into a spin. Adam and I hung tightly to the ropes. A moment of eye contact communicated the exact same thought. "Shit. The car is going over."

Our luck held out. The station wagon did not flip. It did, however, break down somewhere around midnight. Too tired to speak, we helped unload the truck, dragged our tent a few meters away, set it up and climbed in. The last thing we saw was the driver and one of the young men crawling underneath the car. There was a steady banging of wrench against muffler all night long. I couldn't quite determine how hammering the wrench against the muffler for hours on end could possibly help fix the breakdown, but, bestowed with absolutely no mechanical insight whatsoever, I dismissed those doubts with the comforting thought of, *I'm sure they know what they're doing.*

A few hours before dawn, I drifted off into a half-sleep, with the sound of the banging merging into dreams of Janjaweed and Sudanese soldiers attacking the Anka village school.

Villagers from Anka build new shelters

the antonov plane and the wedding

"FIRE FROM THE SKY."

B Y THE TIME the sun rose, the car was pronounced cured. "I guess whatever was wrong, it only needed several hours of someone banging away," Adam muttered as we crawled out of the tent and tried to stretch our fatigue away.

The car was reloaded and we climbed back on. It was the roughest ride yet. I wove my arms through the ropes in such a way that, no matter which direction I might be thrown, the ropes would stop me from being tossed off the car entirely.

The desert was bathed in the early morning light, the sand, hills, and shrubs taking on entirely different colors. The air was crisp and cool, though warming fast. Two ibex ran gracefully across the road ahead of us. I watched them appreciatively as they retreated into the desert beyond. The rebels were struck by the ibex as well, but not for their beauty. A deafening "*Crack!*" filled our ears. The first shot missed the mark but got the attention of the animal, which froze in panic. The second shot hit.

The ibex's throat was slit and it was tied to the back of the car by its legs. The head would have rested against the rear-window, had it existed. Blood drained out of the animal, pooling in a dark circle on the ground. We continued, the ibex slamming against the back of the car in rhythm to the bumps.

Several hours and hundreds of ibex-against-the-car-slams later, Musa's hand reached out from the window of the car, knocking on the roof to get our attention. "We're back in Muzbat!" Two of the rebels untied the ropes holding the ibex and the animal fell to the ground with a resounding thud. They dragged it behind the tree to prepare it for lunch. Dero sank down in the roots of the tree and leaned against it, breathing a long sigh. He probably hadn't slept any better than we had.

"Come," Musa said. "You want to meet some people? See the village?"

Musa led us to the center of Muzbat. We looked around, trying to locate the familiar sites from a few days before: the mosque, school, police station. A middle-aged man wearing a long white *galabiya* and turban approached, welcoming Musa with the long and highly ritualized greeting we had come to expect.

"This is Abdullah," Musa introduced him after the multiple back and forths of *"al-hamdulillah"* and stroking each other on the shoulder. "He is the *omdah* of Muzbat. He would like to show you what happened here."

We gratefully accepted the offer and followed Abdullah to a residential area of the village where circular remains of burned huts were organized. He carried a long, thin stick and walked with an equally long stride. Abdullah waited for us at the edge of a depression in the ground and pointed at it with the stick.

"It is from an Antonov bomb. The bombing here hit all the things in this area." He continued to thrust his stick at multiple other indentations in the sandy ground.

Black soot surrounded the depressions, in stark contrast to the beige sand.

"Over there, over there, over there . . . the planes bombed in four different areas."

A middle-aged man in fatigues joined Abdullah. He greeted us with a nod and a *"Salaam aleikum"* and exchanged some words with Abdullah in Zaghawa. Abdullah paused outside a charred circle of stones, waiting for us to catch up. There was a singed metal gate leaning against what once had been the doorway of someone's home. Abdullah pushed it forward and it fell with a reverberating crash. He stepped over it and inside the destroyed house, Adam, Aisha, and I following silently.

"The owner of this house was killed here and so were his wife and kids," he told us in Arabic. He bent down, slid his stick under a piece of shrapnel, and lifted it up high for us to see and for the camera to record. "This was part of the bomb that hit this home. It exploded on everything all around." The piece of shrapnel dropped to the sand, clanging against another bomb fragment. They were all around.

Abdullah strode out of the burnt house, barely giving us time to refocus the camera on him and follow. He pointed out the carcass of a donkey we passed, telling us that it died from eating the plants that had been covered with a powder from the exploded bombs.

The last time we had been in Muzbat we had only encountered rebels from the SLA. Now there was a handful of old men, women, and children walking around. One little boy wearing a brown *galabiya* kicked a tattered soccer ball made of rags to us. We passed it back and forth with him, careful not to accidentally kick it into the small bomb-crater directly next to us.

Musa answered our questions about the civilians. "They are from Muzbat, but they no longer live in the village itself. Their homes are destroyed and they are too afraid to return. They are living in the *wadi* and under trees, in caves. But the well is the only water source for dozens of kilometers, so they must come to take water."

That explained why we hadn't seen them on our last visit. We had arrived right before sunset and the villagers had already returned from the well to their trees or caves.

"What exactly are they afraid of?" we asked. Muzbat was firmly behind rebel lines; it was not likely that the Janjaweed or Sudanese army could come storming through. The damage here had already been done.

"The airplanes. They could still bomb us from above," Abdullah's companion answered.

"When did an airplane last bomb here?"

Musa, Abdullah, and his friend gave conflicting answers: one month, two months, four months. In any case, it hadn't happened recently. So, why were people still living so far from their village and only water source? Wouldn't it be much easier and more practical for them to return, rebuild, and resume their lives?

He led us to the wracked and twisted frame of a bed that Sheikh Zachariah Madebo had been sleeping in when he was killed by a bomb. The tapping of Abdullah's stick on the burnt metal initially drowned out a low humming noise in the distance. As the humming grew louder and more insistent, Abdullah abruptly stopped speaking. His hand fell to his side. We looked around in confusion.

"Now I am hearing the sounds of an Antonov plane," Abdullah told us, a trace of fear in his voice. "You hear?" He turned on his heels and motioned for us to follow him quickly.

It took a half-minute of squinting into the sun to spot the Antonov, now flying almost directly overhead. "Sit down!" we heard Abdullah shout to villagers as we scanned the sky. "Not over there! Here!" We tracked the plane moving above the village until Abdullah called out urgently, "Aisha! Sit!"

We looked back down. The village appeared to be entirely deserted; everyone seemed to have disappeared into thin air. My eyes adjusted to the scene much as they do when moving from light into darkness. I spotted five children crouched under a tree, an older sister trying to shield her younger brother with her hands. Another tree a few meters away revealed the same. A mother flattened herself against the scarce shadow of a mud-brick wall, restraining her little ones.

We stood in the broad daylight. The drone of the Antonov was the only sound that could be heard. Adam shifted from filming the plane to the people holding each other tightly, trying to find protection under leaves or any other bit of available cover. One of the villagers motioned to us.

"Come, get out of the sun, quickly!" Musa urged us. "You are a target if you continue to stand there."

Adam, Aisha, and I moved under the nearest tree, where the huddled children and their parents made room for us. Children continued to mutely hold onto their mothers and each other long after the plane was out of sight and its droning barely audible. Just five minutes earlier, I had asked myself why people still felt too insecure to return to the village. The question felt ridiculously naïve now.

People emerged again into the sunlight several minutes later, some of them laughing with combined nervousness and relief. Our tour with Abdullah was over. The panic from the plane adjusted his afternoon's priorities.

"Take them to meet Hari," he instructed Musa. "Hari can tell them many things."

Abdullah strode off while Musa led us to homes that were still standing, the only ones in the village. A tiny old man wearing the traditional white *galabiya* and a white skullcap greeted Musa in Zaghawa. He was extremely thin with a head that was too large for his little frame. His body was hunched over and he moved with difficulty. His skin was reddish-brown, a reminder of the complexity of ethnicity in Darfur, and speckled with age spots. He scratched the salt-and-pepper scruff on his chin and cheeks as Musa explained to him who the Westerners with the video cameras were.

He gave each of us a long look with eyes that were both penetrating and lively, but his voice shook with age as he turned to Musa and asked, "These people, they speak Arabic?"

"They can understand," Musa told him.

Satisfied, Hari muttered, *"Al-hamdulillah"* and lowered himself slowly onto a low, wicker stool. His body sunk into the woven threads that gave way under his weight, making him appear somehow shrunken. He placed a small wooden stick with feathers attached to its end next to his wrinkled, calloused feet, waited until we set up the camera, and began to speak.

"I am eighty years old. I've been living in Muzbat and worked for the government at the court since 1956. We didn't have any problem. The Arab nomads came here and grazed their cattle all over the area, moving where the grass and drinking water were, and nobody bothered them. We went to south Darfur to get maize when we had a shortage. We were living very well until the rebellion broke out. The rebels said, 'We need our rights,' and Omar Bashir said, 'You don't have any rights. I won't give you anything. You are slaves. I will finish you. I will give your land to the Janjaweed.' They used poison, planes, cars, and Janjaweed. They took the things from the village, burned the houses, threw small children on the fire, and killed their mothers. In the last two years, all the area became unstable because of the rebels in the Movement and the soldiers of Omar. They made all the area unstable."

I was surprised to hear a criticism of the SLA in the same breath as an accusation against government soldiers, especially voiced in front of Musa. Adam must have had the same thought. He asked Hari if he thought the SLA was part of the problem. The elderly man hastened to explain, echoing the support for the rebel movement we had heard from others.

"No, no. They are going straight. They don't go into anybody's house; they don't take anybody's rights; they don't enter anybody's farm; they don't curse anybody. They say, 'If you come and join us, it is okay. If you don't, we are not going to ask you.' They are facing him," meaning, of course, the Sudanese president.

I thought about other parts of the world where resistance movements were held in high esteem by local populations for the simple act of standing up to their oppressors, whether or not their actions were faultless or effective in bringing about positive change. "They are facing him," Hari had said, a sentiment we had heard echoed from Afghans, Palestinians, Iraqis.

Hari continued. "Did you see those red graves? Everyone buried there, children, elderly people were killed by airplane bombings."

We had heard references to mass graves here and in Furawiya but hadn't seen them.

"Even the animals know that the plane can kill them! When they hear the sound of the aircraft, the goats run under the trees, hiding like this." Hari ducked down, shielding his face with his arm, comically imitating the goats with a half-grin. "The plane bombed on me. I was inside my hut. The area became very dark because of smoke. You couldn't even see. He bombed, bombed, bombed, for three days. He set all the area on fire. My neighbors lost their children and were burned by fire themselves.

"If they fight the rebels out there, nobody will question them. But instead, they left the rebels, came here, and destroyed all the villages.

"When the rainy season came, starvation set in. There is no food. There is nothing in the ground and nothing in storage. They collected and burned all our grain. The water is also finished. That's the way they want to finish all the human beings, through starvation.

"We can't travel. All the routes around this area are mined with roadside bombs. The cars cannot drive on the roads now. We sent ten men with camels south to get food. All ten of them were captured and executed. There is fire from the sky and burning from the ground. We are breathing, but we are like dead people. Our hearts are not stable. Today, the airplane came two or three times. It is still circling around here. No one can return because of the aircraft. The children are scared. We are simply exhausted people. We don't know what to do. We have lost our minds."

Adam asked about life during the British period.

"*Ya salaam,*" Hari answered wistfully. "I served many years in the British time. From here to Khartoum, you could carry only a small whip in your hand and nobody will bother you. The British had justice. If someone stole, he would be fined and jailed. If you killed somebody, you would be executed. They kept all the area clean."

I had never heard people praise former colonial powers the way that Hari was extolling the virtues of the British rule over Sudan. But remembering what life has been like in Darfur since Sudan received its independence, it was easy to imagine why the British regime was recalled as a time of order. His next words underscored my thoughts.

"They didn't bother you at all. They didn't take your things. They didn't go to somebody's house and confiscate it. If their soldiers came to the village, they didn't interfere with anybody. They had to call on a horn to alert the chief to come to them. The chief took them to a *rakuba* (sheltered area) until they left. Listen, today, if the English, Italian, American, French will come, we will welcome them. If the white people rule this country, we will be very lucky."

I shuddered, thinking about what might happen if Hari's wish for a return to European colonization came true. I was willing to wager that Hari's sentiment, though based on nostalgia from a relatively peaceful past, was not shared widely.

Hari looked up at us with a gleam of interest in his eyes. "I just wonder . . . how did you folks get here? If you are able to help execute this man and take him out of power, we will welcome it."

Adam, Aisha, and I tried not to chuckle. Was Hari asking the three of us to overthrow Omar Bashir and the Sudanese government?

"If you stand good and remove this guy from office, we will get a break. Otherwise, he will kill us. He's not going to leave us alive."

Our desire to laugh evaporated.

"We're looking for peace. People should be free. You could take your animals out, you could go to your farm, like before. You could take your kids to the school, or to study Qu'ran. You could go to Mecca. You just needed to take a stick. The remainder of our lives is very short," Hari concluded. "We, the old people, don't care about ourselves. We care about our descendents to live freely."

"Does your stick have any special function or meaning?" I asked. I had been filming it lying by his feet for parts of the interview.

Hari picked the stick up and flicked the feathery end of it in front of his freckled nose. "To keep the flies away from my face!"

He joined us in laughter, though he couldn't possibly have known about our running question which had grown into a joke.

Hari lifted himself off the stool with some effort and gripped our hands as we thanked him for the interview. We headed back to the car, dropping Musa off at the police station-turned-SLA base. We found Dero napping in the shade of the tree. One of the rebels approached us with a tin bowl filled with freshly grilled ibex meat and raw onions, inviting us to join in a meal with those not fasting. We thanked him, and Adam and Aisha partook with great gusto. It was years since I had attempted to be a vegetarian, but after seeing the ibex's pain and fear as it was killed, I couldn't eat it.

MUSA RETURNED AS the shadows grew longer. He relayed an invitation from Kamal, the local SLA commander, to break the fast with him. Musa led Adam, Aisha, Dero, and me to an intact compound and introduced us to Kamal. We recognized him from our first visit.

"Hello, hello, welcome back!" he greeted us warmly. "You have seen many things, I am sure?" We assured him that we had. "Let me introduce you to my wife, Afaf. She just came from Nyala last week."

It would be interesting to learn what was happening in and around Nyala. We hadn't heard many reports coming from the south of Darfur. Afaf was inside the hut, preparing *asida* and stirring lentils in a black pot in the corner of the hut. A small fire danced and crackled under the pot. A ten-month old girl was attached to her back in a sling, playing with her mother's hair as she worked.

"*Asalaam aleikum,*" Afaf greeted us.

The baby turned quickly, looked directly at Adam, and began to shriek in fear. Any thoughts we had about talking more to Afaf were extinguished with the screaming. We left the hut quickly.

Kamal took a seat on a woven mat in the courtyard, next to another fighter named Ibrahim. Ibrahim wore military fatigues and sat cross-legged, a gun across his lap. If it weren't for those visual cues, it would have been hard to believe he was a fighter. His face was round and open, with large cheeks and eyes, and when he greeted us, he was as gentle and soft-spoken as Dero.

Kamal turned on a small transistor radio, and we listened for a few minutes to Arabic news. The commentator on the government-run radio station was discussing the negotiations in Abuja between the Sudanese government and the two rebel groups. The rebels wanted a no-fly zone over all of Darfur, but the government was not willing to agree. The reason the Antonov flew overhead earlier that day suddenly became apparent. The government was sending a message during the middle of the negotiations: they would fly wherever they wanted, whenever they wanted and in the process, intimidate and terrorize whomever they wanted.

The late afternoon sun cast a golden light on Kamal, Ibrahim, and the huts behind them. Kamal shut off the radio. With Dero's help, we began to talk in earnest to the two SLA commanders sitting in front of us.

"Can he tell us where he was born, where his father and grandfather were born?" I asked Dero to ask Ibrahim.

Ibrahim was happy to oblige. "My grandfather was born in Furawiya, and my grandfather's grandfather was born in Furawiya. I was born in the area west of Furawiya called Hangala." Ibrahim tapped Dero on the knee. "Ask them—did they see Hangala burned?"

We had been to Furawiya, we explained, but hadn't seen Hangala.

He continued in his soft voice, telling us about his family's history in the Furawiya region. "They built the area seventy years ago. When the buildings became old and destroyed, we fixed them.

When new people came to Furawiya, we expanded the village. In the past, my grandfathers fought with spears until they died. Now there is no freedom." His sentiments echoed those of the elder Hari.

"Why did you want to be a part of the resistance?" I asked them.

"*Wallahi*, the most important thing in life is freedom," Kamal answered, repeating himself three times to make sure the point stuck. "Not freedom just for Dar Zaghawa or Dar Fur. It should be in all the world."

His words invoked Salih Bob in Amarai. They also reminded me that Darfur received its name because, literally translated, it meant "Homeland of the Fur"; Darfurians themselves subdivided the region not as the government had, into western, northern, and southern Darfur states, (thus reducing the political clout that a unified Darfur would hold) but into tribal areas such as Dar Zaghawa, Dar Masalit, and Dar Fur.

"Since '56, we as a nation want freedom. The world has Internet, and we are still living in these huts since our grandparents' time. We asked and asked and we didn't get anything. So we started carrying the guns." Kamal patted his Kalashnikov, lying across his knee.

"The Janjaweed have been here for a long time. They kept coming and leaving. There was a lot of fighting. I had to do something," Ibrahim added.

"Who are you fighting against?" I asked them.

"Our main target is the government," Kamal answered without hesitation. "The government is behind the Janjaweed. Janjaweed are citizens that the government armed. It's like walking through a mine field. The Janjaweed are in the front and the government is in the back." Kamal used his hands to portray an explosion.

The way he just described it, the Janjaweed themselves were victims of the government, being used as a type of human shield. I recalled our conversation with Dero outside of Anka. He had spoken about the Arabs suffering perhaps equally from government policy. I wondered if this was what he meant. I wished we were able to meet civilians from Arab tribes to find out their take on the situation and how they were affected. Time and access, I knew, would not permit it.

Kamal told us that his home was destroyed.

"Was anyone inside?" I asked, almost dreading to hear the answer.

"My family ran away."

"Isn't that your wife and baby girl with you here?"

"I have two wives. One went to Chad and the other one went to Nyala. The one in Nyala kept moving and came here a week ago."

I thought about the baby who had burst into tears upon seeing Adam. She had been wandering most of her short life. "Your baby girl is beautiful."

Kamal smiled, clearly in agreement with me. *"Al-hamdulillah."*

"What do you want her to do when she grows up?"

"I want her to enter university, *insha'allah*."

"Does your wife feel safe here?" I wanted to know.

"Right now? At this moment, we are safe," Kamal assured us.

"But not with the airplanes coming back," Dero added softly.

"Are you talking about security? Security will come when the African Union is in Darfur and Sudan. But now, with the airplanes coming and bombing us from the sky, we have no security."

"What did you do before you were with the SLA?" Aisha asked.

"I was with the government police," Kamal answered.

"When you were working for the government, how were you treated?" I asked.

Kamal barked a sarcastic laugh. "The reason why I stopped working for them is because they blamed us unfairly for everything. They are like snakes. I was never promoted or paid like the Arab police."

Dero asked Ibrahim what he did before joining the Movement.

"Farmer," Ibrahim answered simply. I had no problem imaging Ibrahim as a farmer.

"What did you grow?" I asked.

"Tobacco."

A short young man with a big gun, loud laugh, and large grin arrived. He threw himself down jovially next to Kamal and Ibrahim, looked at us with our cameras, and then called out with his brightest smile, "Let them tape me, let them tape me!" Kamal waved his hand as if to indicate not now and the young man became silent, watching the proceedings with interest.

I continued talking with Ibrahim, aware that the new arrival was trying to get my attention.

"Can you tell us what your life was like? What you did during the day?"

"I went to my farm to clean it, took care of my animals, camels, and everything I had. That was my work."

"Are you married? Do you have a wife or children?" Aisha asked as Ibrahim waited patiently for the translation. "Yes, I have a wife."

"Do you have any contact with them?" she continued.

"I heard about them, but I haven't seen them for eleven months."

"Where are they now?"

"They are in Kariare. I heard they are with the refugees over there."

We planned to cross back into Chad the next day at Bahai, just half an hour from Kariare. An idea began to dawn on us.

"What is your wife's name?" Adam asked.

"Gassabai," Ibrahim told us. Aisha wrote it down in her notebook.

Adam turned to Dero. "Tell him we will try to go to this camp and find his family. Does he have a message for his wife and kids?"

As Dero translated Adam's offer into Zaghawa, a smile spread slowly over Ibrahim's face. He laughed and shook his head. "Really?" He beamed. "That's great!

If you find them, say hello. Yeah, I am their father. I'm OK," Ibrahim began his recording. We encouraged him to speak directly to his family. He paused, thinking about what words to choose and spoke them lovingly.

"If I die, I die. Otherwise, I will fight until I get freedom. If tomorrow the war stops, that's good. We could dig holes to get water from the near places; now we must go very far. We could live comfortably again." He nodded.

Kamal's other wife and children were in Kariare also, along with most of the refugees from Furawiya. We asked if Kamal wanted to record a message for his family as well. He politely declined.

"One more question to ask," Adam said to Dero as we shut down the equipment. "Is there any symbol on his gun that has a meaning?" Dero looked startled until Adam winked.

Kamal seemed to be considering something as we packed up the camera. He spoke to Dero in Zaghawa.

"He needs to use your pen and paper," Dero told Aisha. "He wants to write a message to his family in Kariare camp."

We put the notebook away with Kamal's letter and the names of his and Ibrahim's family members, hoping we would be able to find them amid the twenty-three thousand refugees in the camp. I thought about the boys we had spoken to at the SLA training camp—had it only been the day before yesterday? I wish we had thought to take messages to their families as well.

As NIGHT FELL, a few other SLA fighters came to the commander's hut to join us for *iftar*. I found myself sitting next to the short man with the bright smile, who told us his name was Ibrahim Jim but to call him Jim, and who grinned at me every time he caught my eye.

When we finished eating, the sky was inky black and dotted with stars. It was Adam's, Aisha's, and my usual time to launch into song, but instead, we asked our hosts if there were traditional Zaghawa songs they would share with us. They took turns singing, alternating between songs of battle and resistance and Zaghawa love songs. The singing was extremely fast and the words, as we learned later from a translator, were free-style improvisation.

"I don't sleep at night and I don't rest in the day. I must confront the challenges. This day is not the day of the cowards. I can tell if you are a warrior or not from how you point your gun. When I go to war, I will do whatever is necessary. I will take all my people. I will not give up. I have a yearning to bring down the black crow [Omar Bashir]. *"*

High-pitched, throaty ululations were the cue to move to the next singer. More fighters came to join the group singing.

"I put on my hijabs for protection. I look at the sun setting. It will be a long night for me, trying to count the stars. I will be like the locust and go through the night. I am tying my sash to prepare for war. I go to the starting line. I can race with the planes. If I see my enemy, I will get rid of him. On all my journey, I didn't find what I want. Why did this happen to me? I don't know why I go. "

The ululations grew stronger and more frenetic as the number of men increased.

"I am fighting because of my little sisters, Numo and Jallaba. I am your older brother. I live outside the village to protect you. I live alone. Let me sleep. I don't know how to speak about this. "

Musa, who had quite a nice voice, took a lead role in the singing. Musa's lyrics, we learned later through translation, took on an element of political analysis as well. *"Omar Bashir doesn't want to accept what I want. I don't want to accept the position of Omar Bashir. Idris Deby doesn't want to accept either. Musa Hilal* [Janjaweed leader] *also has his own position. Until now my heart is suspicious. "*

After the requisite ululations, the next rebel took over the song. *"I turned over every stone, I crossed all the land. I am desperately looking, but I have no solution. I don't know what to do. I don't know how to admit this. So let me rest. "*

We couldn't understand a word of what was being sung at the time, but it hardly mattered. The singing was rich and beautiful, the spirit palpably strong, and the stars, like the rebel fighters who continued to join us, grew progressively numerous.

Ibrahim Jim turned to me out of the blue. "I will give you two hundred camels to marry me." I could barely see him in the dim light of the moon, but I detected a playful tone to his voice.

Dero and Musa eagerly jumped in and helped facilitate the communication.

"Me? Why me? Why not Aisha?"

"You are short. I am short. We would make a good pair. We can do everything together. We can live side by side. We can fight side by side!"

"It's a very good price," Dero advised. "But I get to take ten camels."

"You're taking some of my camels? Why is that?"

"For agreeing to the marriage!"

"Dero After Dark" was back!

We were lying on the mat under the stars, listening to Dero sing "Buffalo Soldier" with his best stab at the lyrics, when someone arrived with the news that a wedding was taking place that night in Muzbat. We were invited.

We piled into two SLA cars and drove a short distance. Two dozen or so villagers gathered inside a compound surrounded by a stick and mud-brick fence. It was dark; there was no electricity, lanterns, or generator. The bride and groom were inside the hut with male family members. Adam and Dero began talking to some of the men who were dancing and singing in the courtyard. Musa led Aisha and me to a woven mat and invited us to sit down. Two young women wrapped in colorful scarves joined us on the mat.

"These are the sisters of the bride!" Musa told us.

We congratulated them as Musa translated and Adam returned to film. The sisters welcomed us in Zaghawa and placed what amounted to the entire wedding feast before us: a plate of fried dough and a bowl of candies.

We asked, with Musa's help, how the bride was doing. Um Bashar, the older sister, answered.

"She is afraid from the planes. Before, she was happy. Now she is on edge. We came from the *wadi* after the sunset. We took her there before the seven days passed. We had to leave the groom and bride over here and spent all the day under the trees. We came only tonight to say hello to them."

We glanced at Musa, confused. He explained to us that traditionally, the wedding celebration should last for seven days without stopping, but because of the planes, the bride and groom were afraid and had shortened the festivities to this one night only.

"We don't have kerosene to make light, so now we are in the dark. We don't have anything to present to the guests. We fast all day, and we are hungry. We slept in hunger when we should have broken the fast and we are very tired," Musa summarized the bride's words.

"We hope we can help with your situation," Aisha said, pausing for Musa to translate. "We want to take your words and bring them to the world, so that people know what you are living through."

Um Bashar responded in Zaghawa.

"Talking is very good," Musa told us she said. "This will be very helpful. Please help yourself to the food."

We were reluctant to take any of such a scarce commodity, but we didn't want to offend our hosts. Aisha and I each took a piece of fried dough and bit into it.

"Delicious, thank you very much!"

Musa translated.

Um Bashar continued telling us what they were living through on a daily basis. "All our donkeys were killed by eating the remains of the bombs. Now, we must carry the water on our heads and we get a headache. What are we to do? Thorns everywhere prick our feet, but we have no place to buy shoes. Look at our hands; this is from drawing the water from the well!"

She held out her hands for us, palms up. I mirrored her, thinking that this was possibly a form of greeting that I hadn't yet encountered, but upon hearing Musa's translation I realized that she was trying to show us the red, chafed welts across her palms from hauling water up from the well.

"I want to go with you because I'm afraid to stay here. I wish I knew English today so I could explain more."

Dero came over. "You're invited to meet the bride and groom," he told us.

We thanked Um Bashar and her younger, quieter sister and followed Dero inside the hut. The hut was filled with ululations and cheering, though the bride and groom were not taking part in the noise making. They were young, no more than twenty years old, with large eyes protruding from their faces and they sat in a corner, completely panic-stricken. I'm sure the plane flying overhead that day was part of the explanation, but this couple looked terrified of more than the plane. We offered our congratulations and watched as the brothers of the bride and groom sang two more traditional songs.

"Rebels, Girls from Dar Gala, you can't get them without a lot of camels. If you marry my sister, you are my brother-in-law. If I want to marry your sister, it takes a lot of wealth," one brother sang, ending in a cascade of ululations, while the other brother picked up the thread:

"I will break his invincibility. I feel all the bullets piercing me like the thorns. If you are my enemy, I will get rid of you like I can get rid of a baby gazelle. The helicopters came from above and the tanks from the ground. The life is not a guarantee. The paths through the badlands are unknown. I thought it's much better but my heart does not feel comfortable."

There was no way to stay long in the hut without being invasive. The space was small and already packed with relatives who focused on us whether we wanted or not. We congratulated the bride and groom again and backed out of the hut, allowing them to be the center of attention once more.

Outside, young men were leaping in the air accompanied by call and response chanting and rhythmic clapping, the whiteness of their robes and turbans shone against the black night. This was the game we observed the young boys from Anka play. It was truly spectacular. Everyone participated, including women, in their own groups. Aisha and Adam joined in immediately. I didn't know how they found the strength. I was exhausted and sore from being nearly bucked off the truck for four consecutive hours after an almost sleepless night. The chanting was hypnotic and trancelike and the frenzy of the jumping produced a tangible energy. I was enveloped in the sights and sounds until Musa poked me on the arm, awakening me from a nearly dreamlike state.

"It is time to go."

We said our good-byes to Um Bashar who clasped our arms and hugged and kissed Aisha and me.

"When are you leaving Muzbat?" she wanted to know.

"Tomorrow morning."

"We will come to say good-bye to you, if the airplane doesn't return. If there is an airplane in the morning, we might not be able to come."

WE WERE INVITED to spend the night in Commander Kamal's courtyard. Tired though I was, I had a hard time falling asleep. I couldn't get the wedding out of my mind. It was the most extraordinary event I had witnessed. Darkness, dancing, fear, singing, anxiety, resilience, all wrapped into one celebration. Given the context, any life-cycle event was its own, remarkable form of resistance. *"You cannot wipe us out!"* the young men singing in the hut seemed to be saying. *"You cannot make us disappear!"* echoed the villagers who were jumping and chanting. I wished I had summoned the energy to jump with them. I would have liked to take part in that form of resistance.

eight

dero

"I CAN'T TELL TO MY KIDS THESE STORIES."

MUSA WOKE US up early with the report that a civilian pickup truck, an extreme rarity, would be driving that day into Chad and he had made arrangements for us to travel on it. Our last view of Muzbat was of women at the well hauling the ropes that had sliced into Um Bashar's hands. They lifted the filled jerry cans onto their heads to lug back to the *wadi*, glancing nervously up at the sky to check for bomber planes.

I WAS SITTING at the rear of the truck next to the exhaust pipe, inhaling more dust and exhaust than oxygen. Adam was next to me. Each time the truck hit a bump, the elderly man next to Adam fell more heavily onto Adam's already-sore shoulder, which was now twisted in an unnatural position to allow him to hold on to the only available rope. It was impossible to talk; I could only hear a grunt of pain with each bump. The truck stopped for a few minutes so the driver could check under the hood. Adam jumped off the side.

"I've had enough of this. I'm riding inside the cab," he barked.

WE ARRIVED IN Shegeg Karo in the late morning where we were told we would stay until after *iftar*—at least five hours. Dero looked happy to be back in his home village. It seemed like a lifetime ago that we had first met Dero in Shegeg Karo. I couldn't believe it was just under a week.

"Do you want to see my school?" Dero asked us, ducking his head modestly.

"Of course! We'd love to!" Aisha said.

He led us through the market to the hut that had been the school. It was where the teenaged Fadi had so eagerly inspected the old rocket launcher. Last week, I hadn't noticed the blackboard leaning outside of the hut.

"So you built and ran this school yourself?" Aisha asked, with some amazement.

Dero rubbed his teeth with the frayed ends of a stick. "Yeah, because no school here in Shegeg Karo. There are more than three thousand people in this area without any school, any hospital. You see now. After I left secondary school, I couldn't go to university. I returned back here to build this school, to run it by effort. No one paid me. I tried to call to people to pay for their children so I could teach them. I didn't care about age. If someone came, more than twenty years, or seven, or eight. My aim was not about age. I wanted to educate people how to read and write. I taught three years without any salary, but after three years this war happened, and now we stopped. I stopped teaching."

Dero took us inside the hut. It was dark, but our eyes adjusted with the help of the light filtering through the cracks in the walls built with mud. Dero painted a picture for us, using his tooth-brushing stick as a pointer.

"The blackboard was there. And the students sat on the ground. Sometimes more than thirty in one class, sometimes less. I tried to teach them how to read and write the alphabet in Arabic. I tried to teach them a few words of English." Dero shrugged, his life's work now abandoned. "Now they use it as a base of the SLA."

"And will you build a new school?" Adam asked, filming the interior of the hut.

"Yeah, if the war is over and the situation gets better, I can try to build a school again. I will call those who have some education to teach the people here." Dero nodded thoughtfully, rubbing his teeth repeatedly with the stick. "Yeah."

WHEN WE WERE last in Shegeg Karo, the old sheikh had told us we could find the graves of his ancestors on top of the nearby mountain. We asked Dero if he would take us there now. With the cameras slung over our shoulders, we started to climb the narrow, rocky path that led to the top of the mountain. We passed clusters of stones lined up and organized in a certain pattern. There were no markings.

"These are more recent graves," Dero explained, showing us how they were aligned to point toward Mecca, in accordance with Muslim burial practice.

We made it to the top, slightly out of breath. We saw huge piles of earth-colored stones and smaller gray and white rocks scattered on the ground. Even without markings, Dero knew exactly which graves were connected to which family. He led us to the rock-covered graves of his own ancestors, which he touched reverently, as well as to the oldest graves on the mountain.

"These graves are from before the time of Islam," he told us.

The view from the top of the mountain was spectacular. A large valley of green and brown patchwork lay below. Trees, rocks and desert stretched for miles in every direction. Dero stood at the edge of the cliff for a long time, gazing silently at the expanse of his ravaged homeland.

Finally, he turned and nodded to us. "Let's go back to the market," he said softly.

We followed him down the rocky mountain path. Dero led us to the same stall where we had sat the day we met him. There was a woman peeling small red onions with a large, sharp knife and tossing them into a black cauldron over a fire. A baby boy with hair that formed a perfect mohawk was strapped with a piece of cloth onto her back. She welcomed us into the space. Dero agreed to talk on film. We knew as we set up the camera that this interview would be different from any other. We had laughed with Dero, sung with him, ridden miles with him across the desert. He was our friend.

Dero began by telling us about the baby and his mother. The boy's father had been killed alongside Dero's brother. He described what happened.

"We depend on our animals. We have here only camels, sheep, cows. There is no agriculture or maize. In southern Darfur, there are many farms. They would bring their maize to Deesa on market day. And we would sell our animals to get what we need: food, clothes, or anything from market. The father of this boy went with his animals on market day to Deesa last January, accompanied by my brother. Suddenly the Janjaweed surrounded the market and killed all the people—hundreds of people killed in one day."

No one spoke for a moment. I wondered whether the atrocity had even been covered in the news. "How did you learn about the attack? Did somebody tell you or did you hear something on the radio?" I finally asked.

"No, no, no, not the radio," Dero answered, looking down and shaking his head. "We haven't phone, but after about five or six days we heard the news that many people were killed on market day in Deesa. And then I began to worry about my brother. Yeah. I tried to tell my mother that he was not killed with them, that he was spared, that he is not what we call *shaheed* here, I don't know in English . . ."

"Martyr," I told him.

"Martyr." Dero mulled the word over in his mind for a moment. "I wanted them not to worry about it. I tried to comfort her—console or condole?"

"Console," I said gently.

"Console," Dero repeated the word, trying to commit it to his memory and then continued. "We waited for more than ten days, and when my brother didn't return, we were sure he was one of those people killed. My mother became crazy, crying all the day, not eating, not drinking. She became ill and thin. My father was patient, not like my mother. Somehow . . . but not like my mother.

"The government troops stayed in Deesa more than six months after the murder. We couldn't go to bury. When the area was liberated by the SLA, I went to search for my brother's body. I couldn't know which was my brother or others, because all the bodies were damaged and destroyed. We couldn't tell by appearance. We gathered all of them and we buried them in Deesa."

Dero began peeling small pieces off the stick he had been rubbing against his teeth earlier.

"You buried everyone together in one grave?"

"Yeah. We could not know the details of who was who." There was silence again. Dero broke it first. "Now when I remember, I feel very bad. It was very hard for me to hear my brother killed in the market without any reason. But there is nothing I can do. Sometimes I remember many times in one day. Also, about this kid's father." Dero pointed to the toddler boy. "Now, when you are asking about my brother, I am also thinking about this kid. His mother needs clothes, food. No one gives it to them. Yeah, I'm thinking about this and about my brother every day. I am feeling very bad now."

"Does it help you to talk about it?"

"When I talk about my brother, I feel very hard. I can't more, I can't more than . . ." Dero didn't finish his sentence. "Yeah." We sat without speaking as Dero arranged the shredded pieces of his stick into rows.

"Why did you choose not to fight with the SLA?" Aisha asked what we were all wondering.

"Because of my father and mother. There is no one to take care of them here. We were only two brothers. If my brother were alive, I could join the SLA. But if I participate in fighting, maybe I would be killed and my mother and father would have no one to take care of them. But I support them in other ways, when it's possible."

"Can you tell us a little bit about your mother and your father?" Aisha asked.

"My father used to have many animals, camels, cows, and sheep. My brother, as I told you, looked after the animals. He brought them to market and brought them hay, grass. But now all the animals died because no one takes care of them. And now my father is very poor. He doesn't have any livestock. My father is more than sixty years old. He can't walk to look after animals. My mother is also more than sixty years old. And that is taking all my attention, how to take care of them, how to make a better situation for my parents. I wanted to go with them to a refugee camp, but they refused. They said to me that they don't want to cross to Chad."

"Why do they refuse to go to the refugee camp?" I asked.

"I don't know. They said they don't want . . . they die here, not in Chad. This is their home."

"But you wanted to go to a refugee camp?" I continued.

"Yeah, if it was possible, because there are no food and services here. It's very hard here. If they would come to the refugee camp, it's better, but they refused."

Very hard here, Dero said, but as he began to speak about the Darfurians fleeing into Chad, his description was harrowing.

"I tried to forget that tragedy. But I can't. Last October, in Shegeg Karo, you had to pass this road to cross to Chad. I saw children die here, suffering, no food. Many people crossed from here. I saw the tragedy. All the people who you saw in the refugee camps in Kari-are, in Iridimi, most of them crossed from here. They were walking on their foot and sometimes they didn't have food, they didn't have water. Some of them tried their way and they died in the desert, thirsty. Many tragedies.

"I felt very, very sad at that time. Sometimes I tried to get water from the well for these suffering, thirsty people. Sometimes I gathered food from my family to give people. But other times I went to another village. I couldn't stay here to see the tragedy. If I didn't have anything to give them, I couldn't watch them crying, thirsty and dying. I had to go away. I couldn't see them like this."

"Do you ever feel angry?" I asked.

"Now angry," Dero answered softly and gently. "If I remember my brother, I feel very angry and sad."

"Do you want revenge?"

"Revenge?"

"When someone hurts you so you want to hurt them back," I explained.

"No, no, no, no. I would try to explain to him that it's wrong. What he's done is wrong. If you have anything against me, you can deal with it, not by killing or by hard thing. You can use another way. Yeah."

"If you saw the one who killed your brother, what would you do?"

He spoke softer still, reconsidering his response, perhaps. "I can fight with him."

"What do you hope for your future, Dero?" Aisha asked.

"I hope to find a good job to take care of my parents."

"What is a good job?" Aisha asked.

"Any work, any salary."

"But what do you dream of doing?" Aisha pursued.

"I dream of being a schoolteacher. If I have the chance to study more, that would be good, but this chance to study is not available. So I try to find work to look after my parents."

"What kind of work do you find?" I asked.

"There is no possible work here now. I tell people to hide."

"Hide from what?" I questioned.

"Like the airplane that you saw this morning. If I gathered students in this school to teach them and suddenly the airplane came to bomb it, then that would be wrong of me. Because of that I call to people to go to Chad or to hide."

"What did you feel when the airplane came yesterday?"

"I feel some fear. But, *al-hamdulillah,* there was no bombing."

"Did you help translate for a lot of journalists before us?" Adam asked.

"Yeah, some journalists come here. I try to help them, to show them the facts and accompany them on their trip, because there are no hotels. They need someone to take care of them. For me, it's good for many reasons. First, I can show all the world what is happening here. Also, I improve my English. And sometimes they give me some fee. Yeah. If it's possible." He avoided our eyes intentionally, not wanting to appear as if he was dropping a hint. "But it's not enough. Because my English is not good. Sometimes I try to explain more, but I can't."

"What would you study if you could?" I asked.

"I want first to improve my English, because English is important to study anything else, anything modern. And then, if it's possible, medicine. Because all this area, from the border of Chad until Kutum, there are no doctors here, no surgery, no medicine."

"Do you want to get married someday and have kids?" I asked.

"In this situation, no. It is a very hard life and I can't take more responsibility. No."

"Is there some special girl you know?" Adam asked.

"Maybe, sometimes, I . . ." Dero broke off, laughing and blushing.

Aisha, Adam and I exchanged grins. "Sometimes?!" Aisha teased him.

"Yeah." Dero tried to meet our eyes but began giggling again and looked down bashfully.

"Does she have a name?" I wanted to know.

"I cannot . . ." he laughed again and shook his head.

"How many camels do you need to marry her?" Aisha joked.

"Usually it would be ten, or more than ten," and then he added with uncharacteristic swagger, "but if I am to marry her, I don't need camels!"

"If you do, you must give camels to us ..." I began with Aisha fin-ishing my sentence.

"For compensation!"

The four of us laughed, enjoying this playful moment together, knowing there wouldn't be many more before we left Dero behind in Shegeg Karo as we continued into eastern Chad. And with the video camera on, we had to capture Dero in his finest moment.

Aisha set the stage. "Dero, what's your favorite music?"

"My favorite is Bob Marley because he's revolutionary."

"You like which song?" she prodded.

"Sit up, sit up don't give up your right . . . stand up for your right . . . don't be survive!" Dero attempted, getting the tune mostly right. "Yeah, that song very good for me."

"Can you sing a little 'Buffalo Soldier' for us?"

"Um . . ." Dero paused, considering the request. He eyed the mother of the little boy with the mohawk. She was stirring soup in the black cauldron, eyeing him back. He laughed, embarrassed. "No, there are many people looking at me."

Aisha didn't give up so easily. "Come on, man." She began singing the song herself, special Dero-style. *"Oi yoi yoi . . ."*

Dero jumped right in without any further encouragement, clearly enjoying himself. *"Oi yoi yoi yoi!"* he continued after Aisha backed out of the singing, giving us his full rendition with gusto. *"I sing on arrival, I sing for survival. A stolen map of Africa in the war on America! I sing on arrival! I sing for survival! Oi yoi yoi!"*

We cheered and clapped when the performance was finished. "*Kor kadai!* (Very good!)" Aisha praised him with a few of the Zaghawa words she had picked up.

When the laughter died down, the discussion turned serious again. "Dero, if you do get married and have kids someday, will you tell them about this time in your life?"

"No," Dero said firmly. "I not tell them this story, because it's very . . . this story can affect him in his mind. People now in Darfur are suffering mentally because they saw many, many crimes. Many people not normal now because they are suffering in their minds from these problems, what happened in Darfur. And so I can't tell to my kids these stories. It's very hard."

His answer surprised me. In other communities that have experienced collective trauma, including other Darfurians, we were told that the telling of the story to the next generation—so the memory lives on—is of paramount importance. Dero was, we continued to discover, unusual in so many ways.

"You said many people lost their minds." I repeated.

"Yeah."

"You did not. You are still so sociable and kind and gentle . . ."

"Yeah." He met my gaze head-on. I wasn't sure if he fully understood what I meant.

"You have managed to keep yourself alive inside of you."

"Yeah."

In every war-torn area I have been, I have met extraordinary people who are able to hold onto their dignity and humanity after living through and witnessing unimaginable horrors. I don't know how they are able to. Adam, Aisha, and I, sitting in front of Dero, were humbled by him.

"*Habibi.* Thank you for telling us your story," I said.

"Yeah. But I'm going to miss you soon. Tomorrow, or after tomorrow." I wasn't sure if Dero realized that we wouldn't be staying in Shegeg Karo. We were supposed to leave right after *iftar*. Our goodbye was only a few hours away.

"We've become good friends." I didn't know how else to verbalize what I was feeling toward him at that moment. "Say it one more time . . . who are you?"

Dero looked confused for a moment. "Dero—"

"No, no, your *other* name!" Aisha winked and Dero laughed. He knew what we were getting at. "Say it like you mean it! Who are you?"

Dero sat up straight and beamed. "I am Mac-daddy!"

WE ATE *IFTAR* with the rebels. The meal was spread out in the middle of the path that cut through the marketplace. After the meal, some of the men got up and began to pray in two straight lines, on small prayer rugs if they had them, or bits of bags that they had procured. *Galabiya*s and turbans glowed white on the praying men as the sky grew darker and darker.

It was almost time to get on the truck and begin the drive back into Chad. I walked into the desert behind the market to find a good place to go to the bathroom. I stepped behind the nearest tree, hoping its branches would provide me with some privacy from the villagers sitting and eating their *iftar*. The moonlit silhouette of the tree, however, didn't reveal that one bough protruded further than the others. As I stepped closer, the extended branch got me directly above and below my left eye. I saw the blood pouring all over my T-shirt before I felt any pain. I grabbed my turban, wrapping it tightly around my head and over my left eye, angry at my own stupidity. Eight days inside Darfur, and we had managed not to get injured, sick, or thrown off the trucks. And then, moments before the final leg of the journey, I walk into a tree and gush blood all over the place.

"Everything okay?" Aisha asked as I woozily climbed up on the truck next to her.

"Yeah, sure," I answered, trying to sound convincing. If I told her and Adam about the injury, they would try to force me to sit inside. It was our last truck ride. I didn't intend to spend it stuffed in the cab because of a run-in with a tree.

We hadn't said good-bye to Dero. I couldn't see him among the other folks who were milling around the truck. I began to get nervous. We couldn't leave without saying good-bye to Dero! We were about to disembark and ask the driver to wait, when Dero came running up. In a maneuver reminiscent of the day we had met him, he tossed a small bundle onto the truck and helped the rebels re-tie the load.

"What are you doing?" Aisha asked him. "You're home now, where are you going?"

"I have to make sure you get back safely into Chad."

"Dero, we'll be fine, you know we'll be," Adam said.

"Maybe you will need help translating in the refugee camp. I should come with you, it's my job."

"It's really not necessary," I protested weakly. It wasn't, and we knew it, but the three of us smiled broadly as Dero ignored our arguments and settled himself on top of the truck.

IT WAS THE smoothest ride yet, or maybe my throbbing eye made me unaware of the bumps. Aisha and I dangled our legs over the side, holding loosely onto the ropes, as she told me about her mother's early years growing up in Haiti. In the distance, with the scant light of the moon, the shrubs and sand dunes almost looked like the beach with the sea in the distance. The truck stopped a few hours later, at the edge of the lake that constituted the border between Sudan and Chad. I surmised that we weren't far from where we had stopped for iftar our first night inside Darfur. Everyone got off the truck to stretch, talking in hushed voices. We would be crossing the border back into Chad near here, Dero told us, at a point further north than where we had entered Darfur.

An hour after crossing the border, Kariare camp came into view. In the daytime, the camp would be teeming with women and children. Now, it was silent, still, surreal. The only sound was the cold desert wind blowing fiercely through ghostly looking tents, discernable only by the truck's headlights. Passengers unloaded their few possessions and slipped between the tents, disappearing into the darkness.

It was midnight when the truck arrived at the UNHCR field site in Bahai. Dero helped us get our gear off the back and said good night.

"Where are you going to sleep? Why don't you stay here with us?"

"I have a friend here, I can stay with him. I will meet you here tomorrow." The UNHCR guards allowed us to pitch our small tent on the premises.

I lay in my sleeping bag with the Air France pillow under my head, trying to warm up from the cold hours on the truck. I was acutely aware of the large, thick tents a few meters from us with the protection from the wind that they could offer and the mattresses that would provide some measure of comfort. At least we had the privilege of knowing we would sleep there the following night. The immediate future was not so clear for the passengers who had accompanied us on our ride and were swallowed by the dark night surrounding Kariare refugee camp.

The boy's father was killed in the same attack as Dero's brother

nine

kariare camp

"I AM ALWAYS THINKING ABOUT HOME."

*A*S MUCH AS we tried to ignore them and keep sleeping, the voices outside were growing stronger and more numerous. The sun was getting hot through the tent. We groggily sat up in our sleeping bags and tried to stretch.

Aisha and Adam looked at me in the daylight for the first time since my incident with the tree. "What the hell happened to your eye? It's all red."

I knew I could never live down the truth. "Don't you remember? Those armed bandits who attacked us yesterday? You forgot how I saved your ass?"

"Come on. What really happened?" I sighed and confessed, to uproarious laughter. We stumbled out of the tent.

"Hey, there! So we meet again!" we heard a voice call out. I blinked in the bright sunlight. Patrice and Ignacio, the UNICEF staff we had met in Abéché, looked right at us. They were sitting in the dining area sipping tea.

"Hey! What are you doing here?" Adam asked.

"Field visit to Oure Cassoni camp," Patrice answered.

We hitched a ride with the U.N. staff to Oure Cassoni/Kariare refugee camp. On the way, we told José, Patrice, and Ignacio about our mission to deliver messages from the SLA fighters in Muzbat. We hoped we could find their families, but we worried that it might be an exercise in futility. Our U.N. *compadres* weren't too optimistic.

The UNHCR car drove into the camp, passing small groups of women and children huddled directly outside the entrance under the shade of scattered, sparse trees. Brightly colored rags and a few containers hung from the lowest tree branches, buffeted by the wind.

"Who are they?" I asked.

"We call them 'spontaneous refugees,'" José explained. "They arrived recently and are waiting to be registered."

The camp was divided into three main blocks. People from the Furawiya area were in Block A. The driver dropped us off and Ignacio wished us luck.

❧

KARIARE CAMP WAS even bleaker than Iridimi. Beige tents with the black UNHCR stamp extended as far as we could see in every direction. There was nothing else but brutal wind. At times, the entire camp disappeared behind a brown wall of sand and dust. The canvas tents buckled and swelled violently against the gale as if they were about to burst. Through cupped hands and squinted eyes, we watched a few people push their way against the squall, their clothes blowing rigidly behind them. From the burned villages we had seen in Darfur, now this new type of hell was their home. The sandstorm abated for a few minutes, revealing classes of young children sitting outside on the ground. Exposed to these elements, how could students see or hear their teacher, let alone learn?

Dozens of children immediately swarmed around us as they had in Iridimi, trying to hold our hands and practicing their only words of French with us: *"Ça va? Ça va?"*

"Legga loo! (good morning!)" Aisha shouted out to them in Zaghawa, above the wind.

"Legga loo!" The kids called back, shrieking with laughter.

"Badi lo cadai? (How are you?)" Aisha hollered to the group.

"Badi lo cadai!" They repeated instead of answering, jumping up and down with excitement. More kids began to run up to see what was happening and join the action. Although there was a large international United Nations and NGO staff in the camps, our presence was a curiosity to everyone, particularly the children. We hadn't

seen any other internationals interacting with them as we were, either here or in Iridimi. I wondered if the disconnect between the international staff and the population they served was due to a philosophy regarding humanitarian work, a consequence of safety regulations imposed on the staff, or a simple lack of time.

A young man stood nearby, observing us with curiosity. He approached, telling us in halting English that his name was Moutassem and asked if he could assist us. Aisha pulled her notebook out of her backpack and showed him the names of the families we were searching for.

Moutassem left and returned a few minutes later, introducing us to a young woman.

"This is Fatima, the wife of Kamal."

I wasn't sure I had heard right. We were in a refugee camp of twenty-three thousand people and within five minutes we had actually found Kamal's wife? We explained to Fatima that we had just come from Darfur, were returning to N'djamena in a few days, and would love to speak to her. We waited to tell her about Kamal until there was some privacy and protection from the whipping, blaring winds. Fatima and Moutassem led us to her tent. Inside were her preschool aged daughter and toddler son.

"Hello," Adam said in Arabic to the little girl. "How old are you?"

"I am five years," the girl stated softly, her eyes fixed on Adam.

A few curious neighbors popped their heads into the tent. Moutassem shooed them away.

"Do you have other kids?" Adam asked Fatima.

Fatima picked up the baby boy and placed him on her lap. He wrapped his little fingers tightly around his mother's index finger and scowled at Adam, as if trying to decide whether or not to cry.

"This is my son. He is the only boy."

Adam took off his red bandana, tied around his forehead as a sweatband, and offered it to the toddler in a gesture of peacemaking. The little boy reached out tentatively, then grabbed it and began to play with it, occasionally looking up at Adam with some, albeit less, suspicion.

Aisha turned to Moutassem. "OK, so tell her that we went to Darfur and we were in Muzbat . . ."

Fatima nudged her daughter. "Face the camera," she told the little girl.

". . . and that we met her husband and have a message for her," Aisha finished.

"Oh. That's good. Is Kamal okay?" asked Fatima.

"He is in good health and he wants to send his family a message," Aisha answered. Moutassem translated.

"Good," Fatima repeated without emotion.

The lack of affect was unsettling. We couldn't determine what Fatima and her daughter were feeling as we tried to provide a link between them and their husband and father.

"When was the last time you had word from your husband?" Aisha asked, with the help of Moutassem's translation.

"It's long ago that I saw him," Fatima answered evenly.

"How long ago exactly?" Moutassem pressed.

"Four months."

"He asked us if we could find you to give you a message," Aisha said.

"Good, thank you." Her voice was flat.

Moutassem took Kamal's note from Aisha and began to read it aloud:

"How are you? How is your situation? How is your health? By the name of Allah, I hope your health is good. Today, I am in good health in Muzbat. A week ago, Afaf came from Nyala . . ."

Moutassem broke away from the letter for a moment. "Who's Afaf?" he asked.

"Afaf is his other wife," Fatima explained, not sounding the least bit aggrieved.

I was relieved. I wasn't sure what the dynamics were between Kamal and the two wives or if it would be painful for Fatima to know that Kamal, Afaf, and their daughter were together in Muzbat, while she was alone with hers and Kamal's children in a refugee camp in Chad. Moutassem continued with the letter:

"I am coming to you, insha'allah, in Eid il Fitr. (the feast to end Ramadan.) *Be in Furawiya. My greetings for all the family. From your husband, Kamal."*

Fatima finally showed emotion: agitation. She said something in Zaghawa.

Aisha turned to Moutassem. "What did she say?"

"The man said here in the letter, 'If you have the way to come to Furawiya.' She said, 'How I go there?'" translated Moutassem.

Discomfort set in. "He did not tell us how she can do this," Aisha said.

There was an awkward silence as Fatima looked at us, searching for guidance, we thought, on how to meet her husband. The communication went from bad to worse.

"She wants to tell him a message by telephone," Moutassem told us, as Fatima shrugged and the baby tried to hook the red bandana over his ear.

"What would she tell him?" Aisha asked, a natural enough follow-up question.

Moutassem translated to Fatima. Fatima looked confused. "There is no phone," he reported her reply.

Aisha tried a different approach. "Today she gets a message from her husband, a surprise. How does she feel?"

The response he translated back was: "Yes. I'm going to send him a letter, if it will reach him."

The baby held the bandana out to his sister, inviting her to take it. As soon as she reached out, he snatched it away again.

"What is she feeling right now, after hearing from her husband . . . ?" Aisha tried again with Moutassem's assistance.

"How will I write the answer?" Fatima replied via Moutassem. "I will write it in Arabic."

Aisha appealed to Adam with her eyes and Adam tried to ask the question one more time in Arabic for clarity, which Moutassem tried, again, to translate into Zaghawa.

All of a sudden, Fatima looked exhausted. "What do they want? What they want, I am going to write."

She thought for a moment while I squirmed uncomfortably. What we want? This shouldn't be about what we want her to say.

"The contents of the letter: I will say, we are here, our health is okay, we feel no pain, but our conditions are bad. *Eid il Fitr*, let him come to meet us. There is no way for us to go there. I will send him a letter like this."

"If your husband comes here, what are you going to say to him?" Aisha asked.

"I'm going to say to him, 'Let us stay together.' " Fatima smiled for the first time. "If our country will be rescued by his efforts, let him go back to Darfur and finish. Then we can return to Darfur and we will be together. If not, and there will be more suffering for the people of Darfur, let him stay here with us."

The baby waved the bandana like a flag and began to babble.

"This is Muzdellifa," Fatima said suddenly, pointing to the five-year-old girl who had been sitting silently all this time.

"Hello, Muzdellifa," Adam said.

"Manal, my older daughter, is not here. She went to bring wood. Muzdellifa, if you saw your father, what would you want to say?" Fatima asked her daughter. Muzdellifa didn't respond. "Do you want to say, 'Father, come and stay with us' or 'Remain there until everything is settled?' "

"I say to him, 'Come,' " Muzdellifa said softly.

"Look at the camera," Fatima and Moutassem simultaneously instructed the little girl.

Muzdellifa obeyed and repeated, "Come."

Fatima picked up the hand of her baby son, and waved it for the camera. Adam then turned it off and we packed up the equipment. I left the tent feeling very uneasy about the exchange, concerned that we had been mistranslated.

"Does Fatima think we are taking her message back to Kamal?" I asked. Had we inadvertently misled her?

"No, of course not," Adam reassured me. "We told her we were heading to N'djamena after Bahai."

I couldn't shake the feeling though. How could we be sure what Fatima really understood when Moutassem's English was so poor?

We struggled through the wind toward a second tent. Moutassem popped his head inside to inform the residents that they had guests and opened the tent flap for us. "You are welcome," he said.

I entered, unsure if it was a good idea after the confusing encounter we had just had with Kamal's wife. Seated were a young woman, an old woman and a six-year-old girl. The young woman was beautiful and gentle, her round eyes bright and youthful. Her head was wrapped snugly in a royal blue cloth. The older woman, draped in a red cloth, peered at us regally through wise eyes. The young girl was thin and shy with large round eyes like her mother. She wore a pink dress with a cloth tied around her head. They greeted us with warm smiles but questioning eyes.

"You are the family of Ibrahim?" Adam asked.

They confirmed that they were Ibrahim's wife Gassabai, daughter Sa'eedah, and elderly mother. Aisha explained that we had a taped message from, respectively, their husband, father, and son. Adam set up our lead camera on the playback function and popped in the tape. Aisha helped Ibrahim's mother place one side of the headphones into her ear with the other side in Gassabai's ear, while I prepared the smaller camera to film them watching their loved one.

They stared at the camera with unblinking, silent amazement as

Adam pressed *Play*. At the sight of Ibrahim talking and smiling at them, his mother gasped, reached out, and stroked the small camera screen. I wasn't sure if she was trying to greet him in traditional Zaghawa fashion or was simply making physical contact with her son, amazed that he could fit into that little square. Sa'eedah squeezed her head into the small gap between her mother and grandmother, staring at the screen and hearing the spillover sound reverberate from the headphones. We took our eyes off them only once, to look at each other in a shared moment of silent gratitude at the opportunity to do this.

They remained speechless for several seconds after Ibrahim's message finished. Ibrahim's mother broke the silence first, with strength, assurance, and glowing eyes. I understood from whom Ibrahim got his gentle manner.

"I saw my son with my eyes. I am happy. My heart became stable." She tapped her heart lightly with her finger.

"He is good. He is still alive. He is not coming here. He is in the war, going forward to liberate the land. That's good. If not, we will see him. What else can we do?"

"*Allah* keep him in peace and to liberate the land. Yes, that's good. I feel good," Gassabai added with a small smile, perhaps still in shock.

"Do you want to speak a letter to the camera?" Moutassem asked them. Aisha hastened to add, asking Moutassem to translate, that we would not be able to return to Darfur to find Ibrahim and deliver it. It's the message they would give to him if they could.

"I am still alive with my children, in peace, in Kariare," Gassabai said, after Adam put in a fresh tape. "*Allah* keep you in peace to take the land. As soon as you are done, come back to me so I can see you with my eyes."

"Speak more!" her mother-in-law commanded her.

Gassabai did, but directed her comments to us. "I was pushed out by the government and we are in Kariare. He knows this. Here, I am like an orphan. We haven't seen each other for a year. I heard that he is still alive. If so, I will see him. Since he left, my children don't have shoes. I don't have clothes. We don't even have a blanket. We are being kept alive by the U.N. If we survive, we will meet each other. I have nothing else to say."

"Say more!" Ibrahim's mother prompted her again.

"I like him. I love him. I was with him. Now I don't see him. We are separated by Omar Bashir, without the right. If I am still alive, I will meet him." She pointed to her heart. "I love him. Ibrahim, I love him." She laughed, perhaps embarrassed by how open she had just been.

"Do you want to say anything, Sa'eedah?" I asked the little girl.

"I love my father so much," she said in a small voice. Her grandmother grabbed her tiny wrist to wave her hand to the camera. "Say hi to my dad. Say hi to my dad. Say hi to my dad."

The women asked us several times if we could stay longer. We had been their only link to Ibrahim in nearly a year. Unfortunately, we had to say good-bye. It was time for us to meet the UNHCR car. We walked to the Land Cruiser feeling uplifted. We had been able to do something real and concrete for people. It wouldn't change their fate but still, for that moment and for the memory created, it was genuine and pure. We had hoped that everything we were doing would ultimately help the people whose stories we were documenting, but that was in the future. This was immediate.

On the way back to Bahai, we passed a small Chadian boy, probably around nine years old, herding a few cows and goats. Our UNICEF friends started making noises about child labor and the need to investigate this. I was baffled. After all the brutal violence they knew the children in Darfur had endured, were they actually concerned about a child practicing the livliehood that had kept his people and culture alive for generations, the same livliehood that was denied those languishing in the refugee camps just a few kilometers behind us?

SLEEP WAS DEEP and dreamless. As we loaded ourselves and our gear into the UNHCR Land Cruiser the following morning to return to Kariare camp, I hopefully climbed up on the roof of the vehicle. The driver didn't seem to mind, but Patrice did. "Against U.N. rules," he told me. I jumped down from the top and slid inside the car without protest, wondering silently if I could ever again stomach a job where I would have to adhere to someone else's idea of safety regulations. My guess was no.

A TEACHER NAMED Rajeb greeted us as we arrived at Block A of the camp. His face was long and gaunt and his eyes were partially concealed under thick eyebrows. He was wearing a button-down shirt rolled to just below his elbows, revealing sinewy forearms. "They told me about your project," he said. "I have found a few boys who want to talk with you."

Rajeb led us to a massive, white tent with large, blue UNICEF letters on the outside that served as a classroom, a relief from the strong winds. He had lined up a different translator as well, one who spoke English slightly better than Moutassem. Dozens of men and boys gathered around, making a small circle for us. All were silent. Their eyes were fixed on the two boys selected for an interview. The first boy was tall and thin. His white turban, *galabiya,* and slightly yellow eyes contrasted sharply with his dark skin. He chewed on his lip, looking down. He seemed nervous.

"My name is Nazir," he said. "I am sixteen years old, from near Abu Gamra."

"What do you remember about the day the Janjaweed came?" I asked.

Nazir chewed on his bottom lip for a moment before answering.

"They murdered the guards at the guard station and entered the village. My father was killed while he was fighting. We saw him the day after he died. After we buried him, they burned our village, took our animals and pushed us from Abu Gamra. We ran away but the army followed us. We fled again to here. We didn't go back."

"Who was with you?" I asked.

"Me and my uncles. I have one brother and some sisters. My brother went to Tine and the girls are here."

"Did you think about joining the SLA?" I asked.

"Yes. I'm going to join the Movement and then I will fight," Nazir answered immediately.

"Why did you decide to come to Chad?" I continued.

"At that time, the Movement was away from us. That's why we fled to here," Nazir explained.

"If you saw the ones who killed your father, what would you do?"

The wind whipped the sides of the tent, and Nazir was talking in a low voice. Even so, his words were crystal clear.

"I will kill them."

"Do you think you will be able to go back home someday?"

"Yes, I will go back very soon. When I do, if I find the people who killed my father, I will kill them." Nazir glanced up at the camera briefly, and then looked back down, biting on his lip intently.

"If you could give a message to your father, what do you want to tell him?"

Nazir looked confused. "Where can I find my father to talk to him?"

I rephrased the question. "Is there something inside your heart that you wish you could say to your father?"

I couldn't be sure if my question was translated accurately, or if Nazir was onto a theme that he didn't want to let go of.

"In my heart, I'm trying to find the person who killed my father, to kill him."

"Are you in school here?"

Nazir nodded.

"What subjects do you study?"

"I'm studying English."

"Do you like school?" I asked the translator to ask him.

"I would like to join the Movement to retaliate for my father."

"Do you have a girlfriend?" Adam asked.

"No."

"Are you sure?" joked Adam.

A smile flickered across Nazir's face. "No."

"Do you want one in the future?"

Another glimpse of a smile, but then Nazir was back on his main subject. "I'm not going to get married unless I fight."

"If someday you do get married and have kids, what do you want to tell your children about this time?" I asked.

"My sons, they will fight," Nazir answered. "They will take the country the same way we are."

We thanked Nazir for speaking to us. He nodded that he had heard but appeared to be drawn inward. He continued to chew on his bottom lip.

Mubarak was next. As he eagerly scooted himself forward for Aisha to clip on the mic, I noticed his green eyes. If there was any doubt as to the blurring of ethnic lines in Darfur, looking at Mubarak's light yellow-brown skin and green eyes while hearing him speak his native Zaghawa tongue put it to rest. Mubarak was younger than Nazir, but open and frank, willing to make eye contact and forge trust with complete strangers.

"When the Antonovs dropped bombs on us, we ran to hide under the trees. My father himself was killed by Antonov. I saw it with my eyes. The bombs severed people's arms and legs. Seventy people were killed. The ones who were not killed ran away. Three days later we came back. We used tools and cut wood from the trees and dug many graves. After we buried the dead bodies, we left."

"What happened to the people who were injured?" Adam asked.

"Some died on the way. We brought the lightly injured ones to Chad."

"Were any of your friends or brothers or sisters injured?"

Mubarak didn't answer directly. Instead he told us, "I wasn't injured." He looked at us with a steady gaze. We saw that his eyes were beginning to well with tears. It was time to change the subject.

"Did you play football in Furawiya?" Adam asked.

"Yes, we played football."

"Where, exactly?"

"Next to the school is the playground. That's where we played."

"Are you a good football player?"

Mubarak smiled. "Yes."

"What do you want to do when you are an adult?" I asked.

"When I grow up, I want to study English and Arabic. I want to be the president of the country." The older boys and men around him smiled, as did we.

"If you were president tomorrow, what would you do?" Adam asked.

"If I become president, I want to kill Arab Janjaweed and the army. All of them."

It was more disarming hearing this from Mubarak who had been so vulnerable with us than it had been coming from angry, brooding Nazir. I wondered again how the community of Darfur could ever hope to resume life as it used to be if the anger, trauma, and desire for retribution weren't dealt with. The SLA had been, by and large, restrained in their actions. I hadn't heard about large-scale revenge attacks on Arab villages. Would that change as more and more of these boys who had experienced such firsthand loss joined their ranks?

"What would you do for your village if you were president?" Adam asked.

"I would build high-rise buildings in Hangala and make an airport and stop the army from operating in the area."

The men around him laughed, perhaps at the combination of his guts and naïveté. Mubarak, slightly embarrassed, broke into a grin himself.

"Will you build a hotel so we can visit?" Adam joked with him.

Mubarak answered earnestly, "Yes, I will. And I will make a gun factory."

"Will you make a big football field?" I asked.

Mubarak had grand dreams. "I will build a full sports facility!"

"And will you find a beautiful girl to marry?" Adam joked.

At that point, Mubarak found it necessary to remind us of his priorities, as Nazir had done. "Country, country, country. When I liberate it from the Janjaweed and army and take the country, then I will marry." He paused, mentally calculating. "In twelve years, I will get married." We laughed with him.

"How many camels will you pay for your wife?" I asked.

"I can pay five hundred!" Mubarak announced boldly with a large and youthful smile.

We had filmed enough testimonies by now to understand that interviews take their own shape, form and length. We instinctively sensed we had only a few more minutes with Mubarak. We wanted to use them effectively.

"The story you told us is hard. What is your feeling?" I asked Mubarak.

"I can't sleep all night long. I also can't eat. I have bad nights. I'm always thinking about back home." Mubarak repeated again, "I'm always thinking about back home."

"We will take your story and share your courage," Aisha told him from behind the secondary camera. "Is there anything you want to say to kids in America?"

Mubarak straightened himself up to deliver his message.

"American kids, I need help from you now. But when we take the country and have liberated ourselves, I will come there and donate to you."

The men and boys around him clapped, showing their support for his words. Mubarak shone with pride. Aisha unclipped the mic and we shook hands with him, thanking him for his courage to be so open and honest with us.

"*Insha'allah*, Mubarak. *Insha'allah* your plans will come true." I raised my eyebrows. "Five hundred camels, huh?" Mubarak blushed. "I hope you will be the president someday."

"Maybe even she looks at you different from the others. She hopes you will be the president," the translator joked with him, shaking his hand.

What did he mean, that I looked at him different from the others? Did he mean Mubarak's light skin and green eyes? Was he treated differently from other kids? I would have loved to ask Mubarak about this—but it didn't seem an appropriate question in the middle of a crowd.

Rajeb, the teacher who had arranged the interviews with the boys, revealed his personal history next. "I was born in Furawiya. I attended primary school in Furawiya, intermediate school in Kornoi and high school in El Fashir. I was a teacher until 2000."

"What was the school like then?" I asked.

"People here loved education. They wanted the best schooling for their kids."

"Was it a government school?" Adam asked.

Rajeb nodded. "The government supported us, but not much. They gave us only the textbooks for the primary school. The chalk was from UNICEF, not the government. There has been a lot of discrimination. Listen, I will explain to you. In Khartoum, the government provides all the school supplies, curriculum, water, snacks for the students. But in Furawiya, we had only books and a teacher.

Sometimes the teachers would go five months without getting paid or we would not get paid at all. We had to ask the students to bring money. It was the parents of the kids who supported us."

Dero had told us the same about his school in Shegeg Karo. But unlike Dero, Rajeb had not been teaching when the conflict erupted.

"The government intelligence had arrested me in El Fashir for three months."

"What happened to you in the prison?" I asked.

"I was tortured. In the morning, they took us out and beat us. When we went back to the cell, they also beat us. There was no food. One time, we didn't have water for three days. They put us inside the cells so we couldn't even reach the water coming from *Allah*. They preferred to use it to irrigate the trees rather than for us to drink."

Rajeb unbuttoned his shirt to show us physical evidence of beatings that he still carried on his back and shoulders.

"They wanted to slaughter me," Rajeb continued. He wiggled his finger along an invisible line on his long neck. "They put the knife on my neck here. Look here."

I tried to locate the mark, but all I could see were protruding veins. With his shirtsleeves now pushed all the way up, however, the scars on his elbows were clear.

"All this area here and this . . ." Rajeb hoisted up his pants' legs for us to see the marking around his knees. "They scraped it with a brick." He rubbed his hand across his knee. It made a rough, scraping sound. I winced. "Then they hit me here until my teeth broke." He opened his mouth and pointed to several severely chipped teeth. "I tried to talk to them. I said, 'I am a teacher in the school.' They told me, 'You are not a teacher, you are nothing. You teachers in Dar Zaghawa are supporting this rebellion. Your mind is the mind of a revolution.' A lot of teachers were captured. Some of them are still in jail. In Abu Gamra, two teachers were killed. One teacher from Kornoi was also killed."

I recalled our conversation with Kareem in Iridimi camp. He had spoken about schools being targeted in attacks as well. But Rajeb was telling us something new: teachers had been specifically rounded up, detained, and tortured. Why? Was the government afraid that teachers in Darfur were educating children to question or challenge the dominance of the ruling elite? Everything we had seen and heard in the camps pointed to how important education was to the people of Darfur. It was viewed as the key to the future in spite of, or perhaps in defiance of, the government's attempts to keep the population ignorant.

Rajeb continued his story: "With the help of *Allah*, I was released. I returned to Furawiya. Many of my family had been killed. The village was destroyed completely. The schoolhouse was burned and the books were burned and torn up. Some people managed to escape. I came with them here to the refugee camp. All my family is here. My mom, my dad, everyone is here."

"Do you have children?" Adam asked.

"I have only one girl. Her name is Deera. I had a baby boy. He became ill. I took my baby for emergency care to Bahai. The doctor gave him medicine, and they transferred him to Iriba. He got better. On the return trip by the will of *Allah*, he passed away. We are for the sake of *Allah* and we return back to *Allah*."

"When was this?" Adam asked softly.

"The day before yesterday."

We sat in silence as Rajeb rolled down his pants' legs and buttoned his shirt, hiding once again the scars from the torture he had endured. Rajeb concluded the interview quietly. "We are just seeking the mercy of *Allah*."

WE HAD AN hour before returning to Bahai. Adam decided to wait in the shade of the tent where our U.N. friends were meeting with teachers from the camp. Aisha and I wanted to talk to the spontaneous refugees, as José had described them. We walked to their trees outside the entrance to the camp. The children ran up to us immediately, eager to see who we were and curious to examine our equipment. They were covered from head to toe in sand, giving them an ashy, ghostlike appearance. They took us by the hand and led us to their mothers. There was so much I wanted to ask them. How long had they been squatting under the trees, waiting to be officially registered inside the camp? Why had they come to Chad now, months after the large influx of refugees had streamed across the border? Had they experienced fresh atrocities? How were they surviving, fully exposed to the harsh desert elements without even the U.N.-provided tent, or daily ration of sorghum to eat and water to drink? Were relatives inside the camp sharing their meager resources with them?

A little boy hopped on one foot in front of us, chewing on a mysterious substance, laughing and pointing to himself, wanting our attention. I smiled at him and then at his mother, hoping that her son's interest in us might open an avenue to sit and talk. When I gestured to my camera, she covered her face and turned away. I put the camera in the bag and Aisha and I winked at the little boy, who was hopping all the more fervently as we walked away. I felt as if we had invaded a very private corner of suffering.

Aisha and I walked back toward the camp. We were followed, and not only by the children. One old woman was trailing us as well. Aisha and I turned to greet her. She wanted to communicate, but was unable to speak. Smiling, but with a sense of urgency, she pointed to her mouth, cupped her empty hands together, and patted her stomach repeatedly.

"Is she trying to tell us that there is no food?" I asked a barefoot little girl in Arabic. She nodded, swaying back and forth with her hands behind her back, but I wasn't sure if she could understand me.

We apologetically left them and slowly returned to Adam.

"Patrice and Ignacio were just filling me in about what's going on with the teachers," Adam told us.

The teachers were upset, he explained, as they had been working so far without pay—something UNICEF hoped to rectify shortly. What made matters worse was that another international NGO was already paying salaries to workers who were cleaning the latrines. What UNICEF would be able to offer the teachers was less than what the other NGO was paying the latrine workers. It had become a matter of pride and, to some extent, class.

Although the same agencies often provide humanitarian relief in crises all over the world, we were beginning to see firsthand the lack of coordination that caused overlap and, in this case, resentment among the population in need.

Minutes later, the UNHCR Landcruiser arrived, José, Patrice, and Ignacio already inside and weary from the confrontation they had just faced with over one hundred teachers in the heat of the tent. They explained the problems further.

"Some folks think it's strange that people whose lives have been devastated would argue over comparative wages," Ignacio told us. "But refugees seek to rebuild their lives and reclaim some element of normalcy in their new circumstances. They organize themselves according to village, clan, and tribe, and try to reestablish community leadership roles. And, in this case, whose work is valued at what price by the international community also matters."

Patrice, Ignacio, and José were concerned that the tensions around this issue might really erupt. I remembered what Gaetan had told us back in Abéché. The trauma that the refugees had endured became evident in overreactions to any inequality or injustice, whether real or perceived. The NGO paying the latrine workers a high wage was surely trying to do something positive. I reflected on my first trip to Kabul, when I learned about Afghans evicted from their homes by landlords who could charge higher rent to the humanitarian agencies coming to Kabul and setting up shop. Humanitarian aid was, at best, an extremely complicated and often highly problematic endeavor.

WE ARRIVED EARLY the next morning at Kariare camp for our final day of filming.

"Legga loo!" a group of women greeted us, the wind whipping their robes around their legs. Slightly baffled, we returned the greeting.

We next encountered a group of unfamiliar children. They also called out to us expectantly, *"Legga loo!"*

"Word must have spread throughout the entire camp that we're the foreigners who know how to say good morning in Zaghawa," Aisha grinned.

Rajeb met us at the school and introduced us to a man named Mahdi. "He will help you today," Rajeb told us.

Mahdi was tall, with a commanding presence. In addition to the turban and *galabiya*, he wore enormous orange-tinted sunglasses.

"You want to meet more people from Furawiya?" he asked us, peering at us from behind the orange shades. There was something unsettling about him, but I couldn't put my finger on it.

"That would be wonderful," we told him.

"I, myself, am from Furawiya and there are many others who want to speak to you. Come!"

Mahdi strode ahead and we had to move fast to catch up. Sand was lifted and swirled by the wind, creating a haze throughout the camp. He led us to a small tent used for storage. Two young women and an elderly man were waiting for us. Rolled up mats leaned against the sides of the canvas flaps and burlap sacks were piled up on top of them. There was scarcely enough room for us all. Mahdi and the old man pulled themselves up on the burlap sacks and Aisha and I did the same.

It was already decided that the two women would speak first. One, wearing a neon green-yellow shawl, with broad features, took the lead. "My name is Hawa. I am from Furawiya. I'm twenty-three years old."

"I'm twenty-five years old," the second woman added in a soft, girlish voice. She was wearing a deep blue shawl and was more petite and delicate. She hesitated to meet our eyes. She said her name, but too quietly to be heard. It didn't help that the fierce wind outside was waging battle with the tent flaps.

Hawa continued speaking before we could ask the woman in blue to repeat her name. "I worked at the school."

"As teachers," the woman in blue added.

"Can you tell us what happened when Furawiya was attacked?" we asked.

Hawa answered first, "The plane came and broke my brother's leg. We ran in different directions. The soldiers came after. We carried our brother with the broken leg. We left the others. The bombs killed them. Now he is sick here." She looked down and became still and quiet.

The woman in blue added her details in a voice barely audible over the wind. "My two brothers were coming from the well. One was five years old and the other was ten years old. Soldiers and Jan-jaweed arrested them. They cut the saddles that were holding the water. They took them to their car. They beat them. We ran to the hills. Other women were beaten, but we were hiding in the hills, so nobody found us."

I wanted her to clarify: Did she specify women for a certain rea-son? By beaten did she mean raped? The woman in blue was looking intently at her hands, one of which was twisting and untwisting a piece of straw around the index finger of the other. There was no sensitive way to address these questions, especially with three men in the tent.

The woman in blue finished her statement. "We are very tired."

Tired not only from everything they had been through, but also from reliving it night after night.

"Last night I had a dream about the Janjaweed and soldiers. They came here and we had to run to another place," the woman in blue continued softly.

"All the kids dream at night and cry," Hawa interjected. "When you ask them 'Why?' they say 'The planes come.' Some of them wake up and run. When you stop them and ask 'Why?' they say, 'Because the soldiers are coming to beat me.' " Hawa's voice grew softer. "Last night I dreamt the Janjaweed and the army came. We fled and carried my brother with the broken leg. The plane came and bombed. It broke his other leg." Hawa took the corner of her green robe and covered her face with it for a few silent moments, crying. She wiped her eyes with her robe, composed herself, and continued, "A bad dream."

Hawa's tears shook me. Was this expression of grief healthy and healing? Or was it damaging for these women to open up their dreams to us and become vulnerable when we would be packing up our cameras and leaving? Could emotional healing ever occur when physical survival was still so tenuous?

"One night I dreamt the planes came and we ran under the trees and to the hills. When I woke up I was so tired. I left my child and ran. I cried," the woman in blue recalled.

"You have a child?" I asked.

"One," she said, still looking down but smiling proudly. "A girl named Mariam."

"Blessings! When was she born?" Adam asked.

"On the way from Darfur to here."

"How did you give birth under those conditions, keep your baby alive, and get here?" I asked in amazement.

The woman in blue continued to wrap and unwrap the blade of straw around her finger, staring at it intently. "I came on foot.

Sometimes I carried my daughter in my arms, sometimes other people carried her for me. It was so difficult."

The conversation turned to the SLA. Not only did they fully support the actions of the young Darfurian men in the rebel group, but the woman in blue looked directly at us and the camera for the first time and stated firmly, "We are ready to fight with them."

Hawa was also prepared to join the rebel movement, which, to my knowledge, was comprised almost only of men, but had something to say about reconciliation as well.

"Bring the peace," was her final message. "The people who are dead are already in the past. We will live with those who are alive."

The elderly man had been perched on a burlap sack silently and without motion. I had almost forgotten he was there.

"This is Uncle Tor'chala," Mahdi introduced him.

Tor'chala had a clipped white beard and eyes that could drill a hole in a plank of wood. He placed himself in the center of the tent and patiently allowed us to clip the microphone, smoothing the creases of his white *galabiya* with his wrinkled hands.

"He was the first witness when the Janjaweed came to Furawiya. They took his clothes off and they tied him and beat him until they left him for dead," Mahdi said.

Tor'chala chose to start his story from an earlier point. "I am from Furawiya. Since *Allah* created me, I was there," he said. "I am eighty years old. Since we were born, we have been in our area. We didn't move at all. We didn't make any problems until the government killed us. They separated children from their mothers and animals from the boys who looked after them. There was fire from the air, the army, Janjaweed, and cars from the ground. If they saw children or women, they abused them. We ran to the mountains and the caves. The children hid under the trees. Some children ran away at that time and we don't know where they went."

I thought about the boys we had met training with the SLA.

"The army of Sudan came to the village. They raped the women. They took our possessions. Nothing is left to us except the empty village and the mountains."

We asked Tor'chala what he thought about the government of Sudan.

"Omar Bashir, he supports the Arabs. He gave them weapons. We were supporting him and he turned his back to us," he spat.

No one else had yet mentioned the role of Darfurians during the decades-long civil war between the North and the South of Sudan. Many had bought into the government's propaganda that it was a war to protect Islam and had fought on the side of the government. I had wondered if all Southerners shared the solidarity that James, the young man formerly from the SPLA, had expressed. But I hadn't considered the betrayal Darfurians must be feeling after they had fought for the government and then found the same tactics used against them.

"Do you have a message you want to give to the international community about how to help Darfur?" asked Adam.

"We are just like orphans. We are looking for someone to help us. And give us emotional support. And take us back so I can stay in my land until I die."

"Come, take your cameras," Mahdi told us after Tor'chala removed the microphone and handed it back to us, his eyes never leaving our faces. "The *omdah* of Furawiya wants to meet you."

MAHDI LED US to a large tent that seemed to function as a community center. A man in his mid-forties stood up to greet us as we ducked inside the opening flap.

"This is Mansour—he is our *omdah*."

Mansour warmly shook hands with each of us. He was the youngest *omdah* we had met by far, but his confidence and poise compensated for what he may have lacked in years. "I hear you have been in my village? Tell me, what did you see there?"

He nodded solemnly as we described the destruction. With Mahdi's help, they began to tell the story of Furawiya from his boyhood until present.

Much earlier, Mahdi told us, there had been a hospital, a Qu'ranic school, and an environmental center. The government took them away and the Darfurians built their own institutions, relying on themselves alone. Mansour spoke about his growing awareness that the increased violence was government policy.

"We went to the government to complain but they called us criminals. 'We have no relationship with you,' they said."

He also spoke about his role as *omdah* during the bombing campaing of Furawiya. He had gathered the residents outside the village and advised them not to go to the well during the day, when the bombing was heaviest. The government realized that the women were going to the well at night and started bombing during the night. The pickup trucks came from the front but still they held on. Finally, they were hit with a full arsenal of trucks, tanks, and planes. They fled to the hills to hide. Mansour sent one person, Ali, back to investigate if the troops and Janjaweed were gone. When Ali got to the village, he was captured and killed. When the news got back to them, they started trekking to Kariare camp.

"What will happen to the children if they can't go back to their homes soon?" Adam asked.

Mahdi contemplated. "We lost this entire generation for an unknown number of years to come."

An older woman entered the tent.

"Ah!" Mansour indicated that she should sit beside him. "This is my mother, Nadifa."

Nadifa settled next to her son, taking us in with her large, deep brown, watery eyes. She was sixty years old, she told us, and began to describe a comfortable life from her childhood; her parents were farmers, and meat and milk were plentiful. She did not feel any racism. "I was a little girl," she said, "but I remember that time very well."

"How old were you when you got married?" I asked.

"Eighteen."

"Can you tell me about your wedding day?"

"Brothers and friends gave a lot of gifts: money, camels, sheep. They played the traditional drum. They gave me everything." I detected a half-smile at the recollection.

"How was the *omdah* as a child? Well-behaved, mischievous . . . ?"

"Smart," She answered decisively. "My son is very good. If he is responsible for something, he does an excellent job."

"What do you think about Omar Bashir?"

"Since the time of Omar Bashir, we live with constant pressure and stress." The top of the tent was drooping so that it almost touched her head. She lifted it up with one hand as if freeing herself from its encroachment. "We are trapped inside our clothes."

WE THANKED THE *omdah* and his mother and followed Mahdi out of the tent.

"Is there someone else you want to talk to? Something else you want to see?"

"Well . . ." Adam hesitated. It was such an unimportant request.

"What?" he questioned.

"The *hijabs* that we see everyone wearing, the leather pouches. Is there anyone in the camp who makes them? Can we buy some?"

"Follow me!" He smiled.

Mahdi strode off ahead, unaffected by the windstorm sweeping through the camp. I was choking on the density of sand in the air.

Mahdi led us to the tent of a craftsman who made and sold *hijabs* in the camp and said his good-byes to us after we assured him we could find our way back. The *hijab* seller had only a few pouches.

"I can make more for you to buy!" he said enthusiastically, sensing a big business opportunity. "Can you come back in a month? I will have many for you then."

In a month we would be back in the United States, well on our way to editing the film, we hoped. We bought the few he had and divided them among ourselves. We certainly hadn't intended to bring souvenirs from Darfur back to family or friends, but these handmade amulets, intended to stave off disaster, felt like a reminder of something important.

We started to push our way back through the sand and the wind when something caught the corner of our eye. About ten meters away we saw a shriveled old man dressed in white rags. He was sitting on the sand, using his hands and legs to scoot himself forward, inch by inch. We approached him. Adam asked in Arabic if he needed help. He couldn't talk, but nodded and gestured his acceptance of assistance, pointing to the direction he was trying to go. Adam handed me the camera bag, and he and Aisha lifted the old man gently and began carrying him.

A younger woman stepped out of her tent after we had gone a dozen meters. "This is my father! Bring him to me, please!"

Adam and Aisha set the old man down inside the woman's tent. He was motioning urgently to his daughter.

"Where was he?"

"Just over there a little way." Aisha pointed to where we had found him.

"He keeps wandering off. He won't stay put. I don't know what he is looking for." She began to tend to her father, wiping sand off his face and clothes, before looking up at us briefly. "Thank you."

As we continued walking, I told Aisha and Adam about a conversation I had had with a documentary filmmaker friend of mine. While studying journalism, she had told me, her teacher once asked his students who would intervene to help the subjects they were filming. My friend raised her hand along with a few others. "You should not be in journalism school," they were told. We didn't verbalize the connections between that story and our role here. We knew we were sharing the same doubts and inner conflicts.

*

I was staring out the window of the Landcruiser on our way back to Bahai, lost in my thoughts. It was a few moments before I realized that the car had stopped. An enormous herd of camels was moving across the desert, crossing in front of us, hundreds upon hundreds of them in a long line guided by a handful of teenaged boys. We jumped out of the vehicle, cameras in hand, to capture their journey north, likely to end up in Cairo. A few years ago Adam had been walking through the City of the Dead in Cairo (where people live in the tombs of the city's past residents) when a similar herd had passed through the tight, squalid alleyways of the ancient city. We were witnessing the start of that one thousand six hundred kilometer voyage here, in the wide-open Sahel desert. The huge animals silently forged the blowing wind. Hundreds of legs moving in unison, their humps swaying up and down, as they were herded along on a timeless journey. Staring at the sea of camels, I thought of the scorched earth that had become Darfur, where centuries of existence were now threatened with extinction. Mahdi's words from earlier that day echoed in my mind: "We lost this entire generation for an unknown number of years to come."

"Spontaneous refugees" outside of Kariare camp

ten

heading home

"IT FELT LIKE WE HAD BEEN GONE FOR YEARS."

DERO WALKED US back to the UNHCR compound after a dinner of goat meat dipped in salt and Pepsi. It was our last evening with him. He was going back home early in the morning and we were catching a U.N. flight to Abéché. He wouldn't be able to toss a bundle onto the Airserv craft and leap aboard to join us, this time. We joked as we always did with "Dero After Dark," but this time the laughter was tinged with sadness. We lingered with him outside the chain fence.

"*Habibi*, it's your last opportunity now. What is your message to Condoleezza Rice?" I asked.

Dero began to blush and laugh. "I don't know!"

"*Yalla,* come on, this is your big chance! We can film it and send her the tape!" Adam joked.

"I can't say. It's not in my job!" Dero laughed.

"How many camels do you think Condoleezza Rice . . ." Aisha started to ask, but Dero cut her off enthusiastically.

"Yeah, if she come here, I can pay to her one hundred camels." His wide smile shone brilliantly in the dark.

"One hundred camels!" Aisha exclaimed. "She'd be very honored. You're too good for her, Dero. She'd be a lucky woman to end up with you."

"And maybe she could send for me political asylum!"

Hugs were exchanged with laughter, and then more hugs, thank-yous, expressed hopes to see each other again, and good-byes. Dero clasped all of our hands in his one final time, then turned to go back to the marketplace. We stood in silence watching him walk away. The white of his robe glowed as he strode further and further into the dark night until we could no longer see him.

The following morning, José asked us if we had a satphone, explaining that Chadian army forces were in the area, confiscating cellular and Thuraya phones, anticipating a possible coup attempt against the President of Chad, Idris Deby. We buried it deep inside Adam's sleeping bag.

I gave José the little red Air France blanket and pillow for the UNHCR compound as we said good-bye and climbed into the Landcruiser to head to the airstrip.

"Why did you do that?" Adam demanded.

"I thought maybe they could use it."

"We were going to film you giving it back to the Air France attendants when you got back on the plane!" Aisha protested.

"Come on, you weren't really going to do that," I responded.

"Hey, you can't make unilateral decisions like that, not when it affects the film!"

The nine-seater plane landed almost on schedule. "Hi folks!" one of the pilots called loudly over the still-roaring engine and propellers. He was a jovial man, short, with white hair and stubble and pot-bellied. "My name is Howard. We've got some good news and some not-so-good news. Good news is: the plane is working fine. During the routine inspection, however, someone forgot to put the fuel plug back into the tank. We've been dumping fuel the entire way here. What's left in the tank now is exactly what it takes to fly from Bahai to Abéché without any reserves to deal with even an unexpected headwind," he stated casually.

Howard and Marianne, the young South African co-pilot with a small frame and long brown hair, laid out our options. We could test our luck and try to make it to Abéché without any reserves in the tank. We could wait here until UNHCR sent another plane, which may or may not happen that day. We could fly the plane to Iriba, almost halfway between Bahai and Abéché, and try to find a car from there or see if another plane could meet us.

"So what should we do, folks?" We stared back at him. "Do you think we should we try to make it?" Howard asked sincerely.

"This is your plane, you're the pilot. Shouldn't you be the one to decide?" Aisha pointed out.

Howard nodded with some uncertainty, retrieved a thick manual out of the cockpit, and began leafing through it. "It says here that the engines can run on paraffin fuel. Can we find that here?"

Adam and Howard got back into the Landcruiser to get a few drums of paraffin while Marianne, Aisha, and I stayed behind to guard the aircraft. Marianne told us about her budding pilot's career. She was working for AirServ to log flight hours so that she could get a job with a commercial airline. She had a quick sense of humor and kept us laughing with anecdotes about flying in remote parts of the world.

"The stories I've heard from U.N. and NGO staff in Chad have been just unbelievable," Marianne said. I expected her to recount tales of the atrocities that the Darfurians had lived through. "The refugees in some of the camps are angry because of the way the U.N. is running things, and how much food they are getting. I mean, aren't they refugees? Shouldn't they be grateful for whatever help they get?"

I sat up, shocked. I might have expected to hear a sentiment like that expressed at my grandmother's country club in Florida, but not here, in the midst of the crisis, by someone engaged in the work, even if only to log flight hours.

Adam, Pauline, Howard, and the driver sped back victoriously with two white drums of paraffin loaded onto the truck.

"Does anyone have a clear bottle?" Howard asked.

I tossed him an empty water bottle. He filled it up partway with the paraffin and held it up to the sunlight, pouring a little on his hands to see how it felt, and smelled it.

"Does anybody know what paraffin smells like?" he asked, wide-eyed. "Is it supposed to have these sediments floating around in it?"

I almost laughed out loud. What if I pretended to be a certified paraffin expert and reassured Howard that this is exactly how paraffin is supposed to smell and look? Would he take my word for it?

"If there's too much sediment, then it can clog the filters and shut down the engine and we'd have to do an emergency landing in the desert," he said matter-of-factly. "So what do you think we should do?"

We decided to fly to Iriba. UNHCR headquarters in Abéché contacted us by radio to inform us that another plane was available to meet us there. We would make it back to Abéché that afternoon and be on target for the next day's flight to N'djamena.

*

ARRIVING BACK IN Abéché felt like returning to some modicum of development—though when we had first been there, we had seen it as a small, dusty, desolate town. We landed on a paved tarmac with an actual building designating it as the Abéché Airport and went through the registration procedures there. We settled our gear at the UNICEF compound, intending to stay for the night at Patrice and Ignacio's invitation and crossed the road to the UNHCR office to get caught up on e-mail correspondence and news from the world beyond.

Aisha was able to talk our way into the French military base yet again. But the base wasn't quite the hub of excitement it had been a few weeks earlier. A large portion of the military stationed there had been flown out to the Ivory Coast crisis. The French planes that usually brought supplies to the base in Abéché were now flying goods into the Ivory Coast. Translation: no Snickers or beer. We stayed only for a little while with a handful of aid workers and the few remaining members of the scaled-down French military.

That night, we spread our sleeping bags out on the concrete floor of a screened porch on the side of the UNICEF compound. I found myself missing the relatively soft sand of Darfur.

OUR FLIGHT TO N'djamena was first thing in the morning. After landing, we headed straight back to the hotel to take a room for the day. We needed to make a list of everything we had to accomplish before the city shut down for *iftar*.

Adam pulled out his notebook as Aisha and I called out items to add to the list: return satellite phone, exchange Chadian dinars back to dollars, locate Fadi's family to show them their son's message, retrieve our "excess of fifteen kilo" luggage from the hotel.

We were able to reclaim our possessions from the storage room easily. More problematic, however, was returning the Thuraya. Adam had been assured on its purchase that he would get back one thousand of the fifteen hundred dollars he had paid. Our mistake was not putting it in writing. Now we were being offered only six hundred dollars. By the time a frustrated Adam had finished arguing with the salesmen, the money market in town was closed. The only exchange rate we could receive for our dinars was ridiculous.

We made it back to the hotel, feeling a bit defeated.

"Maybe we can still reach Fadi's family," Aisha reminded us.

We dug out the notebook where he had written his parents' names and a phone number. It didn't hurt to try. I dialed the number.

A man answered the phone after several rings. *"Salaam Aleikum."*

"Aleikum asallam!" I quickly passed the phone to Adam. What was I thinking, trying to make this call myself?

"Is this Hassan? Your son Fadi is with the SLA?" Adam asked him in Arabic.

"Who is this?"

Adam explained. Half an hour later, the front desk rang our room. "Someone is here to see you."

We came to the lobby, cameras in hand. An elderly man rose from his chair to shake our hand. He was short and squat, with salt-and-pepper hair, and a trimmed beard. He walked slowly with a cane. I remembered that Fadi told us his father had been ill.

We went outside to the veranda, and, inviting him to sit, turned the camera on to the playback feature, giving him the headphones so he could hear his son's voice as he listened to his message.

"Is this him?" we asked, as he looked at the tape. "Is this your son?"

"Ah, Mansour my son," he said.

Mansour? Was there some mistake? The boy we met was Fadi.

Hassan didn't seem concerned by our confusion. He told us about his son leaving home to join the SLA. "He was small, but when he saw the injustice toward his people, he was angry. One day he told me, 'I want to join the revolution.'

"I told him, 'You are still small.'

"He said to me, 'Can't you see that my uncles, my people, are all being killed like sheep? You are an old man; can't you see what is happening to my people? I cannot stay looking at my people in this way.'

"I told him, 'Oh, my son, you are still young, wait until you grow.'

"But Mansour ran away, without telling me. He didn't talk to me. I hope *Allah* may forgive him and support him to achieve his goal.

"It is not my son alone. As time continues and the children are growing and they hear about killing, raping, looting, they will all go and join themselves to the Movement. They will all be against the government. The Prophet Muhammad, peace be upon him, told us that we are all guardians and are responsible for our people. Just like in South Africa, when they suffered injustice from the white men, all the South African people resisted against the oppressors. One day in Sudan, there will be a big revolution against the government. There have been multiple Sudanese governments that have come with hidden agendas for their own benefit. They say they are advocating for Islam and for *shari'a* (Islamic law). I don't know what Islam and what *shari'a* they are talking about. I don't know of any religion that discriminates, kills people, rapes women, especially small girls of eight and nine years. I don't know which *shari'a* they want to apply.

"I want the government to stop the discrimination between North and South or East and West. Not only in Darfur, in all Sudan. There is injustice all over Sudan. People cry, *'Jallaba* (Arab tribes)! *Jallaba!'* But the problem is not from the *jallaba*, it's from the government. Omar Bashir and his group came to power with a specific ideology and gathered a small number of people around them. They use religion as a bargaining tool for material gain. We should not be unfair to *jallaba*. The *jallaba* brought Islam and civilization to Sudan. They have been living with us. The problem is the unjust distribution of development, power, and resources. It's a challenge that all the Sudanese governments faced. None of them managed to evaluate the right share for the other provinces of Sudan. We, all the Darfurians and the Arab tribes, live in the same situation. The problem is created by the government because they want control."

Hassan pushed himself up with his cane and slowly made his way out of the Novotel. We sat on the veranda a few minutes afterward, bewildered. He had provided one of the most astute political commentaries we had heard on our journey. But was he Fadi's father? And who was Mansour?

I SLEPT DEEPLY on the flight to Paris and awoke at five in the morning when we landed, groggy and disoriented. Adam, Aisha, and I sat in the airport coffee shop for several hours, waiting for our connecting flights. We had surprisingly little to say to each other. It felt like we had been gone for years, instead of four weeks. The inner workings of our cameras were clogged with sand. Our clothes were disgustingly dirty. I still had the remnants of my black eye. The pulled muscles in Adam's shoulder were causing him serious pain. We were completely exhausted.

But Adam had forty-five mini-dv tapes in his camera bag filled with interviews, testimonies, and footage. Aisha had thirty-five rolls of film to be developed. And I had the memory of Dero draped in white as he walked away after our final good-bye on the border between Chad and Sudan, heading back to a home and a future that were still so insecure and uncertain, trying to keep my eye on him as long as possible until he melted into the night sky.

eleven

completing the film

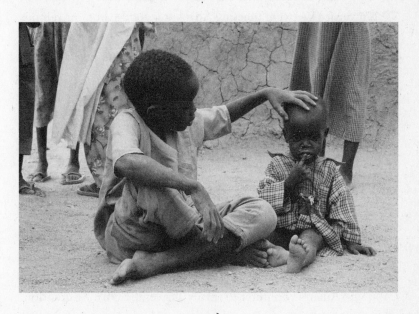

"SO MUCH MORE TO DO . . ."

I MET AISHA OUTSIDE Best Buy to catch the shuttle to American University. We were meeting Adam at a coffee shop on campus for our first post-production meeting. Omer Ismail, who had initially helped us with contacts from the Darfurian community, would be coming also.

It was strange to see Aisha here. She was wearing earrings and was dressed in something other than the lightweight hiking pants that we had all worn in Darfur and Chad.

When we got to the coffee shop, Adam was waiting for us with his laptop. "Hey!" he greeted, as we joined him at his table. "Omer should be here in a few minutes."

"I've got a present for the two of you," I said as I pulled a Tower Record bag from my backpack.

"Oh Lord, you didn't!" Aisha laughed as she pulled the twin-DVDs out of the bag: *Who's the Boss?: The First Season.* We slipped the DVD into Adam's computer to finally answer the burning question: What *was* the *Who's the Boss?* theme song?

When Omer arrived, we were back to business. We briefed him on our trip and showed him the little bit of footage Adam had been able to capture on his hard drive. Omer seemed impressed with what we had accomplished. It also had a sobering effect on him. He whistled low as he caught sight of the bomb crater and unexploded missile in Furawiya.

"I know, of course, about everything that is going on over there. But I never got the chance to see it like this," he said quietly.

"What tribe are you from? Can you understand what they are saying?" It would be wonderful if Omer spoke Zaghawa—we hadn't yet figured out how we would get all this footage translated. The on-the-spot summaries that Dero, Musa, and others had provided wouldn't be nearly specific enough for the word-for-word subtitles we needed on the film.

"I can only understand when they are speaking Arabic. I am from the Berti tribe. But Berti, Zaghawa, Fur, Masalit, it makes no difference. It's the same story for all of us."

The clip we were looking at ended. "Can I see more?" He couldn't right then; we didn't have the five hundred dollars needed to buy an external hard drive to back up the rest of our footage. We'd need to raise more money before we could begin to work.

When Omer left, Aisha and Adam filled me in on the schedule of upcoming meetings and speaking events. We had a presentation at the Institute for Policy Studies in two days, another at the State Department's Bureau for Human Rights, and NPR in Baltimore wanted us for a radio segment the following week. As our goal for the project was advocacy and activism, the attention seemed like a good sign. We would put together a trailer as quickly as possible. In the meantime, we would use photographs, stories from our own experience, and the short clip that Adam had pieced together.

It FELT STRANGE to be asked to speak publicly about Darfur. Suddenly, I was expected to be some kind of expert on Darfur, Sudan, the region as a whole. I felt like an imposter. Yes, I had read everything I could get my hands on about Darfur in the weeks leading up to the trip and had expanded that reading list upon my return to the history of Sudan and eastern Africa, but I still felt as though my background knowledge was patchy. How did I have the right to stand in front of groups of people and authoritatively answer questions about the political complexities of Sudan?

The insecurity faded with time. The firsthand knowledge I had

absorbed while in Chad and Sudan was more significant than I had
realized. I attended multiple Darfur related sessions and panels in
Washington, D.C., and came to a startling realization: I knew as much
as most people who were working on and speaking about this issue.
The authenticity, I realized, came from the people themselves, whose
messages we were communicating.

AISHA, ADAM, AND I rehashed details about the trip in the talks we
gave. Everyone was curious about our personal experience: Weren't
we scared? Were we safe? Was it hard? However difficult those weeks
in Chad and Darfur may have been, from keeping the camera batteries charged to bearing witness to atrocities, it wasn't as challenging as what lay ahead of us. Our real work was only now beginning.
We felt a tremendous responsibility to the Darfurians we had met
whose testimonies were among the forty-five hours of footage
finally backed up on external drives. How were we going to edit it
down to a one-hour film? How would we manage to preserve the
integrity and dignity of the people who trusted us with their stories?
How could we demonstrate the systemic abuses that occurred village after village without creating a repetitive film?

The relationship among the three of us had been surprisingly easy-
going throughout the trip. However, moments of tension over crucial editing decisions arose. An endless stream of questions needed
examination and decisions. We had interviewed many intelligent and
insightful U.N. and NGO staff during our days in Abéché. Should
we include segments of those interviews in the film? Should we uti-
lize narration for background and context? Should our journey and
experience be a part of the film?

We answered no to all those questions. Our film would be a platform for Darfurians, those whose lives had been most deeply
impacted by the crisis, to tell their stories for themselves, in their own

words. Our journey had no place in the film. After much delibera-
tion, we decided to use text screens of information rather than narration. We did not want any outside voices.

How much information and context to put on those text screens
was a harder issue to negotiate. On the one hand, we had no inten-
tion of creating an "A-B-C Primer" about Darfur. Once we stepped
down the path of providing background, it would become an endless web. Yet without any, audiences would have no framework in
which to understand the testimonies. How far back in time should
we go when giving background? Should we stick with April 2003,
the date the media pointed to as the start of the conflict, when the
SLA launched its hugely successful attack against the El Fashir airport? But the people we spoke to testified that oppression and
increasing violence against them were practiced for years, even
decades before 2003. Should we start with the 1989 coup that
brought Omar Bashir into power? Or should we open with Sudan's
independence from Egypt and Britain in 1956? Should we try to
bring in the decades-long civil war between the government and the
SPLA in South Sudan? There were certainly important connections
to be made between the North–South conflict and the current crisis in Darfur. We discovered how quickly the documentary could be
bogged down by information, and background on the background.
We didn't want to spend precious time providing dates and statistics
which could be found on the Internet. It would detract from the
first-person narratives we knew were the heart of the film. We
wanted our viewers to look into the eyes of Darfurians and hear their
stories, hopes, and fears.

We decided that there was no particular character whose story we
would highlight. Instead, the story of Darfur itself would be the narrative through-line: the culture and heritage of the people; the relative tribal and ethnic harmony in the past; the increasing violence
and subsequent founding of the SLA; the eruption of the conflict in

2003; the attacks on villages, leading to the flight of refugees and displaced people and the destruction of homes, schools, and livliehoods; the life of the refugees in Chad and displaced people inside Darfur; the physical and psychological trauma endured by the people, especially the children—all this with a focus on the Darfurians' resilience, demonstrated by their commitment to educate their children, celebrate weddings, and plan for the future. But until we got our footage translated, we could only have a very rough idea of the content and sequence of the film.

We first realized how much we had missed on the ground while we were working with Asadik, a young man from the Zaghawa tribe whom Aisha tracked down in Baltimore. Though his work as an airport security guard combined with his English course at the community college didn't give him much free time, he was able to translate some of the footage we needed more urgently for a few hours a week.

Asadik was going line by line through the tour of Muzbat with us when he stopped and chuckled.

"What?" I didn't remember anything funny about that day.

"They are talking to each other, they are saying something about you guys."

For part of the tour, we remembered, the *omdah* and his friend walked ahead of us, chatting with each other in Zaghawa. The cordless microphone clipped on the *omdah*'s *galabiya* recorded those side comments as clearly as the narration about the village.

"What are they saying?"

"Well, the one in camouflage is saying, 'This is a long walk. They are getting tired.' And the *omdah* is answering him, 'No, these white people are very active, they will never get tired!' "

We laughed. There must have been dozens of side comments and small conversations about the three of us taking place all the time.

After one or two meetings with Asadik, we realized how long and labor-intensive the translation process was going to be. At a pace of just a few hours a week, it would take us a year merely to log our footage. We were hoping to finish the film within a few months. We needed to locate more people from the Zaghawa community who could assist us.

On a snowy day in D.C., I walked to the Howard Law School. As I approached the building, a car with four men inside stopped beside me. One man rolled down the window.

"Hello!" he called out. "Do you know where is the conference on Darfur?"

"I'm heading to the same place. I think that's the main building ahead!"

"Thank you very much. See you inside!"

Judging by their facial features and accents, I was pretty sure they were from Darfur.

I found a seat in the nearly empty auditorium. I hoped that the scant attendance was merely a reflection of the weather and not of dwindling interest in the issue. The men from the car entered and sat down directly behind me. They smiled at me and continued to chat with each other in their native tongue. I immediately recognized the timbre, tone and inflection of the language.

"Legga loo!" I said, leaning over the back of my seat. They stopped speaking and stared at me.

"What did you say?"

I began to lose confidence. "Sorry . . . I thought you were speaking Zaghawa . . ."

"Yes, we were—but how do you know to speak Zaghawa?"

I told them about the film and that we had spent time in the camps in northeast Chad and in villages in Dar Zaghawa.

"What villages did you visit?"

Their eyes grew wide as I ticked off the names. "Furawiya, Muzbat, Shegeg Karo, Amarai, Anka . . ."

"I am from Muzbat," The man who had rolled down the car window and asked directions told me. "My name is Madebo."

"And I am from Anka! My name is Hamza," another man said. "And this guy here, he is from Hangala, just . . ."

"Yes, I know, just west of Furawiya!" I finished his sentence.

"Listen, you must contact us," Madebo said as the moderator for the opening panel stepped behind the podium and checked that the microphone was on. "If there is anything we can do to help your project, please just call." He wrote down their names and his phone number. "We live in Brooklyn, but we would be so happy to help. Please call," he repeated again.

A few weeks later, I found myself ringing the doorbell of a Brooklyn apartment near Coney Island. I had my laptop and a duffel bag filled with VHS tapes. After all, they had offered to help. And we had forty-five hours of footage that needed translation.

Madebo answered the door. "Hello, welcome! Come in!"

I entered their apartment. Several men shared it, but I wasn't exactly sure who lived there and who was visiting. There was a large Zaghawa diaspora in Brooklyn, the second largest in the United States.

We began our first of nine days of translation work. The "Brooklyn guys," as I came to refer to them, drove taxicabs to support themselves and keep their families back in Darfur and Chad alive. Some drove the day shift, some drove the night; they rotated between working in their cabs and working with me on the footage. For up to fifteen hours a day, we pored through the tapes, painstakingly rewinding each small clip over and over to make sure that every word was caught and translated accurately.

There were times that their focus shifted.

"That guy right there," Madebo told me as we watched the tour through Muzbat. "He is my relative."

The group working with me whooped with recognition when we started working on the tape with the founders of the SLA.

"Commander Mohammad Ismail! He was my classmate!" Rahama said. "And Salih Bob—I gave him that nickname—I gave him the name of Bob!"

Hamza happened to be working with me the day we watched the Anka footage. He was quieter than usual; I wasn't sure why. The camera panned over the destroyed village, with nothing remaining except the round circular bases of what used to be homes.

Hamza grabbed my arm. "Please. Can you freeze it? Can you stop the tape?"

I pressed *pause*, remembering at that moment that Hamza was from Anka. Hamza moved to the TV screen and pointed to one of the charred circles of stones. It looked indistinguishable from the rest to me. "That one! Right there! That was my home. That was where I grew up."

We stared in silence at the remains of his childhood home on the TV screen until the VCR un-paused the tape and reverted to the *play* function. Hamza took a deep breath and continued to help me with the translation.

WE HADN'T REALIZED what we actually had on our forty-five tapes until we ploughed through those hours of footage with our new friends. The on-the-spot summaries that Dero and others had offered were, at best, lacking all detail and, at worst, completely mistranslated. I worked with the Brooklyn guys on the delivery of the messages from the SLA fighters in Muzbat to their families in Kariare refugee camp. The feeling I had gotten in the tent of Kamal's family was confirmed. Every word uttered between Fatima and us had been altered in translation by Moutassem.

"She is asking here: 'He is okay? He is in good condition?' " Rahama told me as we sat on his couch in Brooklyn.

Moutassem's translation, captured on the tape, had been: "She said,

'If you have the way to come to Furawiya, how can I go there?' "

"What is she thinking after hearing the message?" Aisha had asked on the tape.

Rahama translated what Fatima said next. "He said come to Furawiya. But if I don't have a way to go there, what can I do? I must forget about it."

Moutassem's translation: "She wants to give him a message by telephone."

"What would she tell him?" Aisha had asked, believing Fatima had requested to give her husband a message by telephone.

"From where you get a phone to talk to him?" Moutassem had translated Aisha's question to Fatima.

Fatima, bewildered, responded, "There is no phone."

The frustration about the miscommunication built on all sides until it led to the moment where Fatima turned to Moutassem and said, "What do they want? What they want, I am going to write."

Most upsetting to me was my discovery as we reviewed the footage of the wedding in Muzbat, when Musa was helping Aisha and me talk to the sisters of the bride, the day the Antonovs returned.

"Talking is very good," Musa had translated Um Bashar's words for us. "This will be very helpful. Please help yourself to the food."

But now sitting in Brooklyn, Madebo was telling us that the bride's sister had actually asked me, "Your talking is good, but can you stop the planes for us? We are very tired from the fires. How about stopping the planes?"

I was certain that Musa had intentionally omitted that request from the translation knowing that we had no power to stop the Antonovs, and wanting to protect us from feeling impotent. So he changed the plea for help to "Please help yourself to the food."

My face burned thinking about the exchange. "Can you stop the planes?" they asked us, and, in response, Aisha and I each bit into a piece of fried dough, exclaiming, "Delicious! Thank you very much!"

That same afternoon, Ibrahim helped me translate the interview with Fadi, the teenaged boy with the SLA whom we had met our first night in Darfur.

"What's your name?" Adam had asked him and Ibrahim translated back the response: "My name is Mansour."

I stopped typing for a moment. "What did he say? Can we play that again?"

Again: "My name is Mansour."

"Mansour? He told me his name was Fadi!" I faltered. "I mean, I thought he told me his name was Fadi." Somehow, that night on the noisy truck, trying to talk to him in my limited Arabic, I thought he had said his name was Fadi. But here it was, on tape. His father was right after all, of course! His name *was* Mansour! We had called him Fadi for days—and he had responded!

Later that week, Tajadin helped us translate the songs from *iftar* at Kamal's compound in Muzbat. The songs were particularly difficult to work with—Tajadin was one of only two people on the East Coast who could help us. The words were extremely fast, rapid-fire, in fact, and were improvised. Every two or three seconds Adam would pause the clip while Tajadin translated a few words that I jotted onto my laptop. *"I'm tying my sash." "I can race the airplane."*

Suddenly, Tajadin looked directly at me. "They're singing about you!"

"About me? What are you talking about?"

"Let me listen more." Adam played the clip again and Tajadin laid his ear down low to the speaker of the computer. As the Zaghawa singing continued, I began to make out the word "Jen" in some of the lyrics. I hadn't noticed it at all the night of the singing.

Tajadin indicated to Adam to stop the footage and looked up at me, grinning. "Did you know that man wanted to marry you?"

"What? That's what they are singing about?"

"Let me translate for you." And Tajadin, listening word for word, began to translate what the rebels had been singing that night, mixed in with the songs of resistance.

"We are here with a purpose," a rebel sang. *"We want Ibrahim Jim to marry the white girl. Those people here, son of Zaghawa, they have nice big teeth, their face are shaped nicely, we have to do something today. All the sons of Zaghawa, you are here, this is a beautiful white girl, we want to give her to Jim."*

"Who?" was asked in song.

And then, as if there was any doubt: *"Her name's Jen. Jen is a white girl from the United States, she came here to Muzbat. We all want to marry Jen, but Ibrahim is the only one lucky enough. The rest of us lost. The people here all agree now, we're going to ask Jen to marry Ibrahim. We are honoring this."*

And then, my suitor sang: *"I thought about this. Jen is in my sight. I feel good! Say more about my sweetheart, Jen! I wear my shoes. I am prepared. I have people behind me. I want to go and tell him that I want to marry the woman."*

"I had no idea that he was serious!" I protested to Tajadin. I had thoroughly dismissed the proposal as a joke at the time. I couldn't even look at Adam. I knew exactly what the expression on his face would be. He and Aisha would never, ever let me forget this.

WITH THE BULK of the footage translated and logged, it was time to select which clips of the footage to use and where. I returned to D.C. late at night and woke early the next morning when Aisha called me.

"You have a land line over there?"

"Yeah, what's up?"

"Dero called me in the middle of the night. He was using someone's satphone. He asked me to call him right back. Can I come over?"

"Sure, come on over!"

Aisha arrived half an hour later, looking distressed.

"What did Dero have to say? How is he?"

"Not good. Shegeg Karo was bombed last night. He wasn't hurt, but some people he knows were killed. He sounded awful. I've been trying to reach him since then on the Thuraya number he gave me, but I haven't been able to get through with my cell phone."

Using the land line didn't help. We couldn't connect to the satellite phone to reach Dero or find out anything more. We had been so wrapped up in the accounts captured in our footage that it had been easy not to pay attention to the atrocities continuing to unfold as we worked on translation and editing. The call from Dero, indicating the beginning of conditions deteriorating, was a call back to reality. The cease-fire that the government had signed with the SLA and JEM had begun to unravel in front of our eyes when the Antonov flew overhead the day we were in Muzbat. But the call from Dero was the first report we had heard of the resumption of the government-led bombing campaign.

We tried over and over again to reach Dero or Suleiman, but with no success. Aisha called human rights organizations to report the attacks and to see if they had heard anything about them. They had not.

AISHA AND I sat late that night in a restaurant, having a drink and sharing our anxiety about Dero and the other people we had grown to care about. In addition to the resumption of the bombing campaigns, there was an outbreak of meningitis in Iridimi refugee camp and, with the oncoming rainy season that made roads impassable, a possible famine was looming.

Our conversation turned to moments in the trip that had caused both of us internal discomfort. I remembered a Joe Sacco graphic novel on Palestine where he sketched himself heading to a demonstration. He depicted himself frightened and coaxing himself into the action by repeating to himself, "It'll be good for the comic … it'll be good for the comic." But it wasn't juxtaposition between fear and what was good for the film that Aisha and I were talking about.

"When we were in Muzbat the day the Antonov flew overhead," I asked Aisha, a few beers into the conversation. "Did any part of you, deep down inside, wish that the plane would bomb?"

"Hell, yes!" Aisha responded immediately. "I mean—I wouldn't have wanted anyone to get hurt of course," she added hastily.

Knowing that we were documenting the horrors in an effort to help stop them didn't eliminate the disgust I felt with myself that I had wished, even for a fraction of a second, that the plane would actually bomb. Realizing that Aisha had had the same impulse alleviated some of my guilt. It must be something all those who document conflict face; if you are documenting a story about atrocities, it is good for your project to have a real live atrocity to film. I was relieved we had verbalized it. But the realization made me question whether I could continue to do this kind of work.

I HAD BEEN logging secondary b-roll footage all day. Hour after mind-numbing hour with my PC on my lap, I recorded every background shot we had filmed. Though the work was extremely tedious, I found myself more affected by the content now, months after our return, than I had been while filming it. I hadn't realized at the time that my defense mechanisms had been in place. But gauging from my reactions to revisiting the footage, it was apparent that while in Darfur and Chad, my emotions had been well protected.

It might not have been a wise choice to watch *Hotel Rwanda* that night, but the movie had just been released to great acclaim and I was still trying to learn as much as I could about the recent history of genocide and Africa.

The film's depiction of U.N. officers refusing to allow Rwandan children on the evacuation bus for internationals only and thus condemning them to the genocide sparked a reaction from audience members. "Damn it!" a woman in the theater yelled out, her voice choked with tears. People around me started to cry. I began to shake and continued shaking throughout the remainder of the film.

The shaking overcame me again late that night when I was finally in bed, trying to sleep. We weren't doing enough. How could making a film possibly give people the protection and the help that they needed? The feeling of inadequacy that we had struggled with in Chad and Darfur threatened to completely overwhelm me now.

WE BEGAN TO screen progressive rough cuts of the film with the triple goals of continuing advocacy, gathering audience feedback on the work in progress, and raising the funds needed to complete the project. After nearly every screening, we were asked, "How can anything we do possibly make a difference?"

"When the horror is so large, there is a tendency to buy into the fallacy that since you can't do everything, then it's pointless to do anything. If we allow ourselves to fall into that trap, we become completely paralyzed. A phone call to your congressperson isn't going to halt the Sudanese government. A letter to the editor of a newspaper isn't going ensure access to humanitarian aid for displaced people. We know this film isn't going to stop a genocide," I answered, speaking as much to myself as to the audience. "But it all feeds into a larger effort. Perhaps it's true that we can't possibly do enough. But what we do does matter. It matters to people in Darfur and refugees from Darfur who are here. It's important for them to know that there are people in the outside world who care about them, who are standing with them and working on their behalf."

We intended for the film to inspire people to activism. We

hadn't planned on audiences asking us what exactly they should do. We didn't want to spoon-feed people by telling them what actions to take. It wouldn't reflect the complexity of the situation, nor would it honor the intelligence of our audiences. We wanted to encourage audiences to first learn all they could about Darfur, going past the simplistic portrayal the mainstream media offered, and then to suggest that they research different organizations in order to determine how they wanted to get involved.

It wasn't difficult to find models of activism to point to for inspiration, especially among students. Student movements that focused on Darfur began cropping up all over the United States and Canada. Groups like STAND (Students Taking Action Now: Darfur) and the Genocide Intervention Network were taking the lead on pressing their universities and local and national government to do more than just pay lip service to the crisis. And they were being effective. Due to student pressure, Harvard University (which was very slow to divest from South Africa during the fight against apartheid) was the first to divest from the stock it held in PetroChina, a company that plays a key role in the Sudanese government's lethal oil business. Other universities, and then state pension plans, followed.

FROM QUESTION AND answer sessions after screenings, it seemed the film successfully communicated that the problem was not, at its core, an ethnic or tribal conflict, but rather a governmental campaign against its own civilians, manipulating tribalism and ethnicity to serve its agenda. "What is the motivation of the Sudanese government?" we heard repeatedly.

It was a tricky question to answer. We hadn't spoken with members of the Sudanese government or the Janjaweed militia. Not only did we not have access to them while in Darfur, but our goal was to give a voice to the victims. We were not, for the sake of some journalistic concept of balance, going to give a platform to the perpetrators. But I was reading the government's statements in written pieces and on their Web site. If asked what their motivation was for the crimes in Darfur, the response usually boiled down to a denial. Rape? Burned villages? Murder of civilians? Those were blamed on the Janjaweed. And about the connection between the government and the Janjaweed? Some articles quoted government spokespeople as saying there was no connection; others admitted that the government had early on armed the proxy militias to fight against the rebels, but have had no control over them since then. Nothing in these statements came close to explaining the use of Antonov bomber planes on civilian populations, or the high level of coordination between the attacks from the air and the attacks on the ground, which was described to us repeatedly as a joint effort of Janjaweed and government soldiers.

The reaction to the film wasn't always a probing for more information. At a screening at Brandeis University, there was a young woman from South Sudan in the audience. She stood up during the Q & A.

"What is happening now in Darfur is what the people in the South endured for decades," she said. "I never felt that my story or my suffering had been given a face or a voice so that people could understand what I and my family lived through. Until now."

It seemed we were meeting our goals.

ADAM, AISHA, AND I needed to begin work on other projects. Aisha graduated from her masters program and took a human rights job that would send her to India and Mongolia for chunks of time. Adam was hired by a human rights organization to work in Afghanistan. I was going to Bosnia–Herzegovina to facilitate a conflict resolution program. The remaining work on the film (graphic design, sound, and introduction) would be worked on alternately by whoever was in the country through e-mail consultation with the other two.

We had a final dinner together, after which Adam gave Aisha a ride home and me a ride to the airport. Adam pulled his car over in front of the National Zoo in Woodley Park across from Aisha's apartment. He pulled three small grayish-white rocks out of his pocket.

"What's this?" Aisha asked.

"They're from the ancient cemetery at Shegeg Karo, on top of the mountain," Adam answered.

"You held on to them for all this time?" I asked.

"I planned to give them to you when the film was done, but since it looks like we won't be together when that happens, I thought I'd give them to you now."

"Look at you, getting all mushy and stuff!" Aisha teased and poked his chest.

"Both of you and this process have been great. We are going to put something out there that will help mobilize opinion, and hopefully action. At least, people won't be able to claim ignorance because of lack of access. We're doing our part." Adam handed one rock to Aisha, the other to me, placing the third on his dashboard. Aisha got out of the car and Adam and I continued on to Reagan National Airport.

SIX MONTHS LATER, the film was finally completed. I went to New York to give copies to the Brooklyn guys. The rock from Shegeg Karo was in my pocket. We had never imagined that it would take us a year to finish the film. We certainly hadn't anticipated that a year after returning from Chad and Darfur, the situation there would be even worse and growing grimmer still.

Madebo spoke to me with concern about the deterioration. Although there had been a lull in the violence in recent months,

people were still dying at an alarming rate. A few estimates I read ran
as high as five hundred people in the IDP camps dying each day from
disease and malnutrition. I thought about Hari in Muzbat telling us
that the government was ending them through starvation. Some ana-
lysts were calling Darfur "genocide by attrition."

And even the brief respite from direct violence had ended; Janjaweed militias were roving and government forces were attacking
civilians again. The African Union troops, their arrival a cause for hope
when we were there, had been largely unable to provide protection.
To make matters worse, the SLA was having its own leadership problems. It was splintering into different factions and engaging in bloody
power struggles internally and with the Justice and Equality rebel
movement. Civilians, as always, were paying the heaviest price.

Madebo's wife and six-month-old baby boy, Musa, entered from
the other room. They had been in a refugee camp in Chad until a
few months earlier, when Madebo had managed to save up enough
money and get visas for them to join him in New York. Madebo gave
me the baby boy to hold and I bounced him on my knee.

"Tell your wife that Musa is beautiful and that I am so happy to
meet them both, please," I said to Madebo, utilizing his translation
skills once more. "You must be so relieved that you were able to bring
them to be with you."

"Sure, I'm relieved!" Madebo said as Musa laughed and pulled my
hair. "Now I know that my wife and son will be safe. They will be
able to eat. If they get sick, we can find medicine or a doctor. My son
will go to school."

I could easily understand why Madebo wanted to get to the
States and then bring his family here. Nearly any place on the planet
is safer than the unstable, precarious refugee camps in Chad or in
Darfur. But millions do remain because they have no choice, or
because, as with Dero's mother and father, it is the only home they
know and they will not leave it, for any reason.

As I rode back to Manhattan, I fingered the Shegeg Karo rock, examining it. I thought about what Madebo wanted for his wife and son: safety, food, health care, education. I pictured ten-year-old Ibrahim showing us the drawings of his village being bombed and his brothers killed, green-eyed Mubarak tearing up as he told us of his sleepless nights, little Tujud in Shegeg Karo lying paralyzed on his mother's lap, and Amira peering silently from behind her mother's skirt, unable to describe the sound of the Janjaweed attacking her school.

WE HAVE NO way of knowing if most of the people we met are still alive or if they have succumbed to disease, starvation, or new violence. I had thought that when the film was completed, our work on Darfur would wrap up as well. But as I put the stone from the ancient cemetery on top of the Shegeg Karo mountain back in my pocket, I knew that telling their stories isn't enough. For those who had shared with us their fears and hopes, nightmares and dreams, there was so much more to do.

Ibrahim holds up his drawings.

afterword

by Adam Shapiro

RETURNING TO THE United States in late November 2004, we found that Darfur was disappearing from newspapers. The government and rebel leaders were holding talks, but the international community had still not taken meaningful action, limiting itself to general statements encouraging peace. Despite mounting evidence and an abundance of testimony from the victims that the attacks were led or supported by the government via Antonov airplanes, MiG fighter jets, and military helicopters, most of these calls for peace focused on the government's support for the *janjaweed* militias and were silent about the government's direct role in the organized violence against Darfurians.

IN JANUARY, AS we worked to translate the dozens of hours of footage and interviews we had collected, the government bombed Shegeg Karo, the village where we had met Dero and others who had decided to stay in their land and not become refugees. Antonovs targeted the village despite the ceasefire that had been announced and despite assurances by the Sudanese government that it was doing all it could to bring peace to Darfur.

STARTING AT THE end of 2004 and continuing for a year, three major events would occur that would seriously effect the humanitarian relief going to Darfur and the political effort to end the fighting. Two of these were natural disasters on a scale unprecedented in modern memory: the Indian Ocean tsunami that affected millions of people in countries spanning Indonesia to Somalia, and the Kashmir earthquake that claimed the lives of tens of thousands of people and destroyed thousands of villages. Despite the abundance of generosity from citizens around the world, both of these events took attention, funds, and energy away from the humanitarian effort to help the refugees and internally displaced people of Darfur, taxing the resources of the international humanitarian community.

THE THIRD EVENT was a peace agreement signed by the government of Sudan and the Sudan People's Liberation Army/Movement, led by John Garang, on January 9, 2005. The negotiations had been going on for a number of years and involved the mediation efforts of a number of African countries, the Intergovernmental Authority on Development (IGAD), and, perhaps most importantly, the United States, through the offices of Special Envoy John Danforth. President Bush's strong support came after he was lobbied by various constituencies in the United States, including some who represent the base of support for the Republican Party. With this high-level U.S. effort and pressure, along with increased estimates of the amount of oil in areas of Sudan along the North-South fault lines of the conflict, both the government of Sudan and the SPLA had new incentives to reach a deal. The SPLA emerged with significant gains in terms of power and resource sharing. In the end, the people of southern Sudan will vote in a referendum on self-determination in 2011.

⁜

THE COMPREHENSIVE PEACE Agreement (CPA), as it was known, was not comprehensive. It did not concern the whole of Sudan. It set up a two-tiered system in which SPLA-controlled territory would share power and resources with the central government, while other areas, including Darfur, were left marginalized and excluded.

⁜

AS NEWS OF the negotiations filtered out, many other Sudanese began to question the logic of their own marginalization. In a number of areas in the country, people started to mobilize to address their political status. In Darfur, locals decided it was time that their discrimination end and took the opportunity to strike out for their share. As the fighting in Darfur exploded and expanded, negotiators at the North–South peace talks worried that the conflict in the west might derail the negotiations. They were not willing to accept that the causes of both conflicts were one and the same. Long used to conceptualizing the North–South conflict as a Muslim–Christian battle, the Sudanese government and Western interlocutors treated the conflict in Darfur as an Arab–African or Arab–black conflict. Rather than seeking to extend the peace talks to the entire country through an inclusive peace process that dealt with the core issues of conflict in the country, the negotiations proceeded based on limited interests and a disregard for Darfur. In fact, by the time the CPA agreement was signed, multiple rounds of talks had been held between Sudanese government representatives and the SLA in Abuja, Nigeria—far away and completely distinct from the other talks. Upon the formation of a joint government with the SPLA in September 2005, President Bush declared: "All Sudanese can be proud of this significant progress, because it demonstrates the parties'

continued commitment to a common vision of a unified, democratic, prosperous, and peaceful Sudan."

THE BLACK/AFRICAN and Arab dichotomy that has been deployed
to define the conflict in Darfur was first put forward by the government of Sudan and quickly adopted by many in the West. This
view is neither historically meaningful to nor useful in helping the
people of Sudan, as it intentionally obfuscates the underlying causes
of the conflict. The promotion of this dichotomy has taken on very
real meaning, however, as a means of organizing support by both the
Sudanese government and those seeking to help the people of Darfur. The government has mobilized political support from the Arab
League, in Arab nations, and among groups in Sudan seeking to identify as an Arab elite. Organized activism in America by institutions
with various political agendas utilizes the demonization of Arabs to
play on the post-9/11 context (where anti-Arab sentiment is promoted by major media outlets such as FOX News and conservative
radio stations), identifying Arabs with terrorism, violence, and a
clash of civilizations. Both sides of this coin are essentially seeking
militarized solutions to the conflict (continued on the part of the
government of Sudan and NATO intervention on the part of those
seeking to save Darfur) and yet neither version offers locally rooted
or meaningful narratives that can offer lasting solutions to the crisis
not just in Darfur, but in all Sudan.

THE PROBLEM WITH the use of the black/African-Arab dichotomy
is exacerbated by the debate over the use of the word and term genocide to label what has happened in Darfur. According to Article II
of the Convention on the Prevention and Punishment of Genocide,
genocide is defined as "any of the following acts committed with

intent to destroy, in whole or in part, a national, ethnic, racial, or religious group, as such:

(a) Killing members of the group;

(b) Causing serious bodily or mental harm to members of the group;

(c) Deliberately inflicting on the group conditions of life calculated to bring about its physical destruction in whole or in part;

(d) Imposing measures intended to prevent births within the group;

(e) Forcibly transferring children of the group to another group."

In the late spring of 2004, the U.S. Congress unanimously passed a non-binding resolution labeling the conflict in Darfur genocide. Later that summer, U.S. Secretary of State Colin Powell said, "acts of genocide had occurred" in Darfur. Activists in the United States picked up on this opening and started organizing into two major coalitions—the Save Darfur coalition and Students Taking Action Now in Darfur (STAND). While both these groups are attempting to raise awareness and stop the bloodshed in Darfur, both have largely accepted the Arab-African/black lens and used this paradigm in mobilizing action in rallies and other public events. The international community, however, has largely held back in its assessment of the conflict as genocide and a special investigatory commission of the United Nations specifically did not use the term in a presentation to the Security Council. Instead the report mentioned war crimes and crimes against humanity, holding off on genocide because the commission could not prove intent on the part of the government. The government of Sudan, itself, has used the accusation of genocide by the United States to drum up support, particularly among Arab countries, seeking to link the Western (particularly American) interest in Darfur to the wars in Afghanistan and Iraq, the crisis with Iran over nuclear energy, and the clash of civilization narrative that is gaining traction in the Arab and Muslim worlds as well. The failure of U.S. intelligence with regard to weapons of mass destruction in Iraq and the bombing of a pharmaceutical plant in Khartoum in 1998 have been used to challenge U.S. government assessments of the situation in Darfur.

NOT ALL INTERNATIONAL efforts have been so politicized or divisive. In early June 2004, the African Union reached an agreement to deploy its first contingent of troops to the region. Ultimately this mission would deploy seven thousand troops as part of an agreement between the government of Sudan and the African Union. However, even this effort is problematic. The mandate of the troops, which was a result of negotiations with the Sudanese government, was limited to an observer mission, without the ability to protect or intervene militarily. This has resulted in African troops standing by helplessly as militias and government forces have attacked civilians in villages and those fleeing toward Chad. Another weakness is in the number of troops, their lack of mobility, and experience. Finally, the African Union, while seeking to provide "African solutions for African problems" nonetheless has neither the funds nor the material needed from its member states to deploy an effective force. Western countries have been hesitant to offer more than the most limited logistical support, and the U.S. Congress even failed to approve fifty million dollars in 2005 (after the genocide resolution) for the A.U. contingent.

IN 2006, INTERNATIONAL efforts toward Darfur began to accelerate. As the situation on the ground worsened, and realization took hold that the African Union effort was largely ineffectual, the United

States, United Kingdom, Egypt, Libya, and other concerned nations tried to support negotiations and determine means to stop the violence. Rebel groups and government officials met again in Abuja, Nigeria, under the auspices of an African Union mediator. The United Nations Security Council, prodded by U.S. Ambassador to the United Nations, John Bolton, began pushing for transforming the African Union force in Darfur to a U.N. peacekeeping force under a Security Council mandate with expanded numbers and support. Earlier the Security Council had agreed to refer the case of Darfur to the International Criminal Court (ICC), a move that the United States did not vote for (due to its opposition to the ICC), but also did not veto.

IN EARLY 2006, the initial report from the chief investigator from the ICC was blocked from being presented to the Council, due to the U.S. opposition to the international court. Once again, larger international politics and policies served to obstruct more significant action on Darfur. The Council instead decided to freeze the assets and impose travel restrictions on four individuals connected to the conflict in Darfur.[1] All four, including two commanders from the rebel groups, were found responsible for the commission of war crimes. The government, *janjaweed* militia, SLA, and other rebel groups are cited for attacks against civilians, and a number of attacks on aid workers committed at different times by all parties. The Council decision was meant to send a message not only to the named individuals, but also to others involved in the conflict. However, the message was quite mixed. The U.N. resolution does not give a sense of scale either of the crimes committed by the different individuals or responsibility for the ongoing crisis. It is quite clear that the government and militias have carried out systematic, widespread atrocities, whereas the rebel groups have been guilty primarily of executing isolated attacks and for impeding the humanitarian effort. While the resolution passed the Council, key countries such as Russia and China (along with Qatar) abstained, indicating that sanctions would have a negative impact on the situation in Darfur. Russia and China have significant business interests in Sudan, including energy and military contracts, and as such have sought to protect the regime from more serious sanctions by the world body.

WHILE DEVELOPMENTS AT the United Nations, in Abuja, Nigeria, and on the ground in Darfur continue to unfold in different directions, life for the people of Darfur—whether they are in refugee camps in Chad, displaced in IDP camps in Darfur, or living in caves and *wadis*—continues to deteriorate. In April 2006, the United Nations announced that due to a lack of funds it would have to cut its food rations for the people of Darfur by fifty percent. In Chad, the political situation has become unstable as rival Chadian factions vie for power, and new armed groups emerge on the political scene. Eastern Chad has now become a dangerous place for the refugees, as Sudanese militias cross the border to attack refugees and Chadian civilians, and as Sudanese army and Chadian army forces exchange fire. From mid-2005 through May 2006, the prospect of wider conflict (with the attendant humanitarian and human costs) in this region became more likely. This has been exploited, in particular, by the government of Sudan that simultaneously claims it has no part in the instability, and warns the international community not to pressure it or else the conflict will spread.

WHAT IS ABUNDANTLY clear to many observers is that the regime in Khartoum is adept at fostering conflict and instability to manipulate the international community. However, when consistent pressure is applied, the government has also shown a willingness to give in, if only as a means of self-preservation. While citizen activism and pressure on the international community to act to stop the bloodshed and preserve human life is important, utilizing a frame of understanding that polarizes and plays into the mobilization of ethnic, religious, or racial hatred (even if fabricated, in this case by the government of Sudan, for the purpose of power) will not help the people of Darfur or Sudan. The politics of power in Darfur and Sudan as a whole cannot be rendered comprehensible by simple, ahistorical notions of Arab and African. Understanding the conflict in Darfur requires acceptance of complexity. That complexity, however, must not undermine calls for protection of human life.

---

[1] The four are: Maj. Gen. Gaffar Mohamed Elhassan, a former commander of the western military region for the Sudanese Air Force; Sheikh Musa Hilal, paramount chief of the Jalul ethnic group in North Darfur; Adam Yacub Shant, a commander in the rebel Sudanese Liberation Army (SLA); and Gabril Abdul Kareem Badri, a field commander of the rebel National Movement for Reform and Development.

glossary

AIRSERV—humanitarian relief organization that provides air transportation.

AU—African Union

CARE—international humanitarian organization

DOCTORS WITHOUT BORDERS—international humanitarian organization

IDP—Internally Displaced Person

IRC—International Rescue Committee, international humanitarian organization

JEM—Justice and Equality Movement (Darfurian rebel group)

NGO—Nongovernmental Organization

SLA—Sudan Liberation Army (Darfurian rebel group)

SPLA—Sudan People's Liberation Army (South Sudanese rebel group)

UNHCR—United Nations High Commission for Refugees

UNICEF—The United Nations Children's Fund

WFP–World Food Program

about the authors

AISHA BAIN is a human rights activist and served as Deputy Director at the Center for the Prevention of Genocide.

JEN MARLOWE spent the past six years facilitating conflict transformation programs with youth from Palestine and Israel, Afghanistan, and Bosnia-Herzegovina.

ADAM SHAPIRO is a human rights activist and founding member of Incounter Productions that produced the documentary film, "About Baghdad".